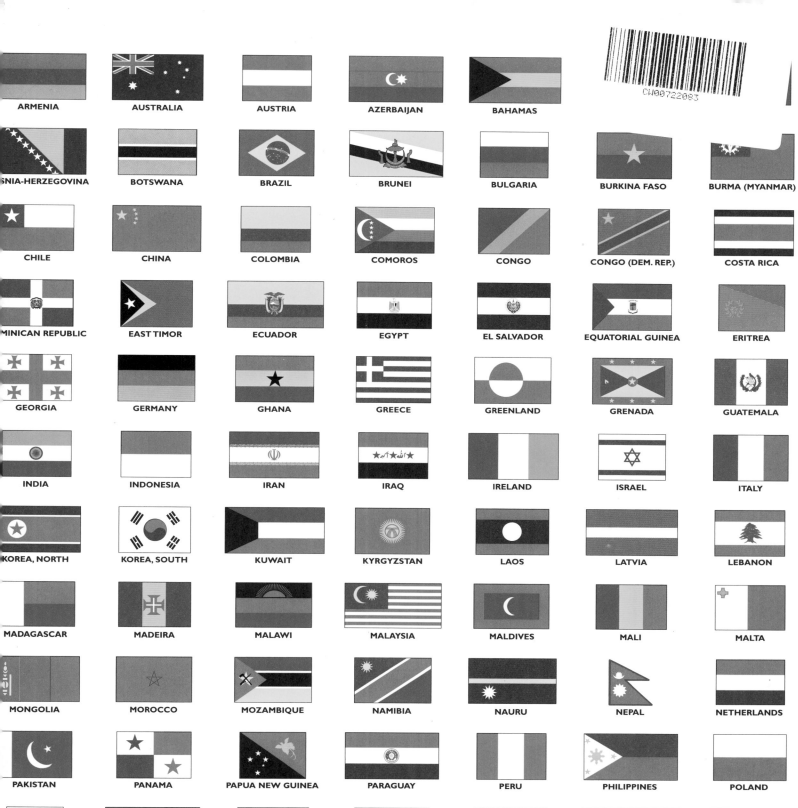

ARMENIA	AUSTRALIA	AUSTRIA	AZERBAIJAN	BAHAMAS
BOSNIA-HERZEGOVINA	BOTSWANA	BRAZIL	BRUNEI	BULGARIA	BURKINA FASO	BURMA (MYANMAR)
CHILE	CHINA	COLOMBIA	COMOROS	CONGO	CONGO (DEM. REP.)	COSTA RICA
DOMINICAN REPUBLIC	EAST TIMOR	ECUADOR	EGYPT	EL SALVADOR	EQUATORIAL GUINEA	ERITREA
GEORGIA	GERMANY	GHANA	GREECE	GREENLAND	GRENADA	GUATEMALA
INDIA	INDONESIA	IRAN	IRAQ	IRELAND	ISRAEL	ITALY
KOREA, NORTH	KOREA, SOUTH	KUWAIT	KYRGYZSTAN	LAOS	LATVIA	LEBANON
MADAGASCAR	MADEIRA	MALAWI	MALAYSIA	MALDIVES	MALI	MALTA
MONGOLIA	MOROCCO	MOZAMBIQUE	NAMIBIA	NAURU	NEPAL	NETHERLANDS
PAKISTAN	PANAMA	PAPUA NEW GUINEA	PARAGUAY	PERU	PHILIPPINES	POLAND
SAN MARINO	SÃO TOMÉ & PRÍNCIPE	SAUDI ARABIA	SENEGAL	SERBIA	SEYCHELLES	SIERRA LEONE
SRI LANKA	ST KITTS & NEVIS	ST LUCIA	ST VINCENT	SUDAN	SURINAME	SWAZILAND
TOGO	TONGA	TRINIDAD & TOBAGO	TUNISIA	TURKEY	TURKMENISTAN	TUVALU
VANUATU	VATICAN CITY	VENEZUELA	VIETNAM	YEMEN	ZAMBIA	ZIMBABWE

FAMILY WORLD ATLAS

Contents

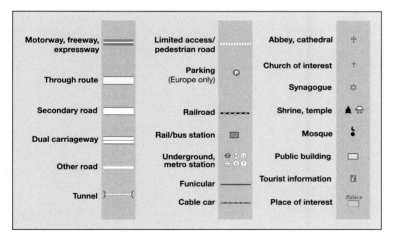

CITY CENTRE MAPS – KEY TO SYMBOLS

Motorway, freeway, expressway	Limited access/ pedestrian road	Abbey, cathedral ✝
Through route	Parking (Europe only) Ⓟ	Church of interest †
Secondary road		Synagogue ✡
	Railroad	Shrine, temple
Dual carriageway	Rail/bus station	Mosque
Other road	Underground, metro station	Public building
	Funicular	Tourist information ℹ
Tunnel	Cable car	Place of interest

Philip's World Atlases are published in association with The Royal Geographical Society (with The Institute of British Geographers).

The Society was founded in 1830 and given a Royal Charter in 1859 for 'the advancement of geographical science'. It holds historical collections of national and international importance, many of which relate to the Society's association with and support for scientific exploration and research from the 19th century onwards. It was pivotal in establishing geography as a teaching and research discipline in British universities close to the turn of the century, and has played a key role in geographical and environmental education ever since.

Today the Society is a leading world centre for geographical learning – supporting education, teaching, research and expeditions, and promoting public understanding of the subject.

The Society welcomes those interested in geography as members. For further information, please visit the website at: www.rgs.org

CITY CENTRE MAPS – Cartography by Philip's
Page iii, Dublin: The town plan of Dublin is based on Ordnance Survey Ireland by permission of the Government Permit Number 8097. © Ordnance Survey Ireland and Government of Ireland.

Ordnance Survey® Page iii, Edinburgh, and page iv, London: This product includes mapping data licensed from Ordnance Survey® with the permission of the Controller of Her Majesty's Stationery Office. © Crown copyright 2006. All rights reserved. Licence number 100011710.

Vector data: Courtesy of Gräfe and Unser Verlag GmbH, München, Germany (city centre maps of Bangkok, Mexico City, Singapore, Sydney and Tokyo).

Published in Great Britain in 2007 by Philip's, a division of Octopus Publishing Group, 2–4 Heron Quays, London E14 4JP

Copyright © 2007 Philip's
Cartography by Philip's

ISBN-13 978–0–540–09034–1
ISBN-10 0–540–09034–4

A CIP catalogue record for this book is available from the British Library.

Printed in Hong Kong

Details of other Philip's titles and services can be found on our website at: www.philips-maps.co.uk

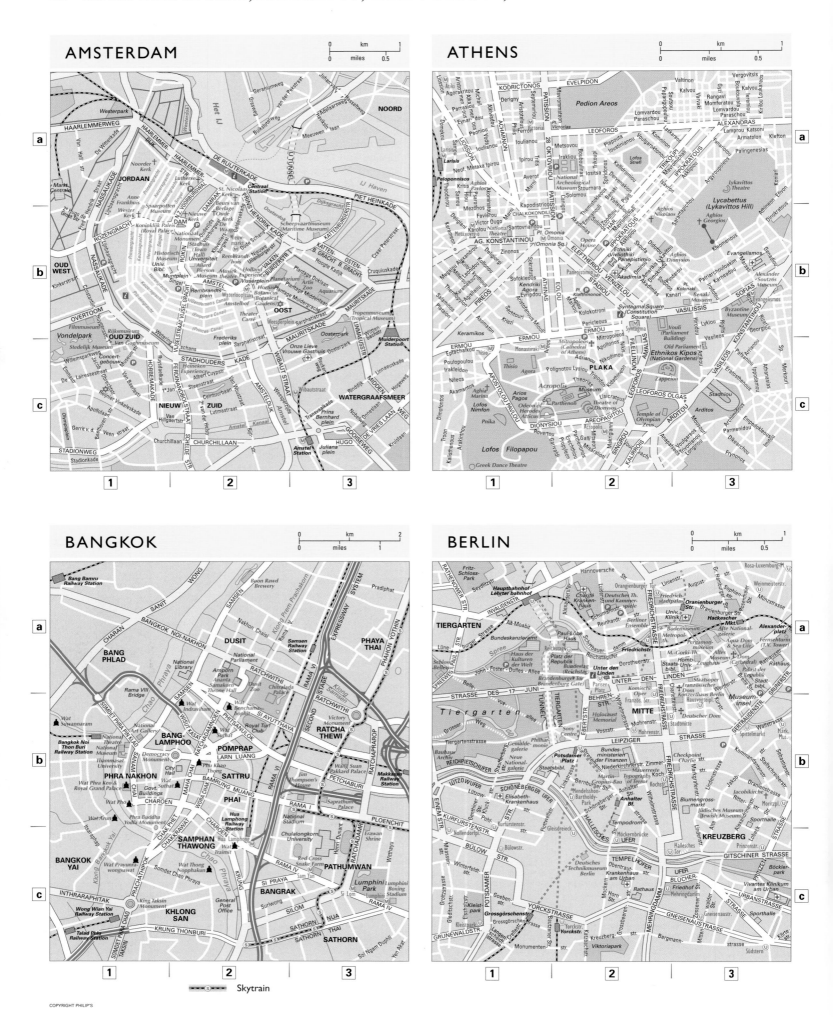

AMSTERDAM

ATHENS

BANGKOK

BERLIN

Skytrain

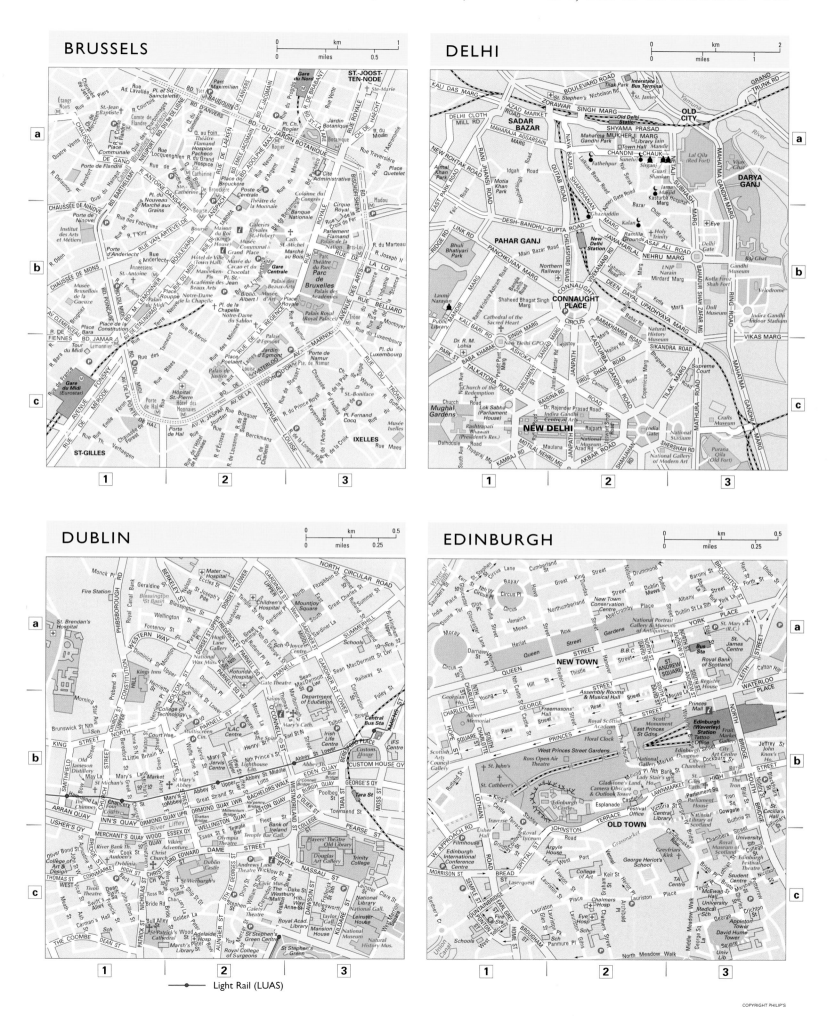

Light Rail (LUAS)

COPYRIGHT PHILIP'S

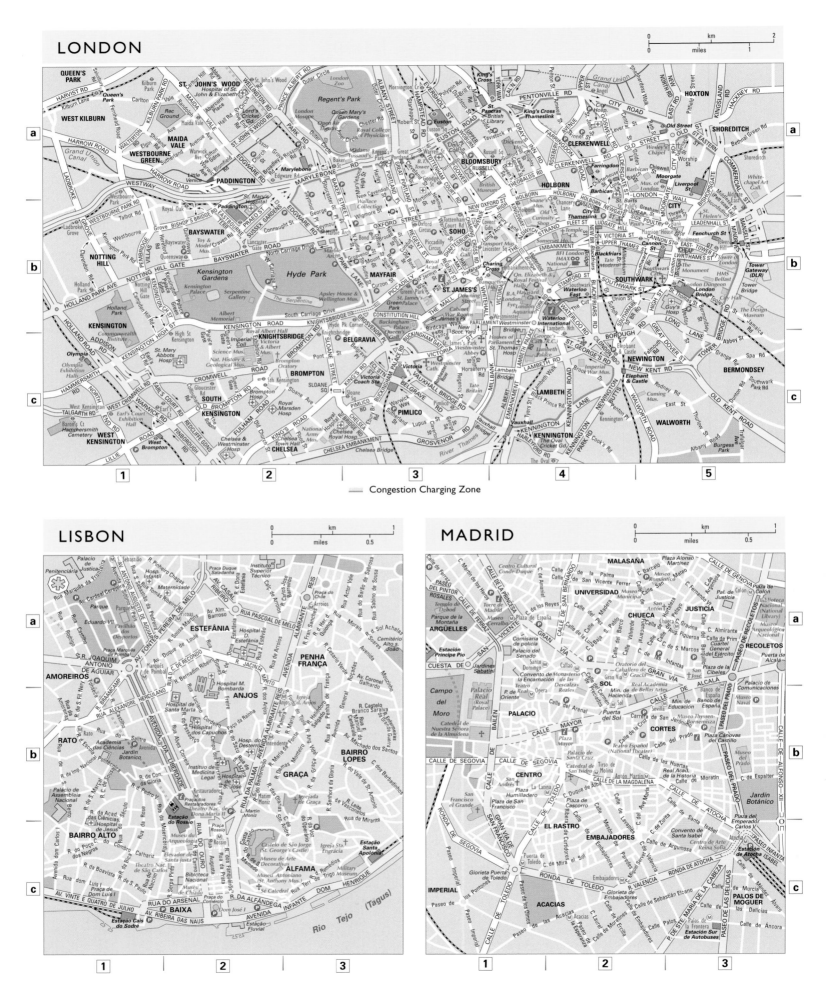

Congestion Charging Zone

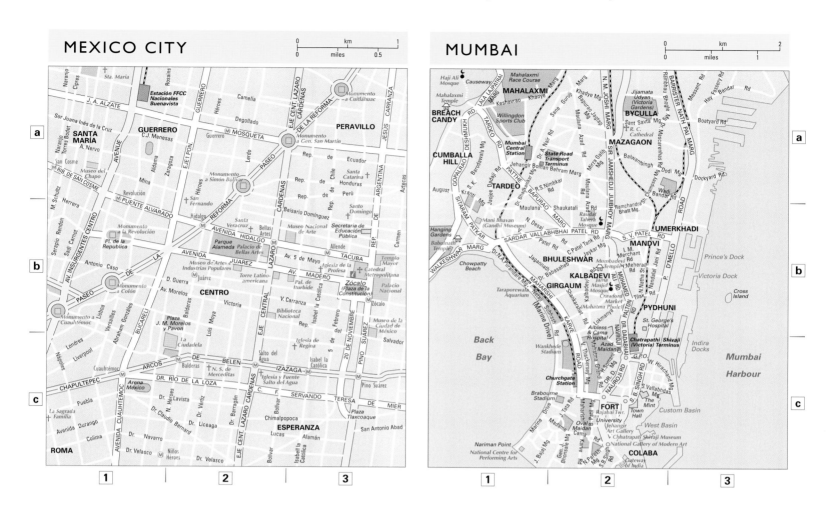

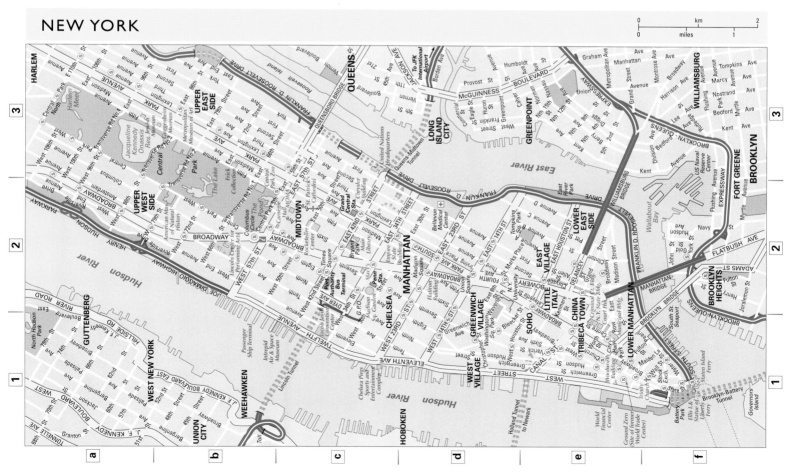

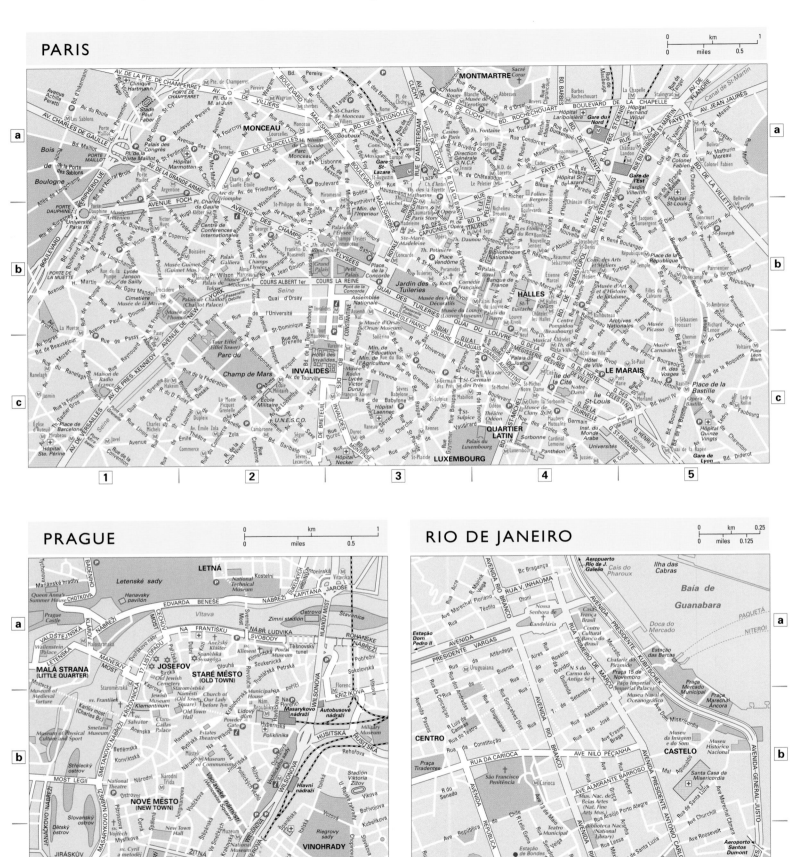

PARIS

PRAGUE

RIO DE JANEIRO

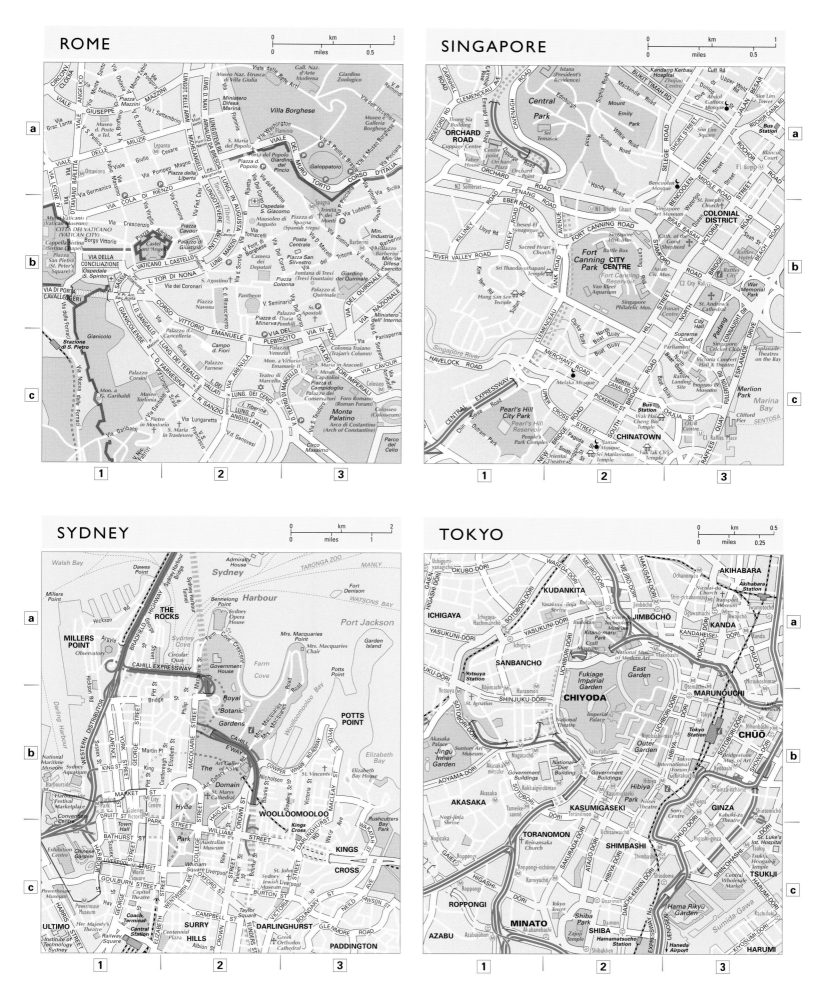

ROME

SINGAPORE

SYDNEY

TOKYO

VIII WORLD CITIES: DISTANCES

The table shows air distances in kilometres and miles between 24 major cities. Known as 'great circle' distances, these measure the shortest routes between the cities, which are used by aircraft wherever possible. The maps show the world centred on six cities, and illustrate, for example, why direct flights from Japan to North America and Europe are across the Arctic regions. The maps have been constructed on an Azimuthal Equidistant projection, on which all distances measured through the centre point are true to scale. The red lines are drawn at 5,000, 10,000 and 15,000 km from the central city.

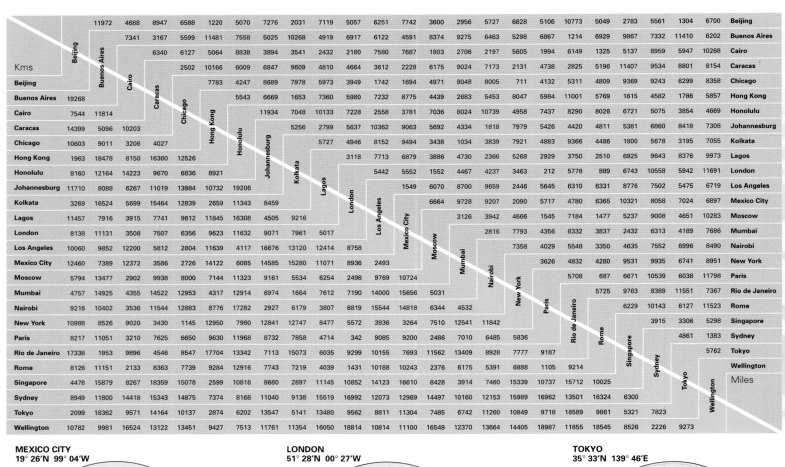

Distances along the diagonal are city names. Values above the diagonal are in Kms; values below the diagonal are in Miles.

	Beijing	Buenos Aires	Cairo	Caracas	Chicago	Hong Kong	Honolulu	Johannesburg	Kolkata	Lagos	London	Los Angeles	Mexico City	Moscow	Mumbai	Nairobi	New York	Paris	Rio de Janeiro	Rome	Singapore	Sydney	Tokyo	Wellington
Beijing	*Beijing*	11972	4688	8947	6588	1220	5070	7276	2031	7119	5057	6251	7742	3600	2956	5727	6828	5106	10773	5049	2783	5561	1304	6700
Buenos Aires	19268	*Buenos Aires*	7341	3167	5599	11481	7558	5025	10268	4919	6917	6122	4591	8374	9275	6463	5298	6867	1214	6929	9867	7332	11410	6202
Cairo	7544	11814	*Cairo*	6340	6127	5064	8838	3894	3541	2432	2180	7580	7687	1803	2706	2197	5605	1994	6149	1325	5137	8959	5947	10268
Caracas	14399	5096	10203	*Caracas*	2502	10166	6009	6847	9609	4810	4664	3612	2228	6175	9024	7173	2131	4738	2825	5196	11407	9534	8801	8154
Chicago	10603	9011	3206	4027	*Chicago*	7783	4247	8689	7978	5973	3949	1742	1694	4971	8048	8005	711	4132	5311	4809	9369	9243	6299	8358
Hong Kong	1963	18478	8150	16360	12526	*Hong Kong*	5543	6669	1653	7360	5980	7232	8775	4439	2683	5453	8047	5984	11001	5769	1615	4582	1786	5857
Honolulu	8160	12164	14223	9670	6836	8921	*Honolulu*	11934	7048	10133	7228	2558	3781	7036	8024	10739	4958	7437	8290	8026	6721	5075	3854	4669
Johannesburg	11710	8088	6267	11019	13984	10732	19206	*Johannesburg*	5256	2799	5637	10362	9063	5692	4334	1818	7979	5426	4420	4811	5381	6860	8418	7308
Kolkata	3269	16524	5699	15464	12839	2659	11343	8459	*Kolkata*	5727	4946	8152	9494	3438	1034	3839	7921	4883	9366	4486	1800	5678	3195	7055
Lagos	11457	7916	3915	7741	9612	11845	16308	4505	9216	*Lagos*	3118	7713	6879	3886	4730	2366	5268	2929	3750	2510	6925	9643	8376	9973
London	8138	11131	3508	7507	6356	9623	11632	9071	7961	5017	*London*	5442	5552	1552	4467	4237	3463	212	5778	889	6743	10558	5942	11691
Los Angeles	10060	9852	12200	5812	2804	11639	4117	16676	13120	12414	8758	*Los Angeles*	1549	6070	8700	9659	2446	5645	6310	6331	8776	7502	5475	6719
Mexico City	12460	7389	12372	3586	2726	14122	6085	14585	15280	11071	8936	2493	*Mexico City*	6664	9728	9207	2090	5717	4780	6365	10321	8058	7024	6897
Moscow	5794	13477	2902	9938	8000	7144	11323	9161	5534	6254	2498	9769	10724	*Moscow*	3126	3942	4666	1545	7184	1477	5237	9008	4651	10283
Mumbai	4757	14925	4355	14522	12953	4317	12914	6974	1664	7612	7190	14000	15656	5031	*Mumbai*	2816	7793	4356	8332	3837	2432	6313	4189	7686
Nairobi	9216	10402	3536	11544	12883	8776	17282	2927	6179	3807	6819	15544	14818	6344	4532	*Nairobi*	7358	4029	5548	3350	4635	7552	6996	8490
New York	10988	8526	9020	3430	1145	12950	7980	12841	12747	8477	5572	3936	3264	7510	12541	11842	*New York*	3626	4832	4280	9531	9935	6741	8951
Paris	8217	11051	3210	7625	6650	9630	11968	8732	7858	4714	342	9085	9200	2486	7010	6485	5836	*Paris*	5708	687	6671	10539	6038	11798
Rio de Janeiro	17338	1953	9896	4546	8547	17704	13342	7113	15073	6035	9299	10155	7693	11562	13409	8928	7777	9187	*Rio de Janeiro*	5725	9763	8389	11551	7367
Rome	8126	11151	2133	8363	7739	9284	12916	7743	7219	4039	1431	10188	10243	2376	6175	5391	6888	1105	9214	*Rome*	6229	10143	6127	11523
Singapore	4478	15879	8267	18359	15078	2599	10816	8660	2897	11145	10852	14123	16610	8428	3914	7460	15339	10737	15712	10025	*Singapore*	3915	3306	5298
Sydney	8949	11800	14418	15343	14875	7374	8168	11040	9138	15519	16992	12073	12969	14497	10160	12153	15989	16962	13501	16324	6300	*Sydney*	4861	1383
Tokyo	2099	18362	9571	14164	10137	2874	6202	13547	5141	13480	9562	8811	11304	7485	6742	11260	10849	9718	18589	9861	5321	7823	*Tokyo*	5762
Wellington	10782	9981	16524	13122	13451	9427	7513	11761	11354	16050	18814	10814	11100	16549	12370	13664	14405	18987	11855	18545	8526	2226	9273	*Wellington*

MEXICO CITY
19° 26'N 99° 04'W

LONDON
51° 28'N 00° 27'W

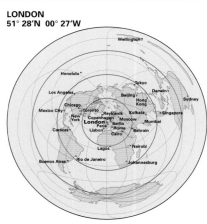

TOKYO
35° 33'N 139° 46'E

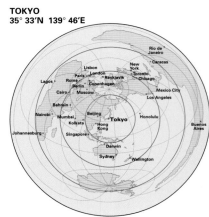

RIO DE JANEIRO
22° 50'S 43° 15'W

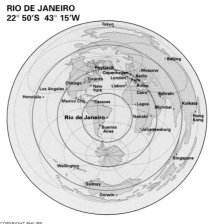

SINGAPORE
1° 21'N 103° 54'E

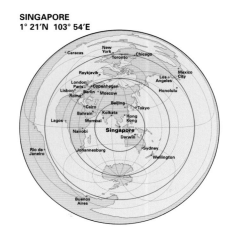

SYDNEY
33° 56'S 151° 10'E

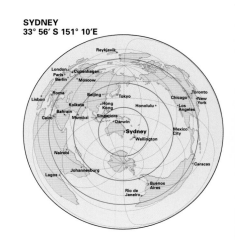

WORLD MAPS

SETTLEMENTS

■ PARIS   ■ Berne   ◉ Livorno   ◉ Brugge   ◎ Algeciras   ○ Frejus   ○ Oberammergau   ○ Thira

Settlement symbols and type styles vary according to the scale of each map and indicate the importance
of towns on the map rather than specific population figures. Capital cities have red infills.

ADMINISTRATION

International boundaries

International boundaries
(undefined or disputed)

Internal boundaries

National park boundaries

International boundaries show the *de facto* situation where there are rival claims to territory

COMMUNICATIONS

Principal roads

Principal railways

Railway tunnels

Road tunnels

Railways
under construction

Principal canals

Passes

Airfields

PHYSICAL FEATURES

Perennial streams

Intermittent lakes

▲ 8848 Elevations in metres

Intermittent streams

Swamps and marshes

▼ 8500 Sea depths in metres

Perennial lakes

Permanent ice
and glaciers

1134 Height of lake surface
above sea level in metres

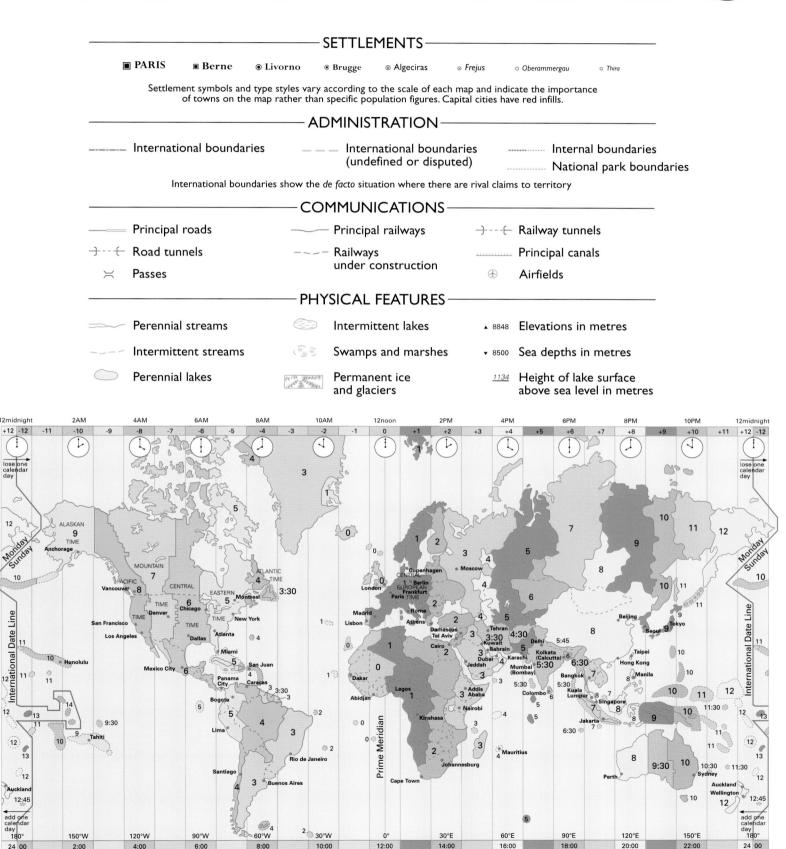

TIME ZONES

Zones using UT
(Greenwich Mean Time)

Zones slow of UT
(Greenwich Mean Time)

Zones fast of UT
(Greenwich Mean Time)

Half-hour zones

10 Hours behind or ahead of UT
(Co-ordinated Universal Time)

International boundaries

10PM Actual solar time
when the time at
Greenwich is
12:00 (noon)

Note: Certain time zones are
affected by the incidence of
'Summer Time' in countries
where it is adopted.

Time zone
boundaries

International
Date Line

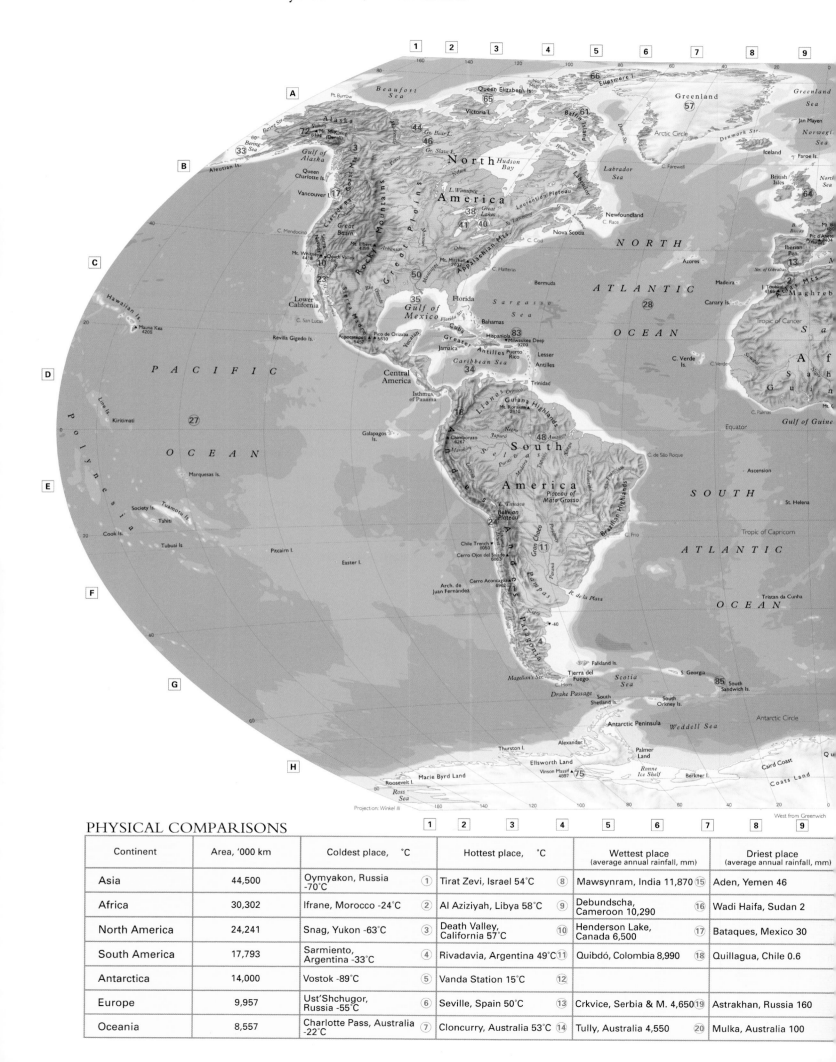

PHYSICAL COMPARISONS

Continent	Area, '000 km	Coldest place, °C		Hottest place, °C		Wettest place (average annual rainfall, mm)		Driest place (average annual rainfall, mm)
Asia	44,500	Oymyakon, Russia -70°C	①	Tirat Zevi, Israel 54°C	⑧	Mawsynram, India 11,870	⑮	Aden, Yemen 46
Africa	30,302	Ifrane, Morocco -24°C	②	Al Aziziyah, Libya 58°C	⑨	Debundscha, Cameroon 10,290	⑯	Wadi Haifa, Sudan 2
North America	24,241	Snag, Yukon -63°C	③	Death Valley, California 57°C	⑩	Henderson Lake, Canada 6,500	⑰	Bataques, Mexico 30
South America	17,793	Sarmiento, Argentina -33°C	④	Rivadavia, Argentina 49°C	⑪	Quibdó, Colombia 8,990	⑱	Quillagua, Chile 0.6
Antarctica	14,000	Vostok -89°C	⑤	Vanda Station 15°C	⑫			
Europe	9,957	Ust'Shchugor, Russia -55°C	⑥	Seville, Spain 50°C	⑬	Crkvice, Serbia & M. 4,650	⑲	Astrakhan, Russia 160
Oceania	8,557	Charlotte Pass, Australia -22°C	⑦	Cloncurry, Australia 53°C	⑭	Tully, Australia 4,550	⑳	Mulka, Australia 100

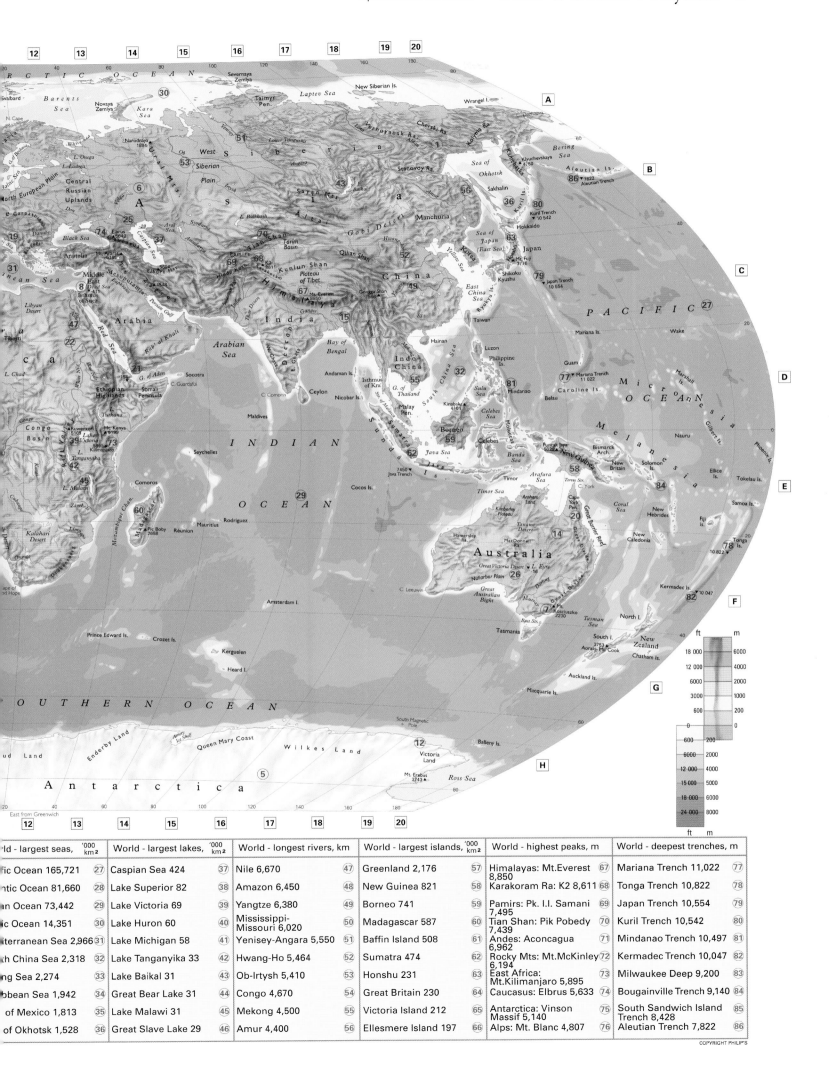

East from Greenwich

World – largest seas, '000 km²		World – largest lakes, '000 km²		World – longest rivers, km		World – largest islands, '000 km²		World – highest peaks, m		World – deepest trenches, m	
fic Ocean 165,721	27	Caspian Sea 424	37	Nile 6,670	47	Greenland 2,176	57	Himalayas: Mt.Everest 8,850	67	Mariana Trench 11,022	77
ntic Ocean 81,660	28	Lake Superior 82	38	Amazon 6,450	48	New Guinea 821	58	Karakoram Ra: K2 8,611	68	Tonga Trench 10,822	78
n Ocean 73,442	29	Lake Victoria 69	39	Yangtze 6,380	49	Borneo 741	59	Pamirs: Pk. I.I. Samani 7,495	69	Japan Trench 10,554	79
ic Ocean 14,351	30	Lake Huron 60	40	Mississippi-Missouri 6,020	50	Madagascar 587	60	Tian Shan: Pik Pobedy 7,439	70	Kuril Trench 10,542	80
terranean Sea 2,966	31	Lake Michigan 58	41	Yenisey-Angara 5,550	51	Baffin Island 508	61	Andes: Aconcagua 6,962	71	Mindanao Trench 10,497	81
h China Sea 2,318	32	Lake Tanganyika 33	42	Hwang-Ho 5,464	52	Sumatra 474	62	Rocky Mts: Mt.McKinley 6,194	72	Kermadec Trench 10,047	82
ng Sea 2,274	33	Lake Baikal 31	43	Ob-Irtysh 5,410	53	Honshu 231	63	East Africa: Mt.Kilimanjaro 5,895	73	Milwaukee Deep 9,200	83
bbean Sea 1,942	34	Great Bear Lake 31	44	Congo 4,670	54	Great Britain 230	64	Caucasus: Elbrus 5,633	74	Bougainville Trench 9,140	84
of Mexico 1,813	35	Lake Malawi 31	45	Mekong 4,500	55	Victoria Island 212	65	Antarctica: Vinson Massif 5,140	75	South Sandwich Island Trench 8,428	85
of Okhotsk 1,528	36	Great Slave Lake 29	46	Amur 4,400	56	Ellesmere Island 197	66	Alps: Mt. Blanc 4,807	76	Aleutian Trench 7,822	86

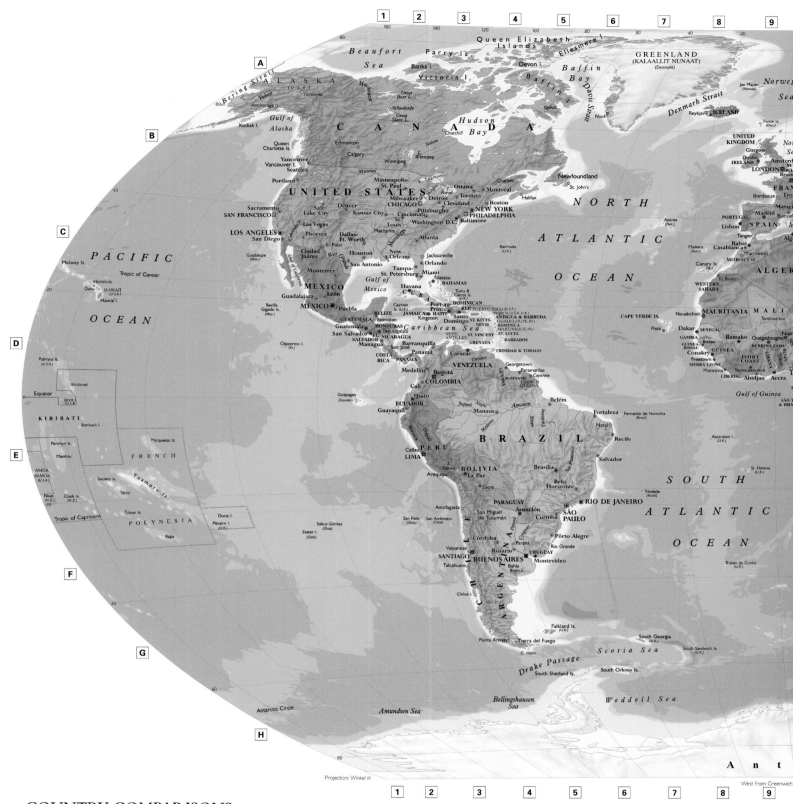

COUNTRY COMPARISONS

Country	Population in thousands 2005 estimate	Area in thous' km²	Country	Population in thousands 2005 estimate	Area in thous' km²	Country	Population in thousands 2005 estimate	Area in thous' km²	Country	Population in thousands 2005 estimate	Area in thous' km²	Country	Population in thousands 2005 estimate
China	1,306,300	9,597	Mexico	106,200	1,958	France	60,700	552	Argentina	39,500	2,780	Uganda	27,300
India	1,080,300	3,287	Philippines	87,900	300	United Kingdom	60,400	242	Poland	38,600	323	Uzbekistan	26,900
United States	295,700	9,629	Vietnam	83,500	332	Italy	58,100	301	Tanzania	36,800	945	Saudi Arabia	26,400
Indonesia	242,000	1,905	Germany	82,400	357	South Korea	48,600	99	Kenya	33,800	580	Iraq	26,100
Brazil	186,100	8,514	Egypt	77,500	1,001	Ukraine	47,000	604	Canada	32,800	9,971	Venezuela	25,400
Pakistan	162,400	796	Ethiopia	73,100	1,104	Burma (Myanmar)	47,000	677	Morocco	32,700	447	Malaysia	24,000
Bangladesh	144,300	144	Turkey	69,700	775	South Africa	44,300	1,221	Algeria	32,500	2,382	North Korea	22,900
Russia	143,400	17,075	Iran	68,000	1,648	Colombia	43,000	1,139	Afghanistan	29,900	652	Taiwan	22,900
Nigeria	128,800	924	Thailand	64,200	513	Spain	40,300	498	Peru	27,900	1,285	Romania	22,300
Japan	127,400	378	Congo, Dem. Rep.	60,800	2,345	Sudan	40,200	2,506	Nepal	27,700	147	Ghana	21,900

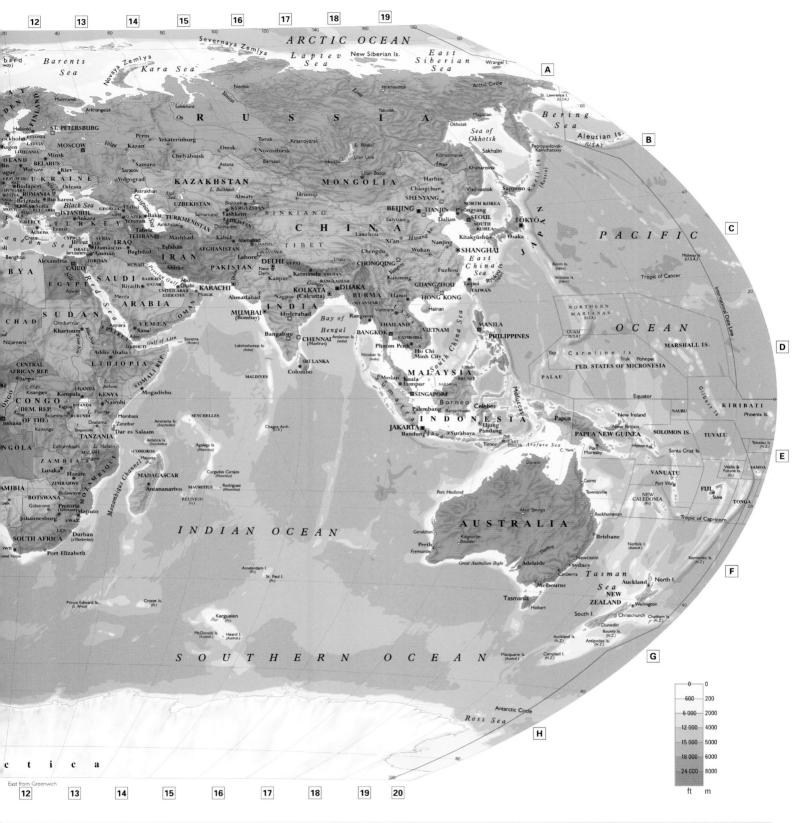

Country	Population in thousands 2005 estimate	Area in thous' km²	Country	Population in thousands 2005 estimate	Area in thous' km²	Country	Population in thousands 2005 estimate	Area in thous' km²	Country	Population in thousands 2005 estimate	Area in thous' km²	Country	Population in thousands 2005 estimate	Area in thous' km²
...n	20,700	528	Kazakhstan	15,200	2,725	Mali	11,400	1,240	Hungary	10,000	93	Azerbaijan	7,900	87
...alia	20,100	7,741	Cambodia	13,600	181	Cuba	11,300	111	Chad	9,700	1,284	Burundi	7,800	28
...nka	20,100	66	Burkina Faso	13,500	274	Zambia	11,300	753	Guinea	9,500	246	Benin	7,600	113
...mbique	19,400	802	Ecuador	13,400	284	Greece	10,700	132	Dominican Rep.	9,000	49	Switzerland	7,500	41
	18,400	185	Malawi	12,700	118	Portugal	10,600	89	Sweden	9,000	450	Bulgaria	7,500	111
...gascar	18,000	587	Niger	12,200	1,267	Belgium	10,400	31	Bolivia	8,900	1,099	Honduras	7,200	112
...Coast	17,300	322	Zimbabwe	12,200	394	Belarus	10,300	208	Somalia	8,600	638	Tajikistan	7,200	143
...roon	17,000	475	Guatemala	12,000	109	Czech Republic	10,200	79	Rwanda	8,400	26	Hong Kong (China)	6,900	1
...erlands	16,400	42	Angola	11,800	1,247	Tunisia	10,100	164	Austria	8,200	84	El Salvador	6,700	21
	16,000	757	Senegal	11,700	197	Serbia	10,100	88	Haiti	8,100	28	Paraguay	6,300	407

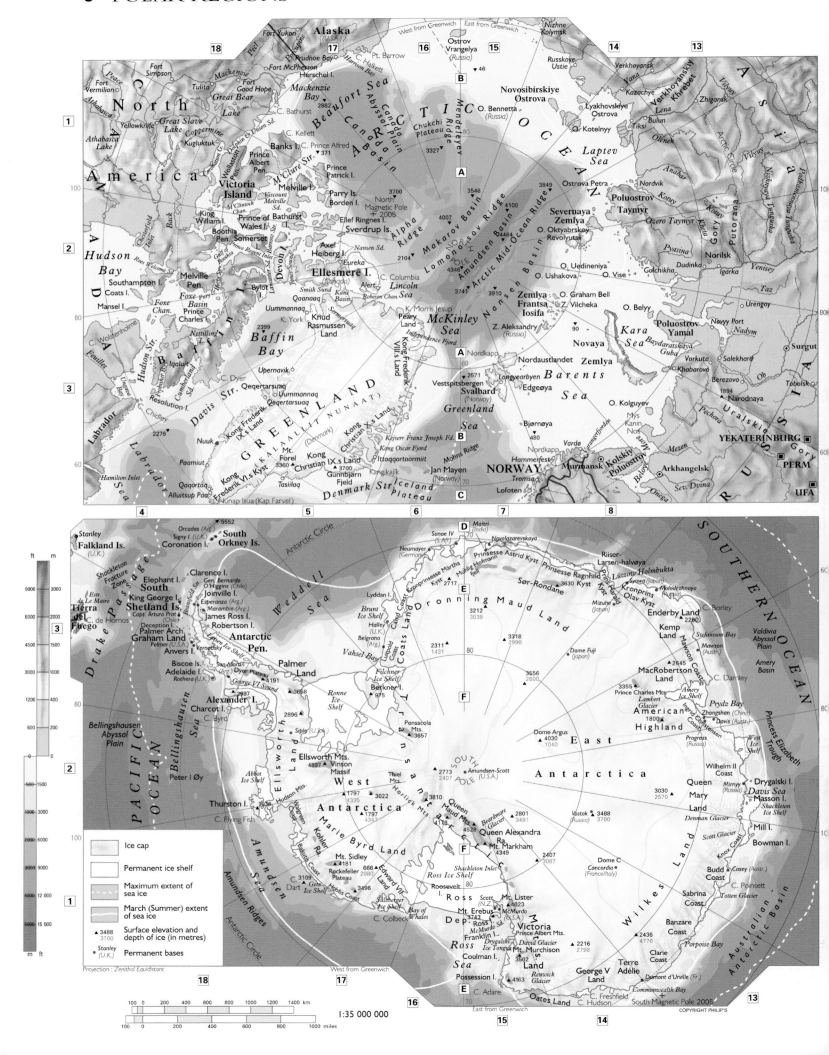

Projection : Zenithal Equidistant

1:35 000 000

COPYRIGHT PHILIP'S

Ice cap

Permanent ice shelf

Maximum extent of sea ice

March (Summer) extent of sea ice

▲ 3488 Surface elevation and
  3700   depth of ice (in metres)

● Stanley Permanent bases
  (U.K.)

1:10 000 000

50   0   100   200   300   400 km
50   0   50   100   150   200   250 miles

ICELAND

ICELAND
on same scale

Ísafjörður · Húnaflói · Siglufjörður · Húsavík
Breiðafjörður · Saudárkrókur · Akureyri · Seydisfjördur
Faxaflói · Hofsjökull · 1355 · 1765 · 2000 · Vatnajökull
Akranes · Langjökull · þjórsá
Reykjavik · Keflavik
Myrdalsjökull · Öræfajökull
1450 · 2119

NORWEGIAN SEA

BARENTS SEA

Nordkapp · Søroya · Hammerfest · Varanger-halvøya · Vardø · Vodsø
Tromsø · Senja · Norvik · Halta · 1328 · Varangerfjorden
Vesterålen · Inarijärvi · Inari · Rybachiy Poluostrov · Pechenga
Lofoten · Lappland · Zapolyarnyy Port Vladimir · Polyarny · Kolskiy Zaliv
Vestfjorden · Torneträsk · 2117 · Porttipahtan · Lokkan · tekojärvi · Severomorsk · Murmansk
Bodø · Kebnekaise · Kiruna · Torne älv · tekojärvi · Kola · Gremikha
Mo i Rana · 1913 · Gällivare · Kemijärvi · Rovaniemi · Monchegorsk · Kovdor · Ozero · 1191 · Kirovsk · Kolskiy
Vega · Horna-van · Storavan · Boden · Haparanda · Tornio · Kemijoki · Imandse · Apatity · Poluostrov · Ponoy
Mosjøen · Storuman · Skellefte älv · Piteå · Kemi · Kuusamo · Kandalaksha · Alakurtti · Kandalakshskiy · Zaliv · Ponoy
Vilhelmina · Umeå älv · Luleå · Hailuoto · Oulu · Pya-ozero · Kestenga · Umba · Kuzomen · Beloye More
Storman · Oujujärvi · Raahe · Top-ozero · Soloveskiye · Kem · Ostrova · Dvinskaya · (White Sea) · Guba · Arkhangelsk
Ostersund · Örnsköldsvik · Umeå · Vännäs · Kokkola · Iisalmi · Kem · Belomorsk · Severodvinsk
Bräcke · Härnösand · Vaasa · Seinäjoki · Pielinen · Kuopio · Nadvoitsy · Onega
Ange · Sundsvall · Jyväskylä · Joensuu · Segezha · Medvezhyegorsk · Povenets · Konevo
Hudiksvall · Pori · Rauma · Hämeenlinna · Kouvola · Savonlinna · Imatra · Suoyarvi · Kondopoga · Pudozh · Kargopol
Söderhamn · Mora · Falun · Uusikaupunki · Lahti · Vyborg · Sortavala · Petrozavodsk · Vytegra
Gävle · Turku · Vantaa · Priozersk · Olonets · Lodeinoye · Voznesenye
Avesta · Sala · Espoo · Helsinki · Kronstadt · Kolpino · Ladozhskoye · Pole · Belozersk
Hamar · Mjøsa · Uppsala · Åland · Hanko · Gulf of Finland · SANKT PETERBURG · Tikhvin · Cherepovets
Lillehammer · Västerås · STOCKHOLM · Hiiumaa · Tallinn · Narva · Novaya Ladoga
Oslo · Drammen · Eskilstuna · (Dago) · Kohtla-Järve · RUSSIA · Volkhov

DENMARK

Holstebro · Randers · Århus · Kattegat · Helsingborg · Malmö
Esbjerg · Odense · Svendborg · KØBENHAVN (Copenhagen) · Lund
Flensburg · Fyn · Sjælland · Bornholm

GERMANY · **POLAND** · **CZECH REP.**

1:2 000 000

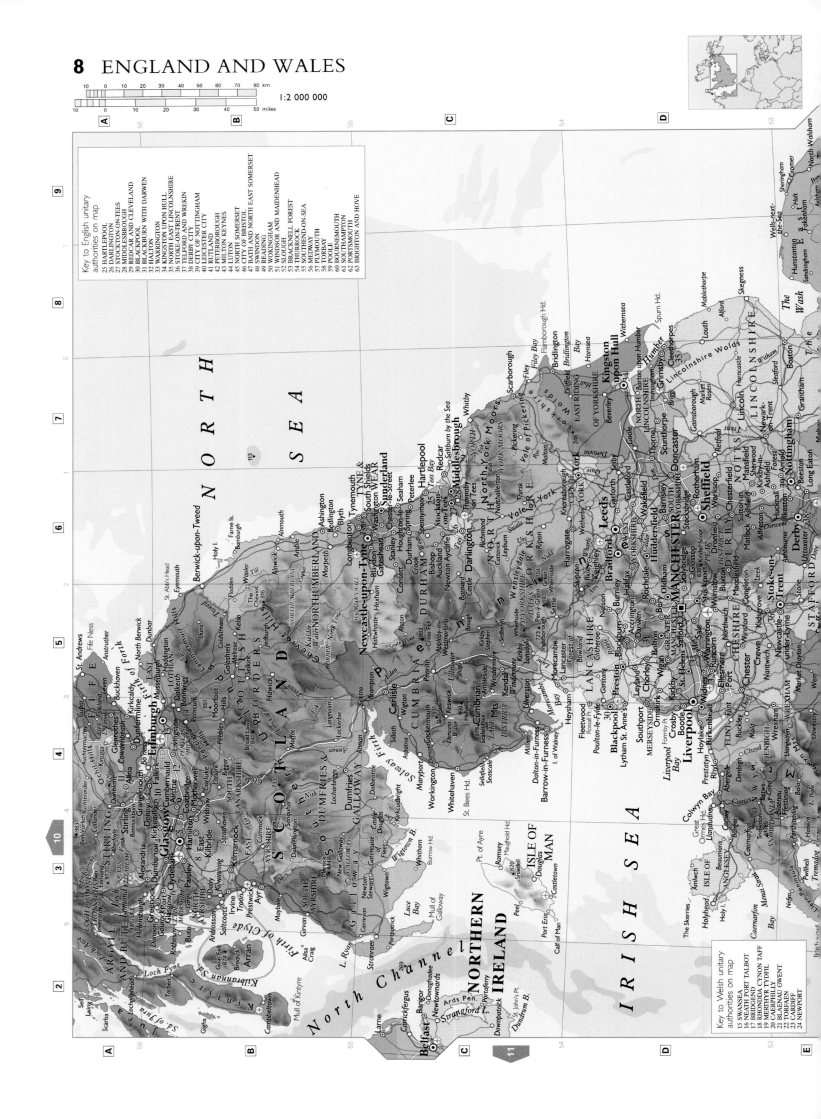

Key to English unitary
authorities on map
25 HARTLEPOOL
26 DARLINGTON
27 STOCKTON-ON-TEES
28 MIDDLESBROUGH
29 REDCAR AND CLEVELAND
30 BLACKPOOL
31 BLACKBURN WITH DARWEN
32 HALTON
33 WARRINGTON
34 KINGSTON UPON HULL
35 NORTH EAST LINCOLNSHIRE
36 STOKE-ON-TRENT
37 TELFORD AND WREKIN
38 DERBY CITY
39 CITY OF NOTTINGHAM
40 LEICESTER CITY
41 RUTLAND
42 PETERBOROUGH
43 MILTON KEYNES
44 LUTON
45 NORTH SOMERSET
46 CITY OF BRISTOL
47 BATH AND NORTH EAST SOMERSET
48 SWINDON
49 READING
50 WOKINGHAM
51 WINDSOR AND MAIDENHEAD
52 SLOUGH
53 BRACKNELL FOREST
54 THURROCK
55 SOUTHEND-ON-SEA
56 MEDWAY
57 PLYMOUTH
58 TORBAY
59 POOLE
60 BOURNEMOUTH
61 SOUTHAMPTON
62 PORTSMOUTH
63 BRIGHTON AND HOVE

Key to Welsh unitary
authorities on map
15 SWANSEA
16 NEATH PORT TALBOT
17 BRIDGEND
18 RHONDDA CYNON TAFF
19 MERTHYR TYDFIL
20 CAERPHILLY
21 BLAENAU GWENT
22 TORFAEN
23 CARDIFF
24 NEWPORT

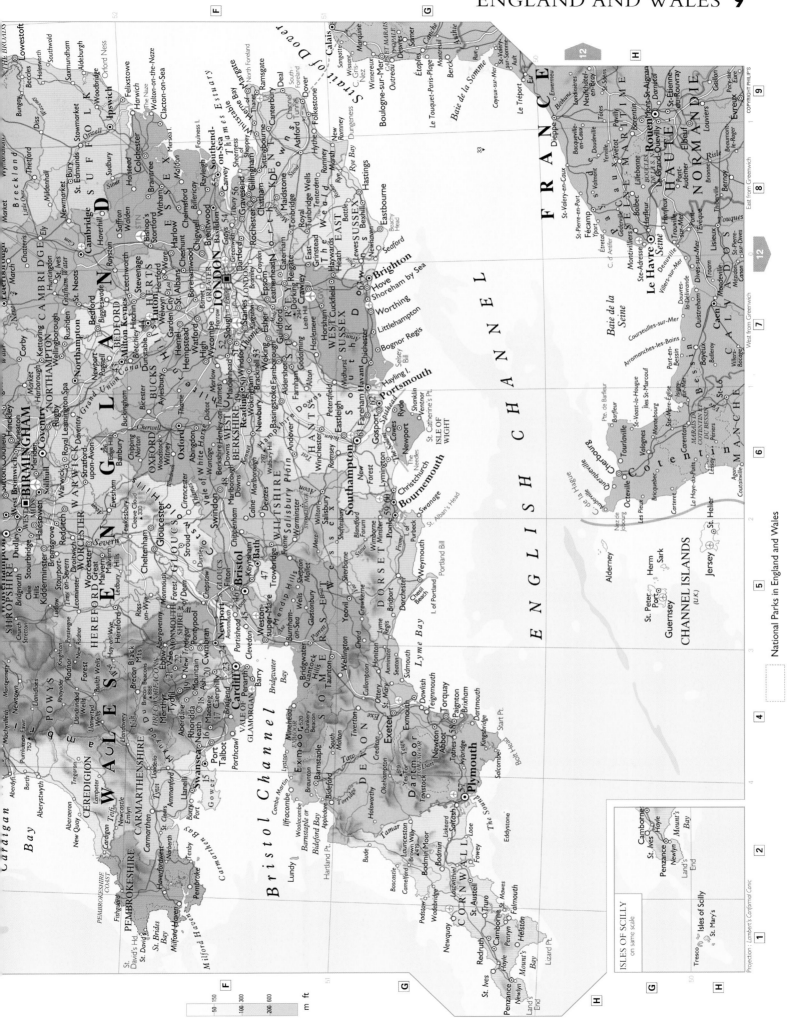

National Parks in England and Wales

ISLES OF SCILLY
on same scale

Projection: Lambert's Conformal Conic

COPYRIGHT PHILIP'S

1:2 000 000

Key to Scottish unitary authorities on map

1 CITY OF ABERDEEN
2 DUNDEE CITY
3 WEST DUNBARTONSHIRE
4 EAST DUNBARTONSHIRE
5 CITY OF GLASGOW
6 INVERCLYDE
7 RENFREWSHIRE
8 EAST RENFREWSHIRE
9 NORTH LANARKSHIRE
10 FALKIRK
11 CLACKMANNANSHIRE
12 WEST LOTHIAN
13 CITY OF EDINBURGH
14 MIDLOTHIAN

ORKNEY IS.
on same scale

SHETLAND IS.
on same scale

SCOTLAND

NORTH SEA

ATLANTIC OCEAN

WESTERN ISLES

NORTHERN IRELAND

ENGLAND

Glasgow
Edinburgh
Aberdeen
Dundee
Inverness
Perth
Stirling
Dumfries
Ayr
Newcastle-upon-Tyne
Belfast

Projection: Lambert's Conformal Conic

COPYRIGHT PHILIP'S

National Parks and Forest Parks in Scotland

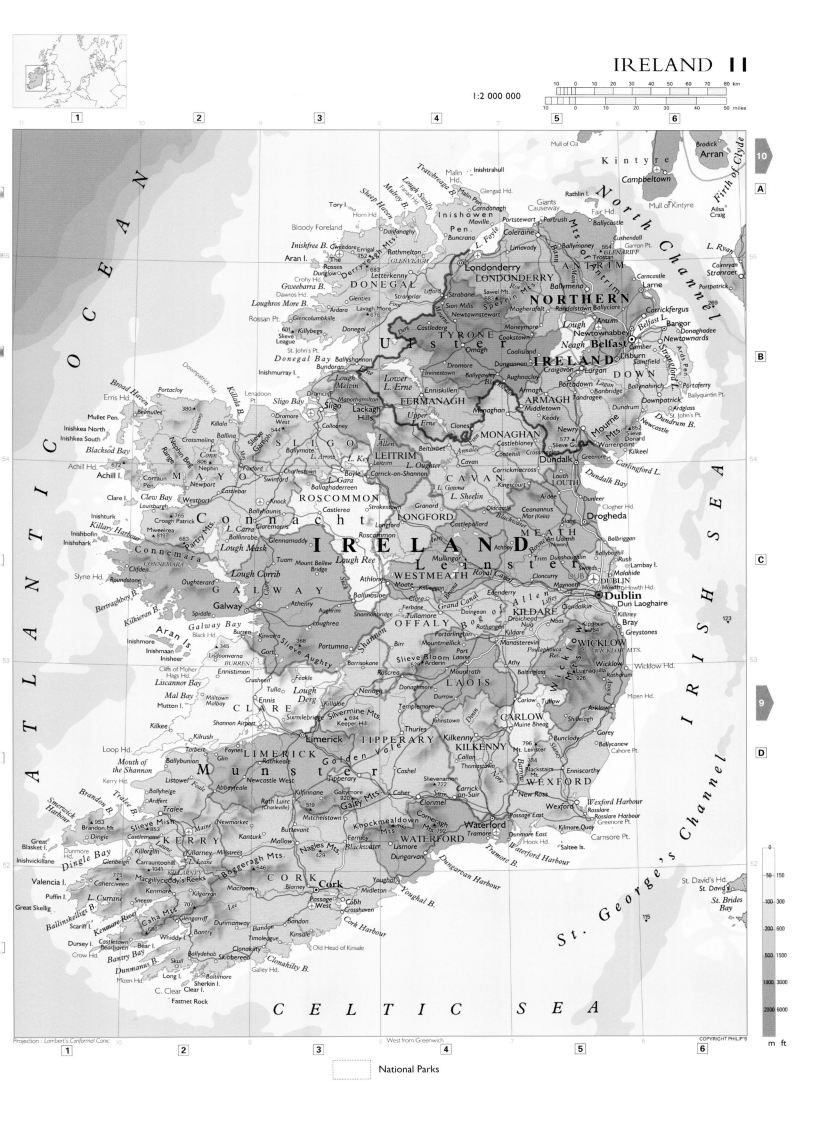

National Parks

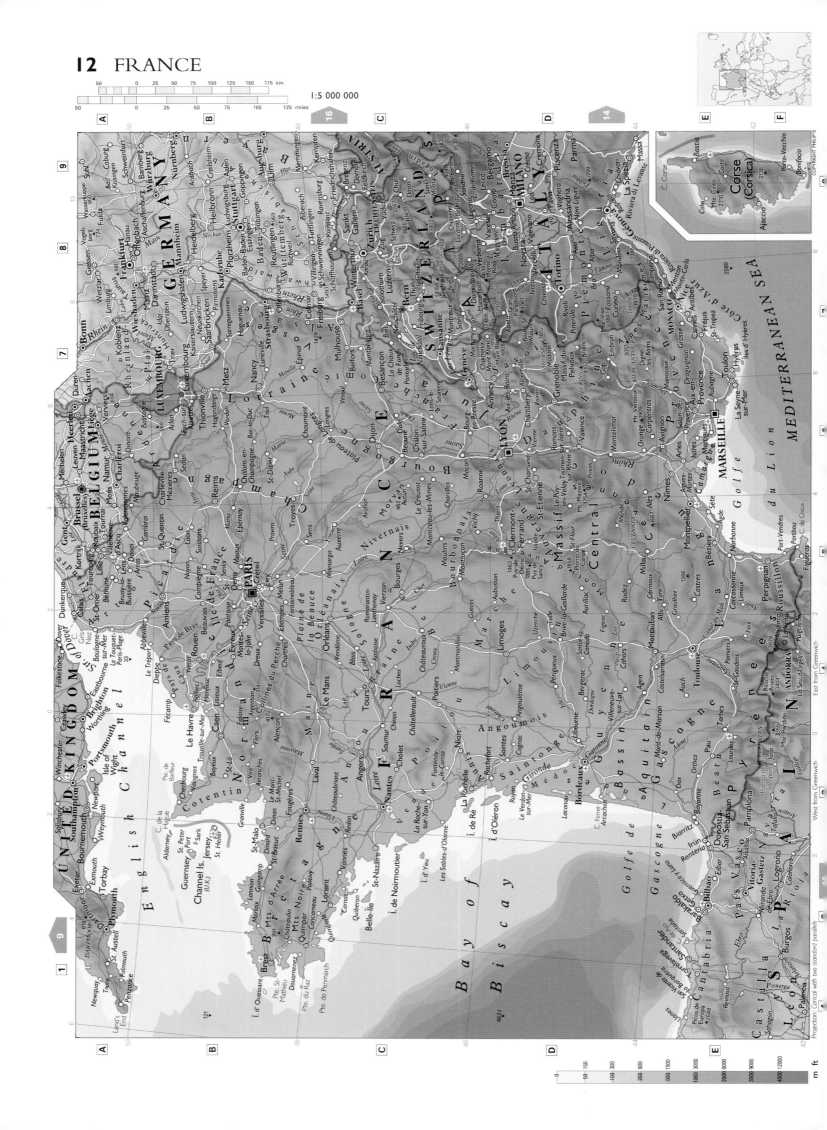

Corse
(Corsica)

1:5 000 000

MEDITERRANEAN SEA

COPYRIGHT PHILIP'S

Projection: Conical with two standard parallels

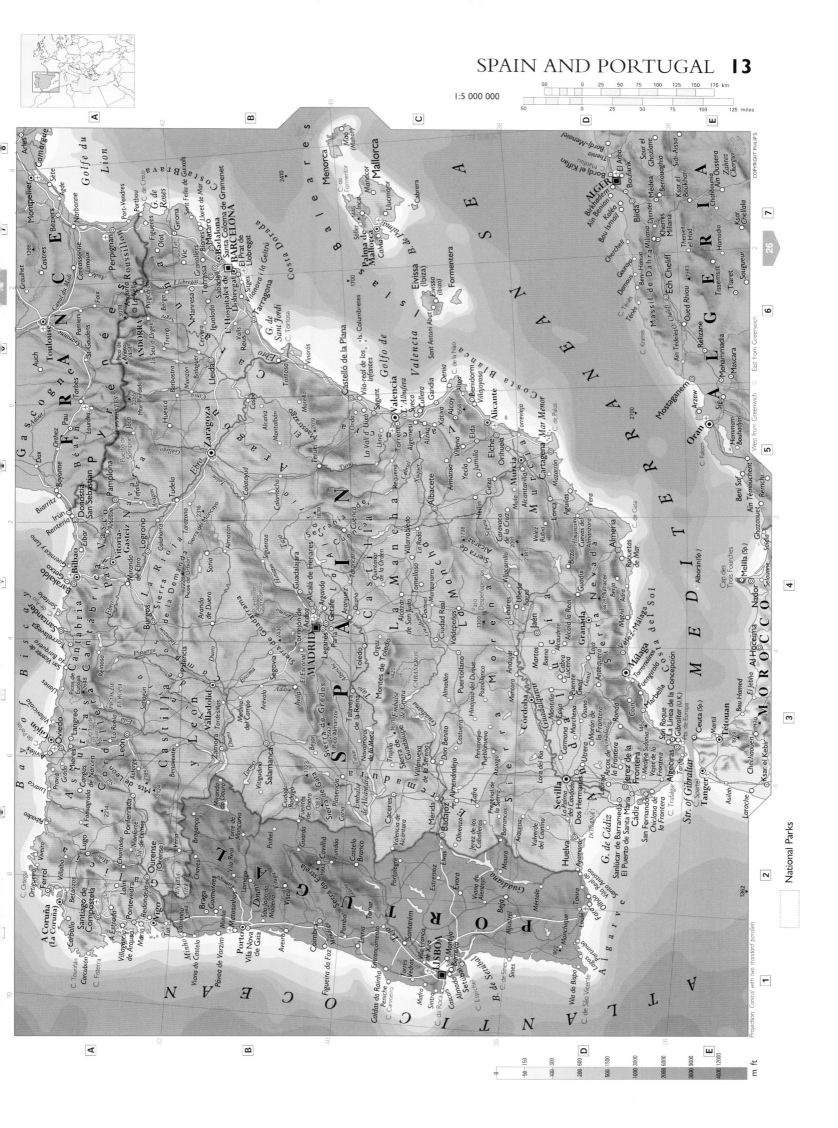

1:5 000 000

National Parks

National Parks

COPYRIGHT PHILIP'S

1:5 000 000

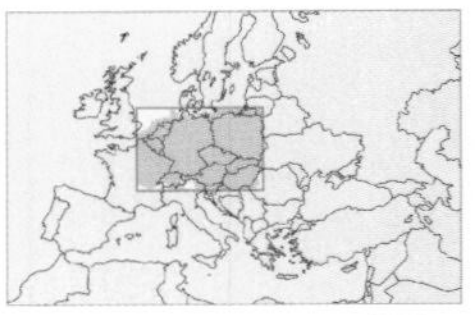

50 0 25 50 75 100 125 150 175 km
50 0 25 50 75 100 125 miles

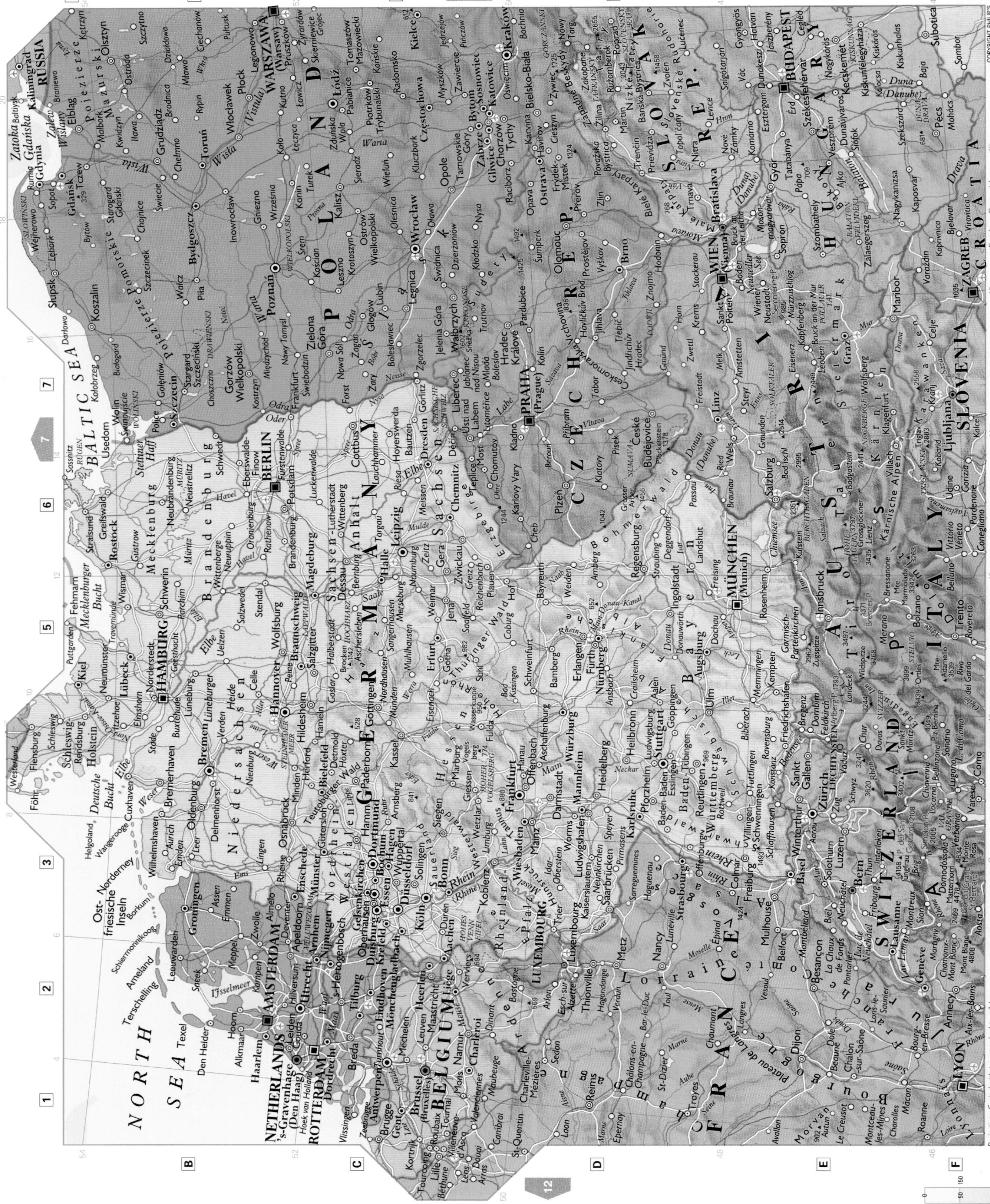

RUSSIA

POLAND

WARSZAWA (Warsaw)

BALTIC SEA

NORTH SEA

NETHERLANDS

BERLIN

GERMANY

HAMBURG

AMSTERDAM

ROTTERDAM

BELGIUM

LUXEMBOURG

FRANCE

SWITZERLAND

CZECH REP.

PRAHA (Prague)

SLOVAK REP.

WIEN

BRATISLAVA

AUSTRIA

HUNGARY

BUDAPEST

SLOVENIA

CROATIA

ZAGREB

ITALY

MÜNCHEN (Munich)

Projection: Conical with two standard parallels

COPYRIGHT PHILIP'S

East from Greenwich

1:10 000 000

50 0 100 200 300 400 km
50 0 50 100 150 200 250 miles

East from Greenwich

Projection: Conic with two standard parallels

CASPIAN SEA

BLACK SEA

MEDITERRANEAN SEA

AEGEAN SEA

Sea of Azov

Countries and regions

RUSSIA · KALMYKIA · DAGESTAN · CHECHENIA · AZERBAIJAN · ARMENIA · GEORGIA · ABKHAZIA · NORTH OSSETIA · SOUTH OSSETIA · KARACHEVO · KABARDINO-BALKARIYA · CHERKESSIA · ADYGEA · INGUSHETIA

UKRAINE · MOLDOVA · ROMANIA · HUNGARY · SERBIA · MONTENEGRO · ALBANIA · MACEDONIA · BULGARIA · GREECE · CRIMEA

TURKEY · CYPRUS · SYRIA · LEBANON · ISRAEL · WEST BANK · GAZA STRIP · JORDAN · IRAQ · IRAN · SAUDI ARABIA · EGYPT · LIBYA

Caucasus Mountains · Zagros Kurdistan · Anadolu · Kuzey Anadolu Dağ · Toros Dağları · Mesopotamia · Bādiyat ash Shām · Stara Planina · Rhodopi Planina · Pindos Oros · Dodekanisos · Cyclades · Ionioi Nisoi

Cities and towns

Astrakhan · Elista · Volgodonsk · Rostov · Taganrog · Donetsk · Makiivka · Horlivka · Luhansk · Mariupol · Berdyansk · Melitopol · Zaporizhzhya · Dnipropetrovsk · Mykolaiv · Kherson · Odesa · Chişinău · Tiraspol · Bălţi · Iaşi · Bacău · Galaţi · Brăila · Buzău · Ploieşti · BUCUREŞTI (Bucharest) · Craiova · Piteşti · Braşov · Sibiu · Cluj-Napoca · Timişoara · Arad · Oradea · Satu Mare · Botoşani

BEOGRAD (Belgrade) · Novi Sad · Subotica · Szeged · Niš · Kragujevac · Kruševac · Priština · Skopje · Bitola · SOFIA · Plovdiv · Burgas · Varna · Ruse · Pleven · Veliko Tŭrnovo · Dobrich · Silistra · Sliven · Haskovo · Edirne · Tiranë · Durrës · Vlorë · Shkodër · Podgorica

Thessaloníki · Lárisa · Vólos · Pátra · ATHINA (Athens) · Pireás · Kalamáta · Spárti · Trípoli · Kérkyra · Irákleio · Chaniá

İSTANBUL · Tekirdağ · BURSA · İzmit (Kocaeli) · Adapazarı · Eskişehir · ANKARA · Zonguldak · Ereğli · Bolu · Çankırı · Kastamonu · Sinop · Samsun · Ordu · Giresun · Trabzon · Rize · Artvin · Batumi · Sukhumi · Sochi · Tuapse · Novorossiysk · Krasnodar · Maykop · Armavir · Stavropol · Cherkessk · Pyatigorsk · Nalchik · Vladikavkaz · Grozny · Makhachkala · Derbent · BAKI (Baku) · Sumqayıt · Gäncä · TBILISI · Kutaisi · Poti · YEREVAN · Gyumri · Vanadzor · Kars · Erzurum · Ağrı · Van · Bitlis · Muş · Tatvan · Malatya · Elâzığ · Diyarbakır · Mardin · Şanlıurfa · Gaziantep · Kahramanmaraş · ADANA · İskenderun · Hatay (Antalya) · Mersin (İçel) · Tarsus · Osmaniye · Karaman · Konya · Niğde · Kayseri · Sivas · Tokat · Amasya · Çorum · Yozgat · Kırşehir · Kırıkkale · Aksaray · Nevşehir · Beyşehir · Isparta · Burdur · Denizli · Aydın · İZMIR (Smyrna) · Manisa · Akhisar · Balıkesir · Çanakkale · Kütahya · Afyon · Uşak · Antalya · Alanya · Fethiye · Marmaris · Bodrum

HALAB (Aleppo) · Hamäh · Ḥimş · DIMASHQ (Damascus) · Tarābulus · BAYRÜT (Beirut) · Ẕaḥlah · Şaydā · Ḥefa · TEL AVIV-YAFO · Jerusalem · GAZA · Nicosia · Limassol · Larnaca · Famagusta

AL MAWŞIL (Mosul) · Arbil · Kirkük · Baʿqūbah · BAGHDAD · An-Najaf · An-Nāşirīyah · Al ʿAmārah · Al Ḥillah · Ar-Ramādī · Al Ḥasakah · Al Qāmishlī · Ar Raqqah · Dayr az Zawr

TABRĪZ · Orūmīyeh (Urmia) · Zanjān · Sanandaj · Kermānshāh (Bākhtarān) · Ardabīl · Maräghen

EL QAHIRA (Cairo) · EL GIZA · EL ISKANDARĪYA (Alexandria) · Dumyāt · El Mansûra · Tanta · Zagazig · Ismāʿilīya · Bûr Saʿîd · El Suweis (Suez) · Marsá Maţrûḥ · Tubruq · Darnah

Physical features / water

Volga · Kuma · Don · Dnieper · Dnister · Dunărea (Danube) · Sava · Tigris (Nahr Dijlah) · Euphrates (Nahr al Furāt) · Jordan · Dead Sea · Kriti (Crete) · Rhodes · Lesbos · Khíos · Samos · Naxos · Cyprus · Tuz Gölü · Van Gölü · Buhayrat al Asad

m ft
0 0
200 600
500 1500
1000 3000
2000 6000
4000 12 000

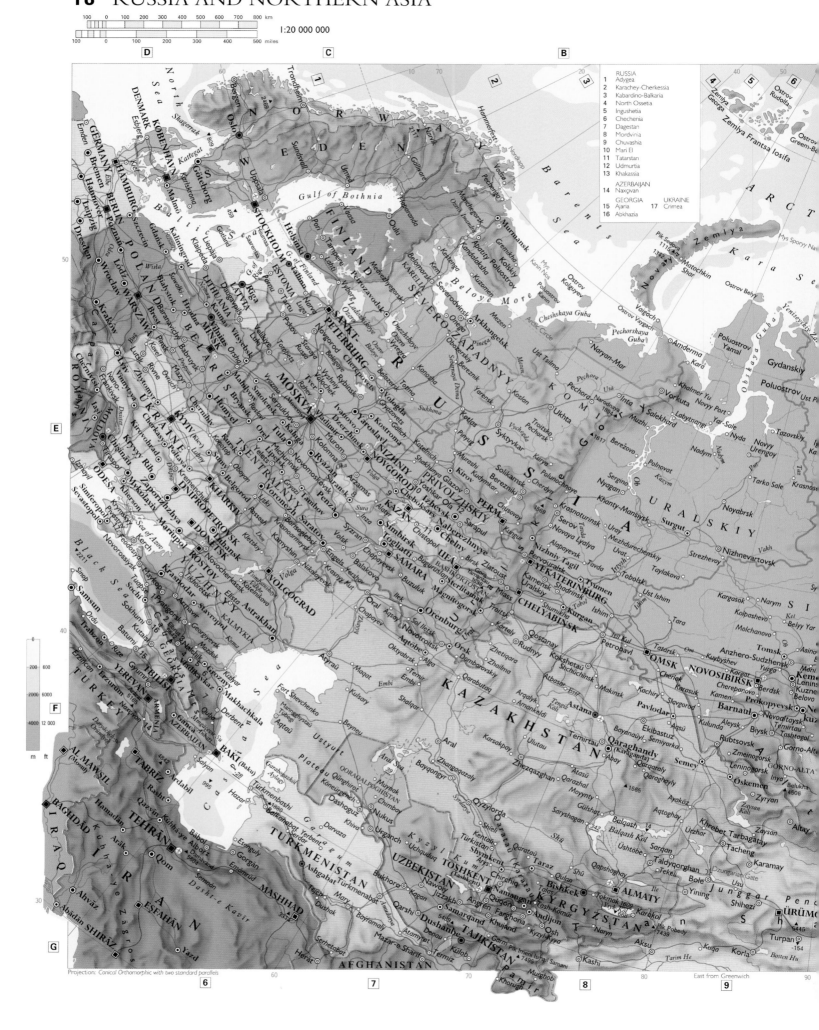

1:20 000 000

RUSSIA
1 Adygea
2 Karachey-Cherkessia
3 Kabardino-Balkaria
4 North Ossetia
5 Ingushetia
6 Chechenia
7 Dagestan
8 Mordvinia
9 Chuvashia
10 Mari El
11 Tatarstan
12 Udmurtia
13 Khakassia

AZERBAIJAN
14 Naxçıvan

GEORGIA
15 Ajaria
16 Abkhazia

UKRAINE
17 Crimea

Projection: Conical Orthomorphic with two standard parallels

East from Greenwich

1:15 000 000

Projection: Bonne

East from Greenwich

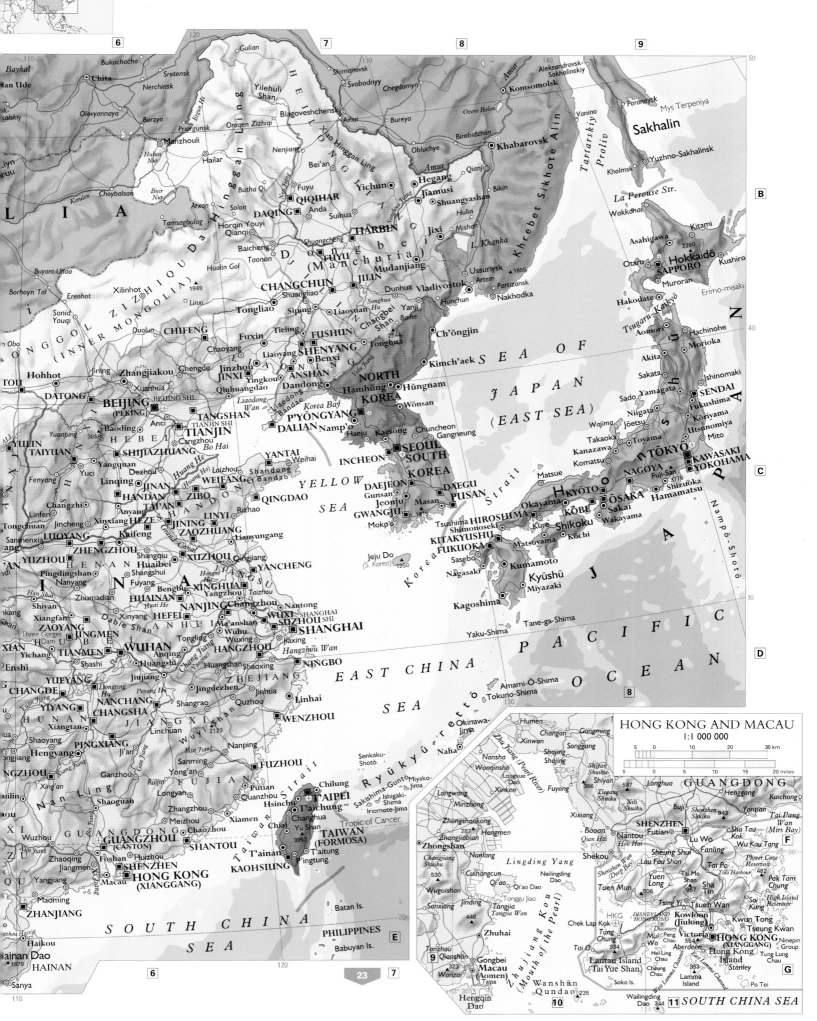

HONG KONG AND MACAU
1:1 000 000

1:6 400 000

50 0 25 50 75 100 125 150 175 km
50 0 25 50 75 100 125 miles

CHINA

RUSSIA

Jixi
Linkou
Novokachalinsk
Kamen-Rybolov
Spassk Dalniy
Suifenhe
Lipovcy
Manzovka
Ussuriysk
Artem
Trudovoye
Vladivostok
Hunchun
Slavyanka
Zaliv Petra Velikogo
Nakhodka
Khasan
Najin
Chŏngjin

Lesozavodsk
Kirovskiy
Ariadnoye
Gornyy
Yakovlevka
Arseney
Lazo
1855
Kavalerovo
Dalnegorsk
Plastun
Terney
Preobrazheniye
Margaritovo

Khrebet Sikhote Alin

NORTH KOREA

SOUTH KOREA
Yeongdeok
Pohang
ULSAN

Ulleungdo (S. Korea)
Liancourt Rocks (Dokdo, Takeshima)
Oki-Shotō (Japan)

SEA OF JAPAN (EAST SEA)

JAPAN

Korea Strait
Tsushima (Japan)
Iki
Katsumoto
Nōgata

FUKUOKA
Karatsu
Imari
Saga
Kurume
Ōmuta
Kumamoto
Nagasaki
Yatsushiro
Sasebo
Isahaya
Gotō-Rettō
Fukue-Shima
Hondo
Amakusa-Shotō
Ushibuka
Koshiki-Rettō
Minamata
Kurino
Sendai
Kagoshima
Makurazaki
Ibusuki
Sata-Misaki

Kyūshū
Kuju-San 1787
Bungotakada
Beppu
Ōita
Buzen
KITAKYŪSHU
Shimonoseki
Ube
Hōfu
Yamaguchi
Tokuyama
Iwakuni
Hagi
Masuda
Hamada
Ōda
Izumo
Matsue
Yonago
Dai-Sen
Tottori
Miyazaki
Miyakonojō
Nichinan
Kanoya
Nobeoka
Hyūga
Yawatahama
Uwajima
Nakamura
Sukumo
Ashizuri-Zaki
Ōzu
Fukuchiyama
Tsuyama
Miyoshi
Fuchū

Chūgoku-Sanchi

HIROSHIMA
Kure
Marugome
Imabari
Matsuyama
Ikeda
Kōchi
Nankoku
Mugi
Anan
Tokushima
Naruto
Takamatsu
Awaji-Shima

Shikoku
Shikoku-Sanchi
Tsurugi-San 1955
Tosa-Wan
Muroto
Muroto-Misaki

Okayama
Fukuyama
Himeji
Nishinomiya
KŌBE
Amagasaki
Higashiōsaka
ŌSAKA
Izumi-Sano
Wakayama
Gobō
Tanabe
Shingū
Kushimoto
Shio-no-Misaki

KYŌTO
Ōtsu
NAGOYA
Yokkaichi
Matsusaka
Kii-Sanchi
Owase
Daiō-Misaki

Biwa-Ko
Ichinomiya
Gifu
Ōgaki
Toyota
Okazaki
Toyohashi
Iwata
Hamamatsu
Shizuoka

Maizuru
Ayabe
Obama
Tsuruga
Takefu
Fukui
Komatsu
Kanazawa
Toyama
Takaoka
Himi
Nanao
Hakui
Wajima
Suzu-Misaki
Nagaoka
Sanjō
Niitsu
Niigata
Shibata

Toyama-Wan
Kusatsu
Takada
Iiyama
Nagano
Matsumoto
Takayama
Ina
Gero
Iida
Kōfu
Fuji
Numazu
Itō
Odawara
Yokosuka
Tateyama
Nojima-Zaki

TOKYO
KAWASAKI
YOKOHAMA
Kawaguchi
Funabashi
Chiba
Ichihara
Kumagaya
Kawagoe
Takasaki
Maebashi
Kiryū
Utsunomiya
Mito
Tsuchiura
Kitaibaraki
Hitachi
Iwaki
Kōriyama
Sukagawa
Shirakawa
Yaita
Tanakura
Abukuma
Fukushima
Aizuwakamatsu
Yamagata
Murakami
Nagai
Sanjō
Tsuruoka
Sakata
Honjō
Akita
Oga
Oga-Hantō
Noshiro
Kazuno
Ōdate
Hirosaki
Goshogawara
Kanagi
Aomori
Mutsu
Ohata
Hachinohe
Kuji
Iwaizumi
Miyako
Morioka
Hanamaki
Kamaishi
Mizusawa
Ichinoseki
Kesennuma
Furukawa
Ishinomaki
SENDAI
Sendai-Wan
Sōma
Haranomachi

Honshū

Ōu Sammyaku
Kitakami
Iwate-San 2041
Hayachine-San
Hanamaki
Chōkai-San 2230
Gas-San 1980
Higashiazuma-San 2024
Inawashiro
Bandai-San
Nikkō
Kantō-Sanchi
Kantō-Heiya

Sado
Ryōtsu
Aikawa
Akō
Shirane-San 3192
Asama
Ontake 3063
Komagatake
Hida Sammyaku
Hodaka-Dake 3190
Haku-San 2782
Ontake 3192
Kiso-Sammyaku
Akaishi-Sammyaku
Fuji-San 3776

Izu-Shotō
Ō-Shima
Nii-Jima
Miyake-Jima
Hachijō-Jima
Aoga-Shima

HOKKAIDŌ
Wakkanai
Rebun-Tō
Rishiri-Tō
Teshio
Embetsu
Haboro
Rumoi
Otaru
SAPPORO
Ebetsu
Iwanai
Suttsu
Setana
Yakumo
Okushiri-Tō
Esashi
Matsumae
Hakodate
Kaikyō
Tsugaru
Tsugaru-Kaikyō

Otoineppu
Ōmu
Mombetsu
Yūbetsu
Engaru
Kitami
Shibetsu
Nayoro
Takikawa
Asahigawa
Daisetsu-Zan 2290
Ishikari-Zan 2077
Akabira
Bibai
Iwamizawa
Ishikari-Wan
Atsuta
Chitose
Shikotu-Ko
Toya-Ko
Uchiura-Wan
Tomakomai
Muroran
Urakawa
Samani
Erimo-misaki
Obihiro
Furano-Sammyaku 2052
Hiroo
Kamui-Misaki

Esashi
Ōmu
Mombetsu
Abashiri-Wan
Abashiri
Shari
Kussharo-Ko
Rausu-Dake 1661
Nemuro
Shibecha
Akkeshi
Kushiro
Nakashibetsu
Poroshiri-Dake

Shiriya-Zaki
Esan-Misaki
Shirakami-Misaki
Henashi-Misaki
Mutsu-Wan

PACIFIC OCEAN

Nampō Shotō

8412
9076
9076

m ft
0
200 600
2000 6000
4000 12 000
6000 18 000
8000 24 000

Projection: Conical with two standard parallels   East from Greenwich

COPYRIGHT PHILIP'S

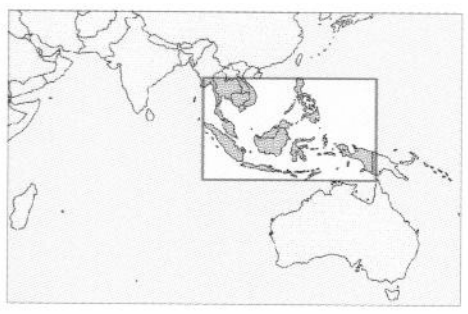

1:20 000 000

100 0 100 200 300 400 500 600 700 800 km
100 0 100 200 300 400 500 miles

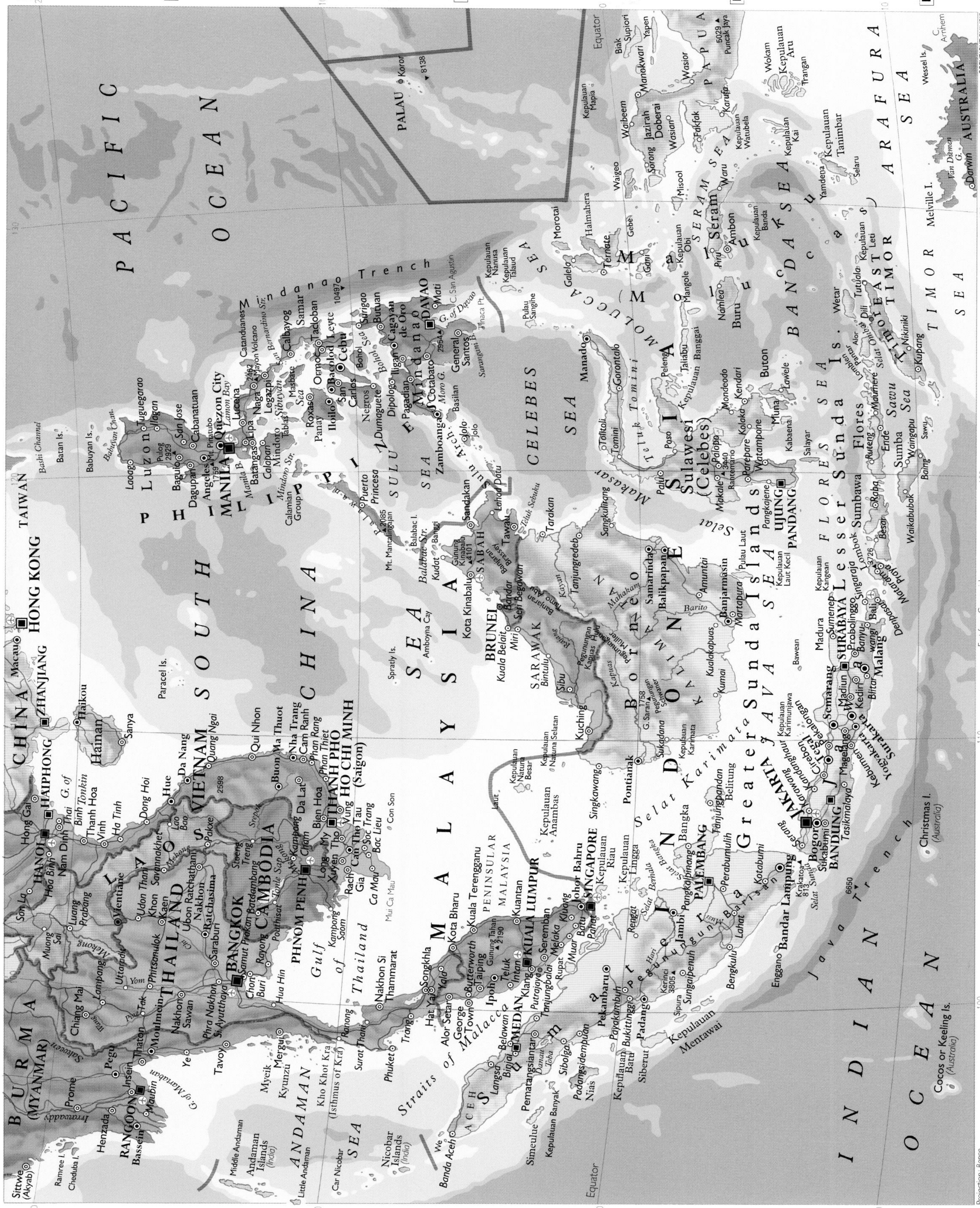

COPYRIGHT PHILIPS

East from Greenwich

Projection: Bonne

PACIFIC OCEAN

INDIAN OCEAN

SOUTH CHINA SEA

CHINA
BURMA (MYANMAR)
THAILAND
VIETNAM
LAOS
CAMBODIA
MALAYSIA
PHILIPPINES
INDONESIA
BORNEO
KALIMANTAN
PAPUA
AUSTRALIA
TAIWAN

TAIWAN HONG KONG Macau Zhanjiang Haikou Hainan Sanya

HANOI HAIPHONG Hong Gai Nam Dinh Thanh Hoa Vinh Ha Tinh Dong Hoi Hue Da Nang Quang Ngai Qui Nhon Buon Ma Thuot Nha Trang Da Lat Cam Ranh Phan Rang Phan Thiet Bien Hoa HO CHI MINH (Saigon) Vung Tau

VIENTIANE Luang Prabang Muong Sai Udon Thani Khon Kaen Nakhon Ratchasima Ubon Ratchathani

PHNOM PENH Battambang Kampong Som

BANGKOK Nakhon Sawan Phitsanulok Ayutthaya Samut Prakan Chon Buri Rayong Hua Hin Chiang Mai Lampang Nakhon Si Thammarat Phuket Surat Thani Songkhla Hat Yai

RANGOON Bassein Prome Pegu Moulmein Tavoy Mergui Sittwe (Akyab)

George Town Butterworth Ipoh Taiping KUALA LUMPUR Klang Seremban Melaka Johor Bahru Kuala Terengganu Kuantan Kota Bharu SINGAPORE

MANILA QUEZON CITY Baguio Dagupan Cabanatuan Angeles Batangas Lucena Legazpi Naga Calbayog Tacloban Cebu Iloilo Bacolod Cagayan de Oro DAVAO Mati General Santos Cotabato Zamboanga Puerto Princesa

BRUNEI Bandar Seri Begawan Kota Kinabalu SABAH Tawau Sandakan SARAWAK Kuching Sibu Miri Bintulu

MEDAN Pekanbaru Padang Palembang Bandar Lampung JAKARTA BANDUNG Bogor Semarang SURABAYA Madiun Yogyakarta Malang Denpasar Bali Pontianak Banjarmasin Samarinda Balikpapan UJUNG PANDANG Manado Gorontalo Palu

CELEBES SEA SULU SEA JAVA SEA FLORES SEA BANDA SEA MOLUCCA SEA SERAM SEA TIMOR SEA ARAFURA SEA CERAM SEA

ANDAMAN SEA Gulf of Thailand Straits of Malacca Java Trench Mindanao Trench

Equator

1:17 500 000

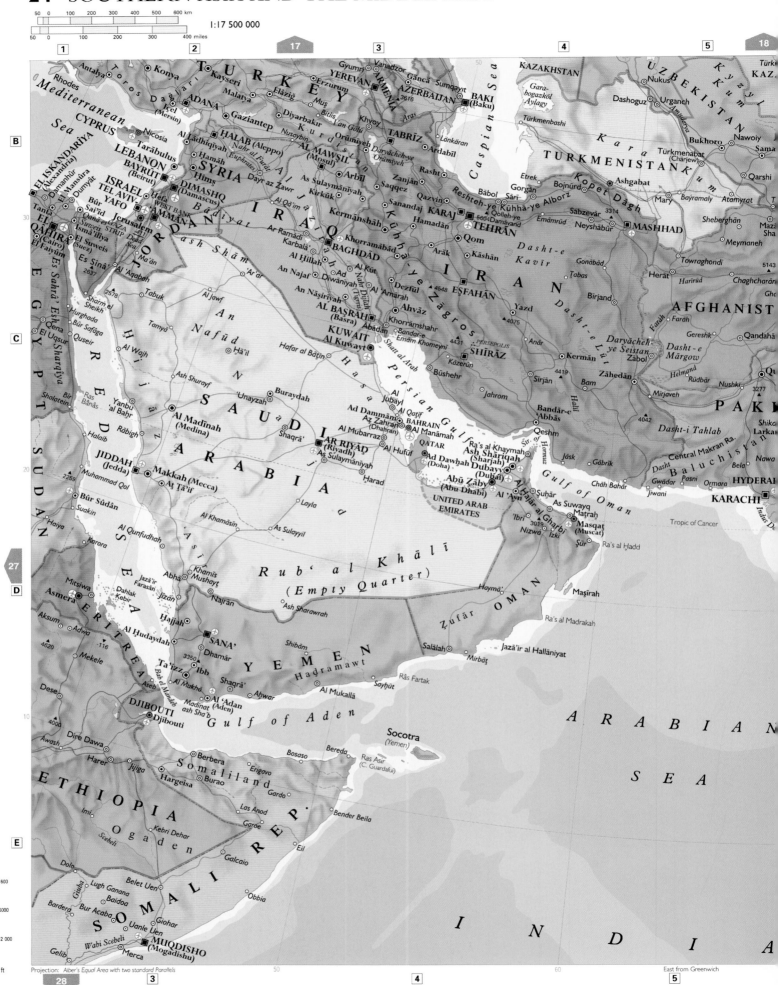

Projection: Alber's Equal Area with two standard Parallels

East from Greenwich

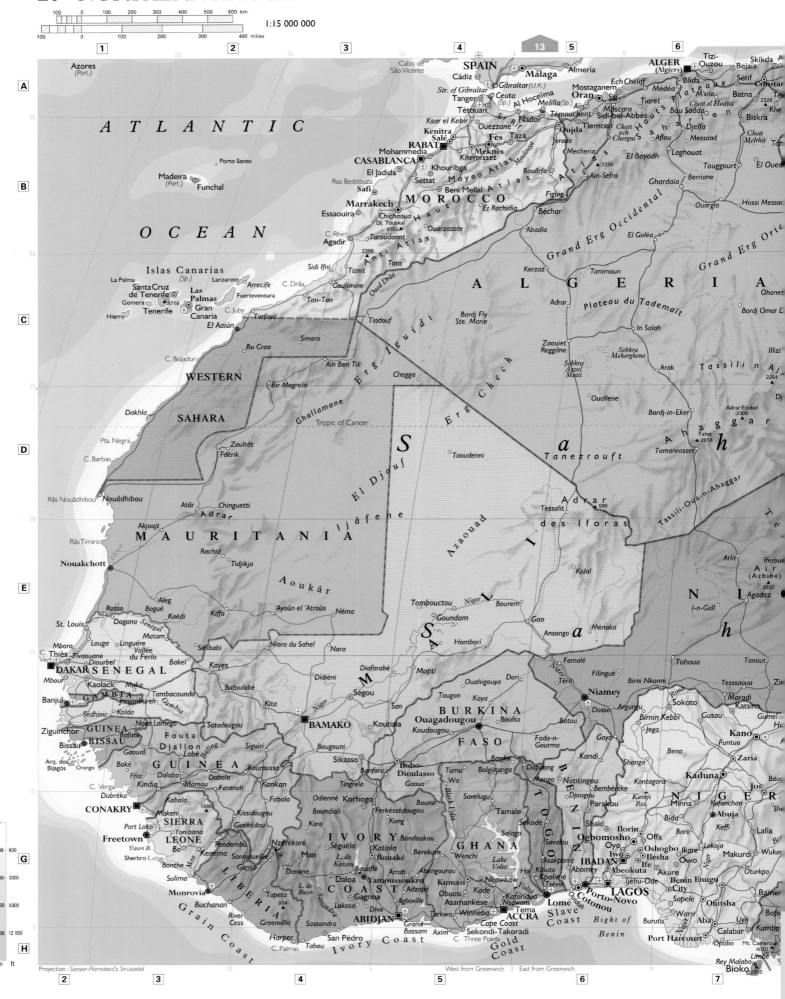

100   0   100   200   300   400   500   600 km
100   0   100   200   300   400 miles
1:15 000 000

Projection: Sanson-Flamsteed's Sinusoidal

ATLANTIC

OCEAN

Azores
(Port.)

Madeira
(Port.) Funchal
Porto Santo

Islas Canarias
(Sp.)
La Palma
Santa Cruz
de Tenerife   Lanzarote
Gomera   Tenerife   Arrecife
Hierro   Fuerteventura
Las Palmas
Gran
Canaria
C. Juby

SPAIN   Málaga   Almería
Cabo de
São Vicente
Str. of Gibraltar   Gibraltar (U.K.)
Cádiz   Ceuta   Al Hoceima
Tanger   (Sp.)   Melilla (Sp.)
Tétouan   Nador
Ksar el Kebir
Kenitra   Ouezzane   Oujda
Salé   Fès   Taza
RABAT   Meknès
Mohammedia   Khenisset
CASABLANCA   Khouribga
El Jadida   Settat
Ras Beddouza   Beni Mellal
Safi   Figuig
Marrakech   Er Rachidia
Essaouira   Chichaoua   Ouarzazate
Dj. Toubkal   Abadla
4165
C. Rhir   Taroudannt
Agadir   2359
Sidi Ifni   Tiznit
Goulimine
Tata
Tan-Tan   Oued Drâa
C. Drâa
Tarfaya
El Aaiún
Smara
Bu Craa
C. Bojador

Mostaganem
Oran   Arzew
Aïn Témouchent
Tlemcen
ALGER
(Algiers)   Tizi-
Ouzou   Skikda
Médéa   Blida   Bejaïa   Sétif
Ech Chéliff   M'sila   Batna   Constant
Tiaret   Bou Saâda   2328
Sidi-bel-Abbès   Bordj   Khe
Mascara   Bou Arréridj
Chott el Hodna
Aïn   Djelfa   Messaad
Mecheria   El Bayadh   Laghouat
Aïn-Sefra   Chott
Melrhir
Abadla   Béchar   Berriane   El Oued
2236   Ghardaïa   Touggourt
Ouarzazate   Ouargla
El Goléa   Hassi Messaoud
Grand Erg Occidental
Kerzaz   Grand Erg Orie
Timimoun
Adrar   In Salah
Plateau du Tademaït
Bordj Fly   Ohanet
Ste. Marie
Zaouiet   Sebkra
Reggâne   Mekerghene
Sebkra
Azzel   Arak
Matti   Illizi
Ouallene   Tassili n'Aj
Bordj-in-Eker   2254
Adrar Edekel
2306
Tamanrasset   Tahat
2918
Ahaggar

Tindouf
Aïn Ben Tili
Erg Iguidi
Chegga
Ghallamane
Erg Chech
Erg Chech

S

a

h

WESTERN

SAHARA

Tropic of Cancer

MAURITANIA

Dakhla
Pta. Negra
C. Barbas
Râs Nouâdhibou   Nouâdhibou
Atâr   Chinguetti
Adrar
Akjoujt
Râs Timiris
Zouîrât
Fdérik

El Djouf
Ijâfene

Taoudenni

Tanezrouft

Adrar
des Iforas
Tessalit   598

Tassili-Oua-n-Ahaggar

Aïr
(Azbine)
Arlit   2022
Iferoua
Agadez

Nouakchott
Aleg
Bogué
Rosso   Kaédi
St. Louis   Dagana
Mboro   Louga   Linguère
Matam
C. Vert   Tivaouane   Sélibabi
DAKAR   Diourbel
SENEGAL
Mbour   Bakel
Kaolack   Kayes
Banjul   Moka
GAMBIA   Tambacounda
Sédhiou   Kolda
Ziguinchor   Nova Lamego
GUINEA   Bafatá
BISSAU
Bissau   Labé
Arq. dos   Orango
Bijagós
C. Verga   Dalaba
Dubréka   Kindia   Mamou
CONAKRY   Kabala
Makeni   1948
SIERRA   Yonibana
LEONE   Port Loko
Freetown   Yawri B.
Bo   Kenema
Sherbro I.   Bonthe
Sulima

Rachid
Tidjikja
Kiffa
'Ayoûn el 'Atroûs
Néma

Aoukâr
Nara

Nioro du Sahel
Sélibabi
Kaédi   Diafarabé

M   A   L   I

Tombouctou
Goundam
Hombori
S
Famalé

Niger
Bourem
Gao   Ménaka
Ansongo

Kidal

I-n-Gall
Tahoua
Tessaoua
Tanout

Séfa
Matam   Nioro du Sahel
Vallée   Nara
du Ferlo
Linguère
Kayes   Diama
Bafoulabé   Didiéni   Ségou
Satadougou   Kita   Koutiala
BAMAKO   San
Siguiri   Bougouni   Sikasso
Kourpussa   Tingrela
Kankan   Odienné
Faranah   Korhogo
Kissidougou   Boundiali
Guékédou   Koro
Nzérékoré   Ségéula
Man   Bouaké
Danané   Katiola
1752   Daloa
Sanniquellie   Gagnoa
Ganta   Yamoussoukro
L. de   Divo
Kossou   Lakota
L. de   Gagnoa
Buyo   Abengourou
914   Adzopé
Tapeta   Agboville
River Cess   Tiassalé
Buchanan   ABIDJAN
Monrovia   Grand
Greenville   Bassam
Sassandra   Axim
San Pédro   C. Three Points
Harper   Tabou
C. Palmas

Tougan   Kaya
Ouahigouya   Dori
BURKINA   Birni Nkonni
Ouagadougou   FASO   Filingué
Koudougou   Boulsa   Niamey
Bobo   Fada-N-   Téra
Dioulasso   Gourma
Banfora   Gaya   Dosso
Tumu   Dapaong   Argungu
Wa   Bolgatanga   Kandi   Sokoto
Bawku   Mango
Savelugu   Natitingou   Birnin Kebbi
Tamale   Parakou   Jega
Salaga   Djougou
Sokodé   Kontagora
GHANA   Wenchi   Kainji   Kaduna
Res.   Bida
Berekum   Kpalimé   Abuja
Kumasi   Atakpamé   Minna
Obuasi   Kloto   Jebba   NIGER
Asamankese   Tsévié   Ilorin   Lafia
Koforidua   Lomé   Offa   Keffi
ACCRA   Cotonou   Ogbomosho   Baro
Winneba   Porto-Novo   Oshogbo   Lokoja
Cape Coast   Lagos   Iwo   Ikare
Sekondi-Takoradi   LAGOS   Ibadan   Ife   Owo
Tema   Ikirun   Oyo   Akure
Abomey   IBADAN   Benin
Kété Krachi   Ijebu-Ode   City
Nkawkaw   Enugu
Bénin   Sapele
Bight of   Onitsha
Benin   Warri   Aba
Burutu   Port Harcourt
Opobo   Calabar
Mt. Cameroun   Uyo
4070
Rey Malabo   Limbe
Bioko   2850

SENEGAL   Bafing   Niger

GUINEA
Fouta
Djallon
Goual   Boké
Fria
Kindia
Faranah
Fabala
Kabala   Odienné
LIBERIA

IVORY

COAST

Grain

Coast

Ivory   Coast

Gold
Coast

Slave
Coast

West from Greenwich   0   East from Greenwich

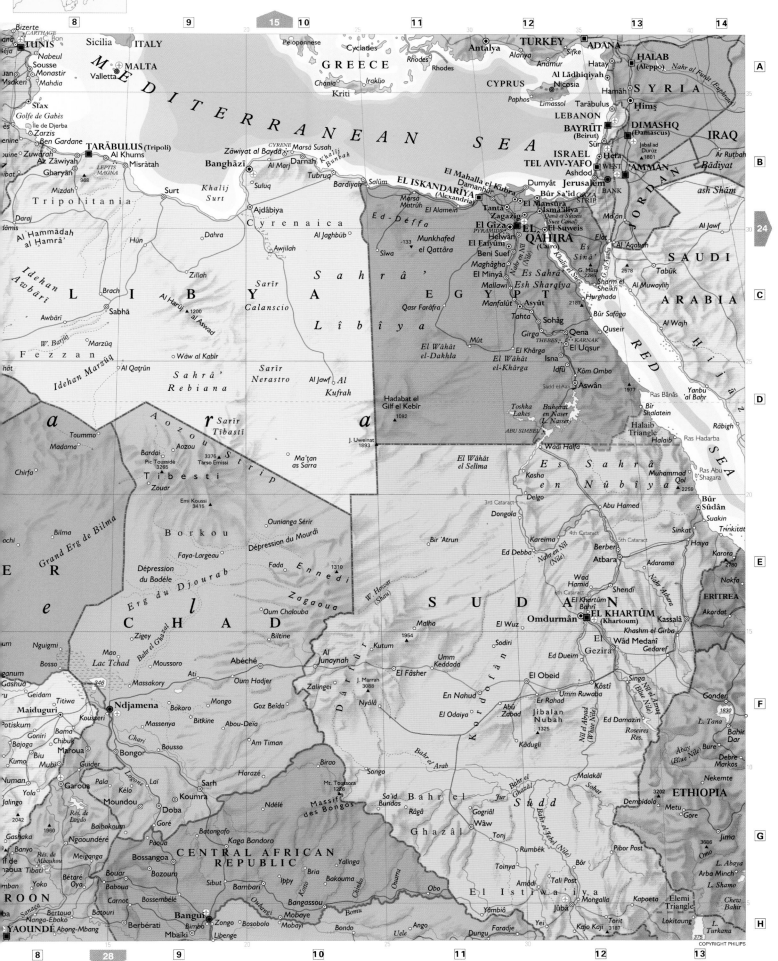

MEDITERRANEAN SEA

GREECE
Peloponnese
Cyclades
Rhodes
Chania
Kriti
Iraklio

ITALY
Sicilia
MALTA
Valletta

TURKEY
Antalya
Alanya
Anamur
Sifke
Adana
Hatay
Al Lādhiqiyah
Nicosia
CYPRUS
Paphos
Limassol

HALAB
(Aleppo)
Nahr al Furāt (Euphrates)

SYRIA
Hamāh
Ḥimṣ

Bizerte
CARTHAGE
C. Bon
TUNIS
Nabeul
Sousse
Monastir
Mahdia
Sfax
Golfe de Gabès
Île de Djerba
Zarzis
Ben Gardane
Zuwārah
Az Zāwiyah
Gharyān

TARĀBULUS (Tripoli)
Al Khums
Misrātah
LEPTIS MAGNA
968

LEBANON
BAYRŪT (Beirut)
Ṣūr
Ṭarābulus

ISRAEL
TEL AVIV-YAFO
Ashdod
Ḥefa
WEST BANK
GAZA STRIP
Jerusalem
Dumyāṭ
Būr Sa'īd

DIMASHQ
(Damascus)
Jabal ad Durūz
1801

AMMĀN
Ar Ruṭbah
Bādiyat
ash Shām

IRAQ
Al Jawf

Mizdah
Tripolitania
Daraj
tāmis
Al Hammādah al Ḥamrā'

CYRENE
Zāwiyat al Baydā
Marsā Susah
Darnah
Al Marj
Tubruq
Khalīj Bunbah
Salūm
Bardiyah

EL ISKANDARIYA
(Alexandria)
Marsā Matrūh
El Alamein
El Mahalla el Kubra
Damanhûr
Tanta
Zagazig
El Mansûra
Ismā'īliya
Qanâ es Suweis (Suez Canal)
El Suweis
El Faiyûm
Beni Suef
Maghâgha
El Minyâ
Mallawi
Manfalût
Asyût
Tahta
Sohâg
Girga
Qena
THEBES
KARNAK
El Uqsur

Banghāzī
Suluq
Ajdābiya
Surt
Khalīj Surt
Hūn

Cyrenaica
Al Jaghbūb
Dahra
Awjilah

Sahrâ'
Lîbîya

EGYPT
Es Sahrâ
Esh Sharqiya
Sînā'
G. Mûsa
2285
2578
Tabūk
Sharm el Sheikh
Hurghada
Būr Safâga
Quseir
Al Wajh

SAUDI
ARABIA
Al Muwayliḥ

Zillah
Sarîr Calanscio
al Ḥarūj
al Aswad
1200

Qasr Farâfra
El Wâhât el-Dakhla
Mût
-133
Munkhafed el Qattâra
Sîwa
El Kharga
El Wâhât el-Khârga
Isna
Idfû
Kôm Ombo
Aswân
1977

RED

Ḥijâz
Ras Bânâs
Bîr Shalatein
Yanbu 'al Baḥr

LIBYA
Idehan Awbāri
Brach
Al Harûj
Awbāri
Sabhā

Sarîr Nerastro
Al Jawf
Al Kufrah
Hadabat el Gilf el Kebîr
1082

Sahrâ' Rebiana
J. Uweinat
1893
Ma'tan as Sarra

Toshka Lakes
Buheirat en Naser
(L. Nasser)
ABU SIMBEL
Sadd el Aali
Wadi Halfa

Halaib Triangle
Halaib
Ras Hadarba
Muhammad Qol
2259
Ras Abu Shagara

SEA
Rābigh

Fezzan
W. Barjūj
Marzūq
Idehan Marzūq
Al Qaṭrūn
Wāw al Kabir

a
Toummo
Madama
Bardai
Pic Toussidé
3265
Aozou
3376
Tarso Emissi
Chirfa

Aozou Strip
Sarir Tibasti
Tibesti
Zouar
Emi Koussi
3415

Es Sahrâ en Nûbîya
3rd Cataract
Delgo
Dongola
Kareima
Berber
4th Cataract
5th Cataract

Būr Sûdân
Suakin
Trinkitat
Sinkat
Haiya
Karora
2780
Nakfa

r
Sarir Tibasti
Grand Erg de Bilma
Bilma
Borkou
Ounianga Sérir
Faya-Largeau
Dépression du Mourdi

Bir 'Atrun
Abu Hamed
Ed Debba
Nahr en Nil (Nile)
Atbara
Adarama

ERITREA
Akordat

e
achi
Nguigmi
Bosso
Gashua
Geidam
Titiwa
Maiduguri
Potiskum
Gashaki
Bama
Chibuk
Biu
Mubi

Dépression du Bodéle
Erg du Djourab
Mao
Lac Tchad
346
Ndjamena
Kousseri
Massakory

CHAD
Zigey
Biltine
Moussoro
Ati
Abéché
Oum Hadjer

Ennedi
1310
Fada
Zagaoua
Oum Chalouba

W. Howar (Shau)
Malha
1954
Kutum
El Wuz
Sodiri
Umm Keddada
En Nahud
El Odaiya

SUDAN
Ed Dueim
El Obeid
Er Rahad
Umm Ruwaba
Abū Zabad
Jibalan Nubah
1325
Kâdugli

Wad Hamid
Shendî
El Khartûm Bahrî
Omdurmân
EL KHARTÛM
(Khartoum)
El Gezira
Wâd Medanî
Singa
Kôstî
Ed Damazin
Roseires Res.

Kassalâ
Khashm el Girba
Gedaref
Nahr Atbara

ETHIOPIA
Gonder
1830
L. Tana
Bahir Dar
Âbay (Blue Nile)
Bure
Debre Markos
Dembidolo
Metu
Gore
Jima

Nil el Abrag (Blue Nile)
Nil el Abyad (White Nile)

Garoua
Marova
Guider
Pala
Kélo
Laï
Sarh
Moundou
Doba
Goré
Baïbokoum
Ngaoundéré
Réf. de Lagdo
2042
1960

Bokoro
Mongo
Massenya
Bitkine
Abou-Deïa
Am Timan
Bongor
Bousso
Goz Beïda
Harazé
Birao
Songa

Mt. Toussora
1276
Ndélé
Massif des Bongos
Sa'id Bundas
Râga
Gogriâl
Waw
Tonj
Rumbêk
Amâdi
Tali Post
Yambio
Jûba
Kajo Kaji
Yei
Torit
Faradje
Uele
Dungu

El Wâhât el Selima
Kosha
3202
Sobat
Malakâl
Bahr el Jebel (Nile)
Bôr
Pibor Post
Toinya
El Istiwa'îya

3686
Omo
L. Abaya
Arba Minch
L. Shamo
Metu
Gore

Bahr el Arab
Bahr el Ghazâl
Sudd
Kordofân
Darfur

CENTRAL AFRICAN REPUBLIC
Bouar
Bozoum
Bossangoa
Batangafo
Kaga Bandoro
Bossembélé
Sibut
Bambari
Ippy
Bria
Bakouma
Yalinga
Bangassou
Obo
Ouarra

Bétaré Oya
Yoko
Bertoua
Nanga-Eboko
YAOUNDÉ
Abong-Mbang
Batouri
Carnot
Berbérati
Nola
Bangui
Bimbo
Mbaïki
Mbaïki
Zongo
Bosobolo
Libenge
Mobaye
Mobayi
Bondo

Elemi Triangle
Kapoeta
Lokitaung
L. Turkana
375

1:15 000 000

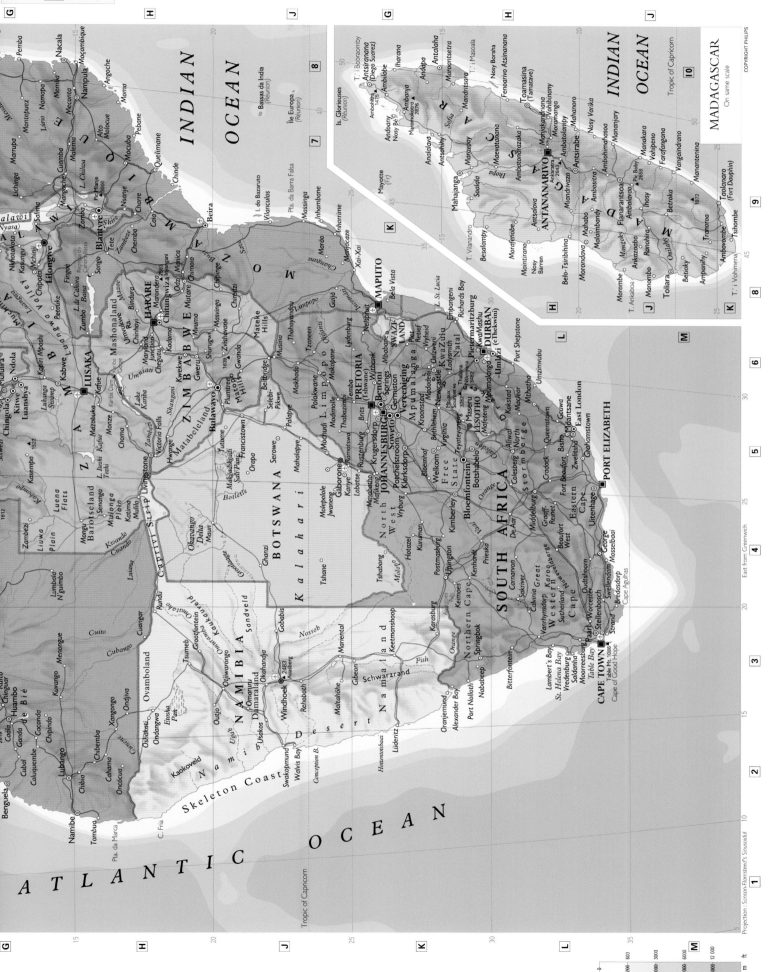

INDIAN

OCEAN

ATLANTIC OCEAN

MADAGASCAR
On same scale

INDIAN
OCEAN

MOZAMBIQUE

ZIMBABWE

ZAMBIA

BOTSWANA

NAMIBIA

Kalahari

SOUTH AFRICA

LESOTHO

SWAZILAND

Namib Desert

Skeleton Coast

Caprivi Strip

Ovamboland

Barotseland

Matabeleland

Mashonaland

Western Cape

Northern Cape

Eastern Cape

Free State

North West

HARARE

LUSAKA

PRETORIA (Tshwane)

JOHANNESBURG

MAPUTO

BULAWAYO

Bloemfontein

CAPE TOWN

DURBAN

PORT ELIZABETH

ANTANANARIVO

Tropic of Capricorn

East from Greenwich

COPYRIGHT PHILIPS

Projection: Sanson-Flamsteed's Sinusoidal

ft
12 000
6000
4000
2000
1000
600
200
0
m

1:20 000 000

100 0 100 200 300 400 500 600 700 800 km
100 0 100 200 300 400 500 miles

Projection: *Lambert's Equivalent Azimuthal*

East from Greenwich

Ontong
Java
Plateau

160　Solomon Rise

Bougainville

Balbi
Island Is.

Choiseul

Lavella

SOLOMON

Santa Isabel

New
Georgia Is.

Vangunu

Russell Is.

Florida Is.

Honiara ▲ 2439

Guadalcanal

Bellona

Rennell

ISLANDS

Malaita

San Cristóbal
(Makira)

Pocklington
Reef

Reef Is.

Duff Is.

Nendo

Santa Cruz
Is.

Vanikoro

Tikopia

Fataka

9165 ▼

7223

South Solomon Trench

Vitiaz Trench

Tabiteuea　Beru　Nikunau

Gilbert　Tamana

Is.

Arorae

K I R I B A T I

Baker (U.S.A.)

Equator

▪ 6195

170

McKean

Abariringa
Birnie

Enderbury

Nikumaroro

Phoenix Is.

Orona

Rawaki

Carondelet

Manra

Namumea

Nanumanga

Niutao

Nui

Vaitupu

TUVALU
(Ellice Is.)

Funafuti

Fongafale ⊙

Nukulaelae

Niulakita

Rotuma

Atafu

Nukunonu

Fakaofo

Tokelau Is.
(N.Z.)

M e l a n e s i a

Is. Torres

Vanua Lava

Is. Banks

Gaua

Espíritu Santo ▲ 1879

VANUATU
(New Hebrides)

Malakula

Epi

Shepherd Is.

Port Vila ⊙ Efate

Erromango

Tanna

Aneityum

7569 ▼

Mata-Utu ⊕ Uvea

Wallis & Futuna

Horn　(Fr.)

Alofi

Niuafo'ou

Niua
Group

Niuatoputapu

SAMOA

Savai'i

'Upolu

Apia ⊙

Pago
Pago ⊙

Tutuila

American
Samoa
(U.S.A.)

M i c r o n e s i a

West
Fiji
Basin

Vanua Levu

Viti Levu

Taveuni

Suva 1323 ▲

FIJI

Kadavu

Lau Group

Lau
Ridge

Vava'u Group

Late

Lau

Ha'apai Group

Basin

TONGA

Nuku'alofa ⊕ Eua

Tongatapu
Group

Ata

Niue
(N.Z.) ⊙

Îles D'Entrecasteaux

Îles Bélep

Îles Chesterfield

Lord Howe Seamount Chain

New
Caledonia
(Fr.)

4628 ▲

Î. Lifou

Î. Maré

Nouméa ⊙

Î. des Pins

Îles Loyauté

South New Hebrides Trench

Î. Matthew

Ceve-i-Ra

Caledonia Ridge

Norfolk Ridge

5303 ▼

P A C I F I C

O C E A N

Tonga Trench

10 882 ▼

Tropic of Capricorn

South
Fiji
Basin

Lord Howe Trough

Norfolk I.
(Austral.)

Norfolk
Basin

Lord Howe I.
(Austral.)

734 ▼

T a s m a n   S e a

Kermadec
Is.
(N.Z.)

Raoul I.

Macauley I.

Curtis I.

10 047 ▼

Colville Ridge

Kermadec Trench

Southwest

Pacific

Basin

North C.

Kaitaia

Whangarei

AUCKLAND ▣

Hamilton

Bay of
Plenty

Tauranga

North Island

Rotorua

Gisborne

Ruapehu
▲ 2797

Napier

Palmerston
North

Challenger

Plateau

New Plymouth

NEW

ZEALAND

Wanganui

Masterton

Wellington

Nelson

Blenheim

Greymouth

Cook Strait

South Island

Aoraki Mt. Cook
3753

Southern Alps

Christchurch

Chatham

Rise

Chatham I.

Pitt I.

Chatham Is.
(N.Z.)

Queenstown

Timaru

Invercargill

Dunedin

Stewart I.

International Date Line

5267 ▼

Lord Howe Rise

a

e a

170

160

N e w

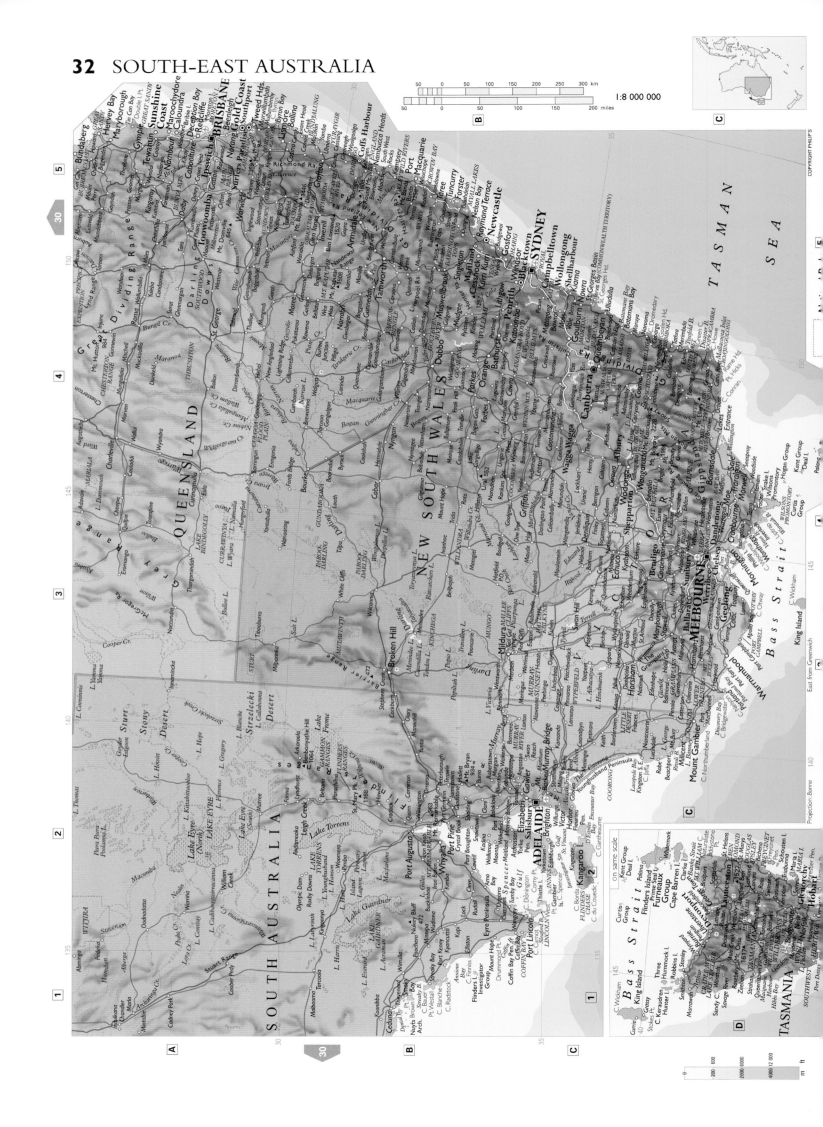

1:6 000 000

50   0   50   100   150   200 km
50   0   50   100   150 miles

| 1 | 2 | 3 | 4 | **31** | 5 | 6 | 7 |

168   170   172   174   176   178

C. Reinga
C. Maria van Diemen
North C.
Houhora Heads
Rangaunu B.
Doubtless B.
Mangonui
Whangaroa Harb.
Ahipara B.
Kaitaia
Okaihau
Waitangi
C. Brett
Opua
B. of Islands
Tauroa Pt.
Rawene
Kaikohe
Hikurangi
Hokianga Harbour
Waipoua Forest
Whangarei
Whangarei Harb.
Bream Hd.
Bream B.
Dargaville
Waipu
Little Barrier I.
Warkworth
C. Rodney
Great Barrier I.
Kaipara Harbour
Helensville
Hauraki Gulf
Cuvier I.
C. Colville
Takapuna
Coromandel
Whitianga
■ **AUCKLAND**
Whangamata
Manukau
Papakura
Thames
Mayor I.
North
Island
Waiuku
Pukekohe
Mercer
Waihi
Te Aroha
Tauranga Harb.
Waikato
Huntly
Mount Maunganui
Tauranga
Whakatane
Whakaari (White I.)
Runaway
Raglan
Te Awamutu
Cambridge
Te Puke
Bay of Plenty
Hamilton
Morrinsville
Kawerau
East C.
Kawhia
Otorohanga
Putaruru
Rotoiti
Taneatua
Raukumara Ra.
Hikurangi 1752 ▲
Kawhia Harbour
Waitomo Caves
Te Kuiti
Tokoroa
Rotorua
L. Tarawera
Murupara
Waipiro
Mokau
Mokai
Waikite
L. Rotorua
Ruatahuki
Motu
Tolaga Bay
North Taranaki Bight
Ongarue
Taumarunui
L. Taupo
Taupo
Rangitaiki
UREWERA
Ormond
Waitara
WHANGANUI
Turangi
Kaimanawa Mts.
Waikaremoana
Gisborne
New Plymouth
Inglewood
Whangamomana
Tarawera
Nuhaka
Poverty Bay
Mt. Taranaki or Mt. Egmont 2518 ▲
C. Egmont
EGMONT
Stratford
Ohakune
Ruapehu 2797 ▲
TONGARIRO
Bay View
Wairoa
Waikokopu
Mahia Pen.
Opunake
Eltham
Raetihi
Waiouru
Hawke Bay
Kapuni
Rohine Ra.
Napier
C. Kidnappers
Hawera
Waverley
Taihape
Mangaweka
Hastings
South Taranaki Bight
Patea
Wanganui
Marton
Halcombe
Waipawa
Waipukurau
Bulls
Palmerston North
Feilding
Dannevirke
Foxton
Woodville
TASMAN
Shannon
Pahiatua
SEA
C. Farewell
Levin
Eketahuna
C. Turnagain
Otaki
Paraparaumu
Masterton
Golden B.
Kapiti I.
Collingwood
ABEL TASMAN
D'Urville I.
Carterton
Takaka
Tasman B.
Greytown
KAHURANGI
Tasman Mts.
Pelorus Sd.
Featherston
Martinborough
Upper Hutt
Wairarapa
Karamea
Motueka
Petone
Lower Hutt
Karamea Bight
Nelson
Havelock
Wellington
Seddonville
Richmond
Picton
Granity
Wakefield
Cook Strait
PACIFIC
Westport
Lyell
NELSON LAKES
Blenheim
Maruia Ra.
Murchison
L. Rotoiti
Seddon
OCEAN
Inangahua
Rotoroa
Ward
PAPAROA
Mt. Travers 2338 ▲
Tapuae-o-Uenuku 2895 ▲
Reefton
Punakaiki
Spenser Mts.
Clarence
Blackball
Grey
Lewis Pass
Kaikoura Ra.
Greymouth
Runanga
Hanmer Springs
Kaikoura
Kumara
L. Brunner
Waiau
Hokitika
Jacksons
ARTHUR'S PASS
Culverden
Ross
Waikari
Hurunui
Waiau
South
Abut Hd.
Waipara
Island
Amberley
Oxford
Rangiora
Pegasus Bay
Kaiapoi
WESTLAND
Coleridge
Springfield
New Brighton
Aoraki / Mt. Cook 3753 ▲
Whitecliffs
Christchurch
Westland Bight
Riccarton
Lyttelton
Mount Cook
Methven
Lincoln
Banks Pen.
Jackson B.
Staveley
MT. COOK
Rakaia
Akaroa
L. Ellesmere
Okuru
Southern Alps
Tekapo
Little River
(Tiritiri o te Moana)
Southbridge
Canterbury Plains
MOUNT ASPIRING
Mt. Aspiring 3027 ▲
Fairlie
Temuka
Ohau
Mt. Earnslaw 2818 ▲
L. Wanaka
Timaru
Canterbury Bight
Milford Sd.
Haast
St. Andrews
Sutherland Falls
Wanaka
Waimate
Bligh Sound
Arrowtown
Kurow
George Sound
Cromwell
Tokarahi
Ngapara
Secretary I.
Queenstown
Clyde
Naseby
Oamaru
Doubtful Sd.
Wakatipu
Alexandra
Maheno
FIORDLAND
L. Manapouri
Kingston
Roxburgh
Hampden
Danback
Breaksea Sd.
Mossburn
Dunstan Mts.
Waikouaiti
Palmerston
Dusky Sd.
Manapouri
Lumsden
Edievale
Port Chalmers
Resolution I.
Te Anau
Kelso
Otago Harbour
Nightcaps
Tapanui
Dunedin
Chalky Inlet
L. Southland
Clifden
Ohai
Winton
Lawrence
C. Saunders
Preservation Inlet
Te Waewae B.
Tuatapere
Orepuki
Milton
Riverton
Gore
Balclutha
Solander I.
Invercargill
Mataura
Kaitangata
Bluff Invercargill
Wyndham
Owaka
Tahakopa
Foveaux Str.
Tokanui
Nugget Pt.
Halfmoon Bay
Stewart I. (Rakiura)
RAKIURA
Ruapuke I.
Port Pegasus
South West C.

Projection : Conical with two standard parallels
East from Greenwich

166   168   170   172

National Parks

SAMOAN ISLANDS
1:12 000 000

| | | 12 | 13 | 14 |

SAMOA
AMERICAN SAMOA
Savai'i
Apia
Upolu
Pago Pago
Tutuila
West from Greenwich

172   170   168

| | 8 | 9 | 10 | | 11 |

Futuna
Wallis & Futuna (Fr.)

Niuafo'ou (Tonga)

Thikombia
Labasa
Vanua Levu
Yasawa Group
Taveuni
Koro
Vanua Balavu
FIJI
Lautoka 1323 ▲
Viti Levu
Levuka
Ovalau
Lau Group
Nandi
Koro Sea
Gau
Lakeba
PACIFIC
Suva
Moala
OCEAN
Kadavu
Vatoa
Vava'u
Tofua
TONGA (Friendly Is.)
Tongatapu
Nuku'alofa

178   East from Greenwich   180

FIJI AND TONGA
1:12 000 000

50   0   50   100   150   200 km
50   0   50   100   150 miles

178   176 West from Greenwich   174

COPYRIGHT PHILIP'S

| 7 | 8 | 9 | 10 | 11 |

0
200   600
2000   6000
4000   12000
6000   18000
m   ft

Equatorial Scale 1:54 000 000

B

Moskva
Volga
Yekaterinburg
Ob
RUSSIA
Novosibirsk
Lena
Irkutsk
Oz. Baykal
Chita
Blagoveshchensk
Amur
Khabarovsk
Sakhalin
Sea of Okhotsk
Okhotsk
Poluostrov Kamchatka
Shirshov Ridge
Aleutian Basin
Ber
Se
Near Is.
Andrean

Astana
(Aqmola)
Semey
Ulaanbaatar
Harbin
Changchun
SHENYANG
Vladivostok
La Perouse Str.
Kuril'skiye Ostrova
(Russia)
Kuril-Kamchatka Trench
10,542
Petropavlovsk
-Kamchatskiy
7822
Aleutian Trench

KAZAKHSTAN
Balqash Köl
Almaty
Ürümqi
MONGOLIA
Changchun
Sapporo
Hokkaidō
Hakodate
Northwest
Chinook R
Emperor Trough

Aral Sea
Toshkent
TAJIKISTAN
MONGOLIA
Beijing
Tianjin
NORTH KOREA
Dalian
SOUTH KOREA
Seoul
Sea of Japan
Honshū
Sendai
Shatsky Rise
Pacific
Seamount Chain

AFGHANISTAN
Kabul
Srinagar
PAKISTAN
CHINA
Kunlun Shan
Lanzhou
Xi'an
Huang He
Qingdao
Yellow Sea
Nagoya
Kyōto
Fuji-San 3776
Tōkyō
Yokohama
JAPAN
10,554

Lahore
Delhi
Kanpur
Mt. Everest 8850
NEPAL
Lhasa
XIZANG
Chengdu
Chongqing
Wuhan
Hangzhou
Shanghai
East China Sea
Okinawa
Ryūkyū-rettō
Iwo-Jima *(Japan)*
Ogasawara Gunto *(Japan)*
Minami-Tori-Shima *(Japan)*
Midway Is. *(U.S.A.)*

Ganga
Brahmaputra
Irrawaddy
BURMA
Kunming
Changsha
Fuzhou
Taipei
TAIWAN
Taiwan Str.
Kyushu-Palau Ridge
Kazan-Rettō (Japan)
Wake I. *(U.S.A.)*
Lisianski I. *(U.S.A.)*

Kolkata (Calcutta)
Dhaka
Mandalay
Salween
Guangzhou
Macau
Hong Kong
Philippine Sea
NORTHERN MARIANAS *(U.S.A.)*
East Mariana Basin
P A
A

INDIA
Hyderabad
Bay of Bengal
Rangoon
THAILAND
Hanoi
Hainan
Luzon
Paracel Is.
Manila
West Mariana Basin
Tinian
Saipan
GUAM *(U.S.A.)*
MARSHALL IS.
Enewetak Atoll
Rongelap
Bikini
Majuro
Ralik Chain
Ratak Chain

Chennai (Madras)
Andaman Is. *(India)*
Bangkok
VIETNAM
CAMBODIA
Phnom Penh
Mekong
South China Sea
Mindoro
Samar
10,497
PHILIPPINES
Challenger Deep 11,022
Yap
Mariana Trench
Kwajalein

SRI LANKA
Colombo
Nicobar Is. *(India)*
G. of Thailand
Thanh Pho Ho Chi Minh
Palawan
Sulu Sea
Mindanao
Davao
Philippine Trench
Koror
Caroline Is.
Truk
Pohnpei
Palikir
Micronesia
Jaluit
Majuro

MALAYSIA
4101
BRUNEI
SABAH
Celebes Sea
Maluku
FED. STATES OF MICRONESIA
PALAU
West Caroline Basin
Eauripik Rise
East Caroline Basin
Solomon Rise
Melanesian Basin
Butaritari
Tarawa
Gilbert Is.
Howland I.
Baker I.
Pacific

Kuala Lumpur
PEN. MALAYSIA
SARAWAK
Borneo
Sulawesi
Ujung Pandang
Buru
Seram
Puncak Jaya 5029
PAPUA
New Guinea
Admiralty Is.
Bismarck Arch.
Yaren
NAURU
Banaba
Melanesia
Phoenix Is.
Abariring
Enderbu
KI

Singapore
Sumatera
Sunda Ridge
INDONESIA
Palembang
Jawa Sea
Java Sea
Jakarta
Surabaya
Bali
Flores Sea
Flores
Banda Sea
7440
EAST TIMOR
PAPUA NEW GUINEA
Lae
Rabaul 8940
Bougainville
New Britain
Port Moresby
New Ireland
SOLOMON IS.
Honiara
Guadalcanal
Santa Cruz Is. 9165
Fongafale
TUVALU
Tokela *(N.Z.)*

INDIAN
Selat Sunda
Sunda Trench (Java Trench)
Christmas I. *(Austral.)*
Sumbawa
Sumba
North Australian Basin
Arafura Sea
Torres Strait
C. York
Louisiade Arch.
Coral Sea Basin
Rotuma
Is. Wallis & Futuna *(Fr.)*
SAMO
Api

Cocos Is. *(Austral.)*
Ninetyeast Ridge
Wharton Basin
Broome
Exmouth Plateau
Darwin
C. Arnhem
Gulf of Carpentaria
Cairns
Townsville
Coral Sea
Espíritu Santo
VANUATU
Port Vila
Is. Chesterfield
West Fiji Basin
Vanua Levu
Viti Levu
Suva
FIJI
Nuku'alofa
TO

OCEAN
Broken Ridge
Geraldton
Perth Basin
North West C.
Mount Isa
Rockhampton
NEW CALEDONIA *(Fr.)*
Nouméa
Is. Loyauté
7570
10,822
Tonga Trench

Nouvelle Amsterdam *(Fr.)*
Îs. St. Paul *(Fr.)*
Naturaliste Plateau
Perth
AUSTRALIA
Alice Springs
L. Eyre
Murray
Darling
Brisbane
Middleton
Lord Howe I. *(Austral.)*
New Caledonia Ridge
Lord Howe Rise
Norfolk I. *(Austral.)*
South Fiji Basin
Kermadec Is. *(N.Z.)*
10,047

Great Australian Bight
Albany
South Australian Basin
Adelaide
Sydney
Canberra
Mt. Kosciuszko 2230
Tasman Sea
NEW ZEALAND
Auckland

Kerguelen *(Fr.)*
Heard I. *(Austral.)*
Kerguelen Plateau
Bass Str.
Melbourne
Tasmania
Hobart
East Tasman Plateau
South Tasman Rise
Tasman Basin
Aoraki Mt. Cook 3753
Christchurch
Chatha *(N.Z.)*
Chatham Rise *(N.Z.)*
Wellington
Dunedin
Bounty Trough
Invercargill
Bounty Is. *(N.Z.)*
Cook Strait

SOUTHERN OCEAN
Îs. Crozet *(Fr.)*
Macquarie Is. *(Austral.)*
Antipodes Is. *(N.Z.)*
Auckland Is. *(N.Z.)*
Campbell Plateau
Campbell I. *(N.Z.)*

12 13 14 15 16 17 18 19 20

Arctic Circle

ALASKA
(U.S.A.)
Anchorage
Bristol Bay
Gulf of Alaska
Juneau
5959

Prince of Wales I.
(U.S.A.) Prince Rupert
Queen Charlotte Is.
(Canada)

Tufts
Abyssal
Plain

Vancouver
Vancouver I.
Victoria
Seattle
Portland
Boise
Snake

CANADA
Edmonton
Calgary
Winnipeg
L. Winnipeg
R O C K Y

Northwest Atlantic
Mid-Ocean Canyon

Newfoundland

NORTH
ATLANTIC
OCEAN

St. Lawrence
Québec
Montréal
Ottawa
Toronto
Detroit
L. Ontario
Boston
St. John's
Grand Banks
of Newfoundland

Northeast

C. Mendocino
Mendocino Fracture Zone

Sacramento
San Francisco
4418

Minneapolis
L. Superior
L. Michigan L. Huron
Chicago
Pittsburgh
Cincinnati

New York
Philadelphia
Baltimore
Washington D.C.

Murray Fracture Zone

6741

Pacific

Los Angeles
San Diego

Phoenix

UNITED STATES
Oklahoma City
Memphis
Dallas
Atlanta

Denver

Salt Lake
City

C. Hatteras

Bermuda
(U.K.)
Bermuda Rise

Sohm
Abyssal
Plain

Ciudad
Juárez

Houston
San Antonio
New
Orleans

Mississippi

Jacksonville

Miami

Sargasso Sea

Guadalupe
(Mex.)

Molokai Fracture Zone

Monterrey
Gulf of Mexico

3504
Sigsbee
Deep

BAHAMAS

Tropic of Cancer

Basin

C. San Lucas

M E X I C O

La Habana
Canal de Yucatán
CUBA
HAITI

9200
DOMINICAN REP.
Leeward
Is.

Honolulu
O'ahu
4205
HAWAI'I
(U.S.A.)
Hawai'i

Clarion Fracture Zone

Is. de
Revillagigedo
(Mex.)

Guadalajara
Mexico
5610
Puebla
Acapulco

Mérida
7680
JAMAICA
Kingston
PUERTO
RICO
(U.S.A.)
BARBADOS
Windward Is.
5059

C I F I C

Clipperton
(Fr.)

Middle America Trench
GUATEMALA
Guatemala
San Salvador
EL SALVADOR
Managua

HONDURAS
BELIZE

Caribbean
Sea

Clipperton Fracture Zone

Guatemala
Basin

NICARAGUA
COSTA
RICA
Colón
PANAMA
San José
Panamá

Barranquilla
San José
Maracaibo
Caracas
Orinoco

Cooper Ridge

Cocos Ridge
I. del Coco
(Costa Rica)
Panama
Basin

Medellín
Bogotá

VENEZUELA

Palmyra I.
(U.S.A.)

Teraina
Tabuaeran
Kiritimati

I. de Malpelo
(Colombia)

Cali
COLOMBIA

Jarvis I.
(U.S.A.)

Equator

Galapagos Fracture Zone

Galápagos
(Ecuador)
Carnegie Ridge
Quito
ECUADOR

Amazonas

E A N

Malden I.
Starbuck I.

Guayaquil
C. Paliñas

Iquitos

BRAZIL

Caroline I.
(Millennium I.)
Nuku
Hiva

Îs. Marquises
Hiva Oa

Trujillo
6369

PERU

Manihiki
Pukapuka
Manihiki
Plateau

Penrhyn
(Tongareva)

Vostok I.
Flint I.

Marquesas Fracture Zone

Yupanqui
Basin

Mendaño Fracture Zone

Lima
Cuzco

Suwarrow Is.

Îs. de la
Société
Bora Bora
Huahine
Raiatea
Papeete
Tahiti

Rangiroa

Îs. Tuamotu

Peru Basin

Nevado Ancohuma
6550
Arequipa
L. Titicaca
6866
Peru-Arica

La Paz
BOLIVIA

Cook Is.
(N.Z.)
Aitutaki
Atiu
Rarotonga
Mangaia

FRENCH POLYNESIA

Îs. Gambier
Mururoa

Nazca Ridge

Iquique
Chile
Chile
Basin

Îs. Tubuai

Tropic of Capricorn

Antofagasta
8064
Trench

PARAGUAY
Asunción

Oeno I.
Henderson I.
Pitcairn I.
(U.K.)
Ducie I.

Easter Fracture Zone
Sala-y-Gómez
(Chile)
I. de Pascua
(Chile)

Sala y Gómez Ridge

Easter Fracture Zone

San Félix
(Chile)
San Ambrosio
(Chile)

San Miguel
de Tucumán

Pôrto
Alegre

Rapa

Roggeveen
Basin

Arch. de
Juan Fernández
(Chile)

Córdoba
Aconcagua
6960
Valparaíso
Santiago
Rosario
Buenos
Aires

URUGUAY
Montevideo
Río de la Plata

Southwest

Challenger Fracture Zone

Chile Rise

Concepción

ARGENTINA

SOUTH
ATLANTIC
OCEAN

Argentine
Basin

Pacific

Menard Fracture Zone

114

Falkland
Plateau
6212
Falkland Is.
(U.K.)

Georgia Basin

South Georgia
(U.K.)

Basin

Pacific-Antarctic Ridge

Punta Arenas
Est. de Magallanes
Tierra del Fuego
C. de Hornos
4402

Southeast
Pacific Basin

Drake Passage

West from Greenwich

COPYRIGHT PHILIP'S

ft	m
12 000	4000
9000	3000
6000	2000
3000	1000
1500	500
600	200
0	0
200	600
1000	3000
2000	6000
4000	12 000
6000	18 000
8000	24 000
m	ft

1:15 000 000

Projection : Bonne

ALASKA
1:30 000 000

West from Greenwich

NORTHERN CANADA

Continuation northwards on same scale as main map

COPYRIGHT PHILIP'S

1:6 000 000

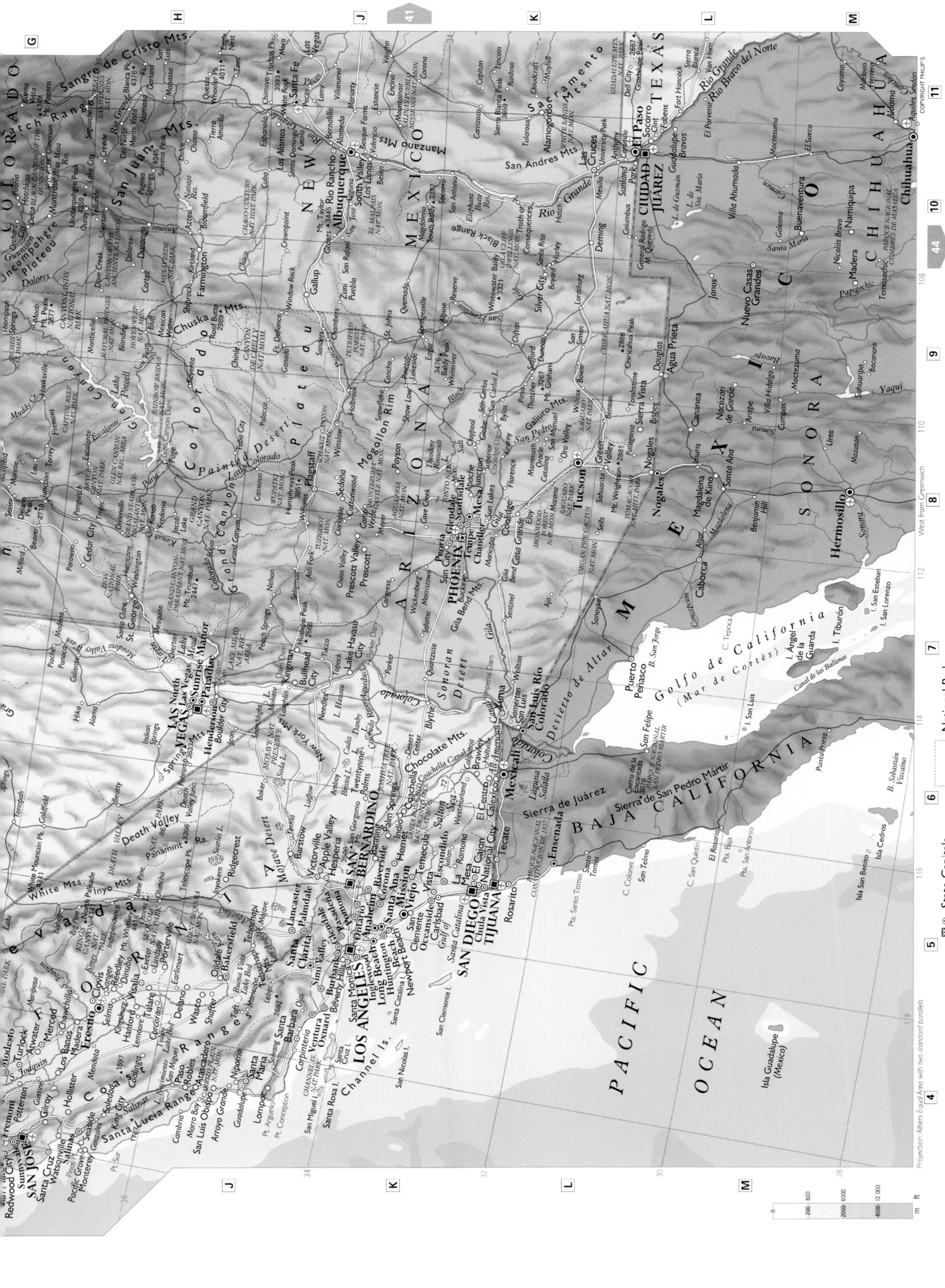

COLORADO
NEW MEXICO
ARIZONA
TEXAS
CHIHUAHUA
SONORA
MEXICO
BAJA CALIFORNIA
PACIFIC OCEAN
Golfo de California (Mar de Cortès)
Colorado Plateau
Sangre de Cristo Mts.
San Juan Mts.
Sacramento Mts.
Mojave Desert
Sonoran Desert
Desierto de Altar
Channel Is.
LOS ANGELES
SAN DIEGO
TIJUANA
PHOENIX
Tucson
Albuquerque
Santa Fe
El Paso
CIUDAD JUÁREZ
Chihuahua
Hermosillo
Mexicali
LAS VEGAS
SAN BERNARDINO
SAN JOSE
Fresno
State Capitals
National Parks
West from Greenwich
Projection: Albers Equal Area with two standard parallels
COPYRIGHT PHILIP'S
m ft

1:6 000 000

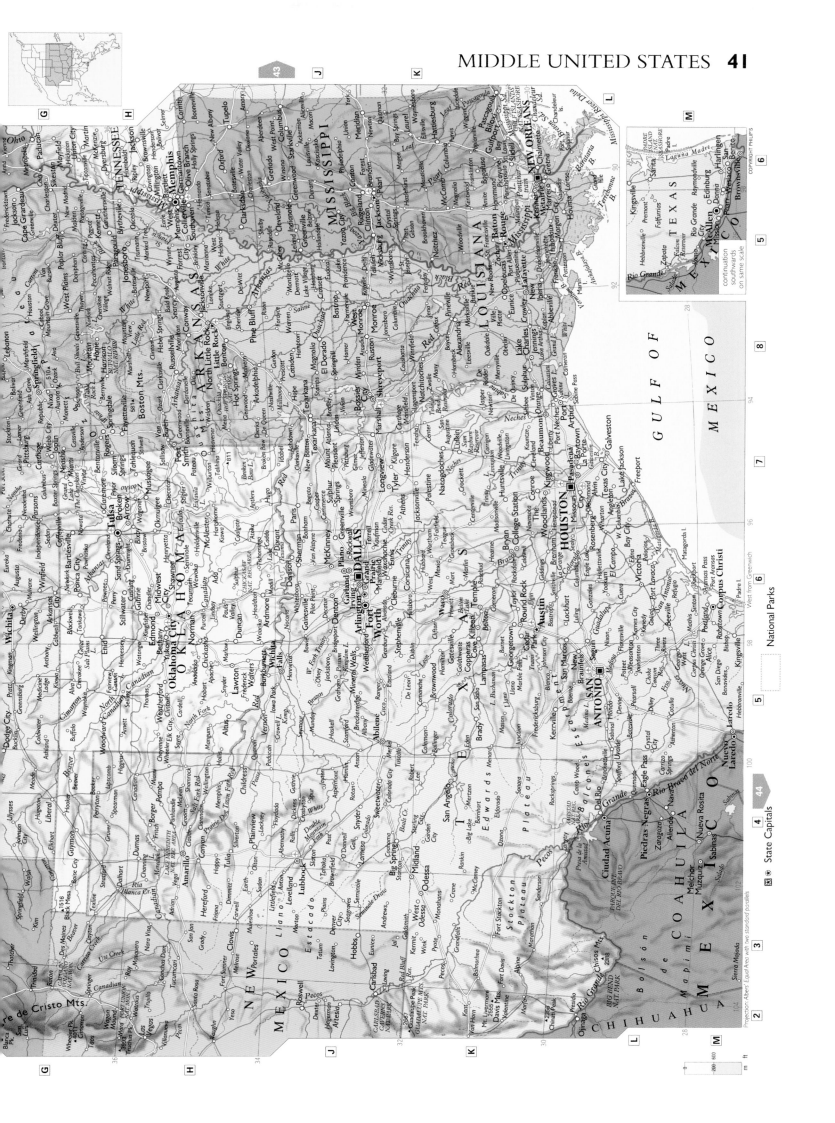

State Capitals

National Parks

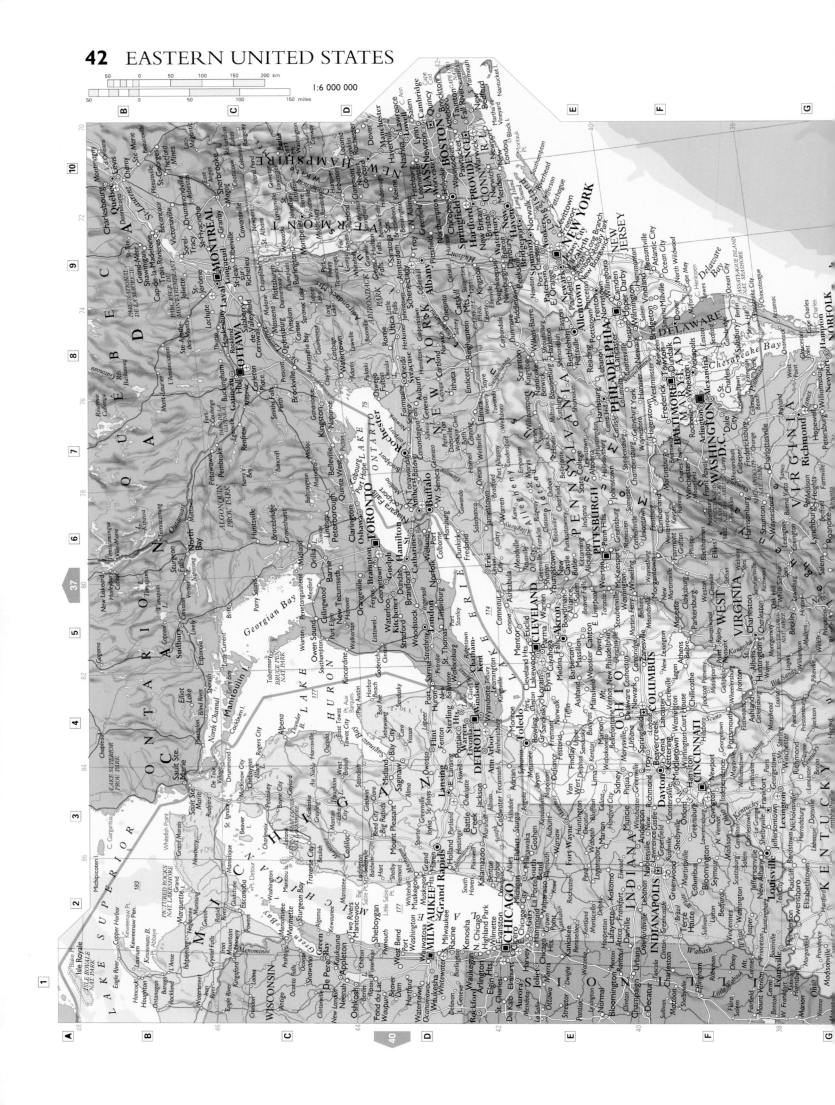

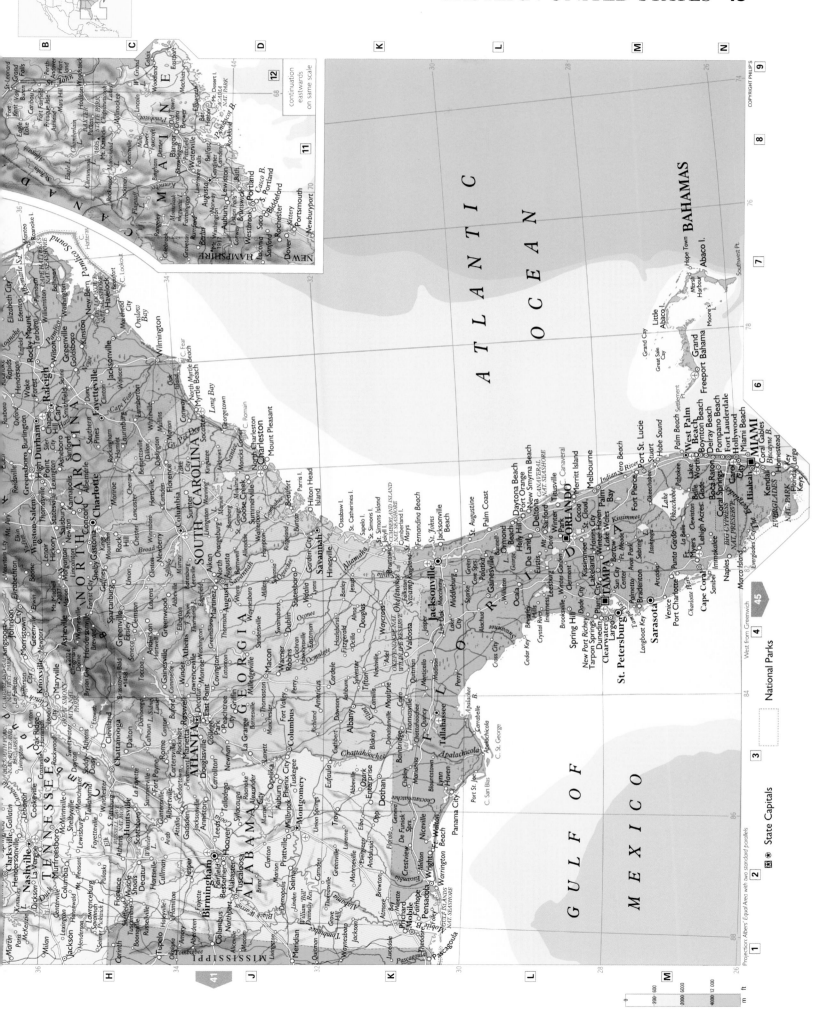

1:15 000 000

100   0   100   200   300   400   500   600 km
100   0   100   200   300   400 miles

| 1 | 2 | 3 | 4 | 39 | 5 | 6 | 7 |

SAN DIEGO
TIJUANA
Mexicali
Ensenada
San Felipe
3078
Baja California

PHOENIX
Tucson
Casa Grande
Deming
Las Cruces
El Paso
CIUDAD JUÁREZ

UNITED STATES

Roswell
3659
Lubbock
Wichita Falls
Little Rock
Huntsville
Birmingham

Sonoita
Nogales
Cananea
Nacozari
Douglas
Agua Prieta
Nuevo Casas Grandes
Villa Ahumada
Carlsbad
Pecos
Fort Stockton
Odessa
San Angelo
Abilene
FORT WORTH
DALLAS
Tyler
Shreveport
Monroe
Greenville
Tuscaloosa
Montgom

Caborca
I. Angel de la Guarda
I. Tiburón
Hermosillo
Madera
Chihuahua
Cuauhtémoc
Ojinaga
Rio Grande
Ciudad Acuña
Del Rio
SAN ANTONIO
Austin
Bryan
HOUSTON
Beaumont
Lake Charles
Baton Rouge
Jackson
Natchez
Alexandria
Meridian
Hattiesburg

Bahía Sebastián Vizcaíno
Pta. Falsa
Santa Rosalía
Guaymas
Empalme
Ciudad Obregón
Navojoa
Huatabampo
Delicias
Ciudad Camargo
Jiménez
Piedras Negras
Nueva Rosita
Sabinas
Nuevo Laredo
Laredo
Victoria
Corpus Christi
Galveston
Port Arthur
Mobile
Pensacola
NEW ORLEANS
Mississippi River Delta

GULF OF MEXI

Loreto
Los Mochis
Topolobampo
Guasave
Guamúchil
Gómez Palacio
3050
Hidalgo del Parral
Tepehuanes
Monclova
San Pedro de las Colonias
TORREÓN
Saltillo
MONTERREY
Reynosa
Matamoros
McAllen
Brownsville
Padre I.
Laguna Madre
Matagorda I.

B. de La Paz
La Paz
2164
Culiacán
El Salto
Durango
Sombrerete
Concepción del Oro
Linares
Montemorelos
San Fernando
Falcon Res.
Sabinas Hidalgo

C. San Lázaro
C. San Lucas
Cabo San Lucas
Mazatlán
Rosario
Escuinapa
Acaponeta
Jerez
Zacatecas
Presnillo
Matehuala
Charcas
Ciudad Victoria
3540
TROPIC OF CANCER
3664

Islas Marías
Tuxpan
Tepic
Rio Grande de Santiago
2980
Aguascalientes
San Luis Potosí
Ciudad Mante
Ciudad Madero
Tampico
Ciudad Valles

Is. de Revillagigedo (Mex.)
Puerto Vallarta
C. Corrientes
GUADALAJARA
LEÓN
Guanajuato
Irapuato
Celaya
Querétaro
Pachuca
Tulancingo
Poza Rica
Papantla
Tuxpan
Nogozal
C. Rojo

Ameca
L. de Chapala
Zamora
Morelia
MÉXICO
TOLUCA
Cuernavaca
PUEBLA
Pico de Orizaba
5610
Xalapa
Veracruz
Orizaba
Córdoba

Golfo de Campeche

Progreso
Mérida
Motul
Tizimín
C. Catoche
Cancún
Valladolid
Cozumel
I. de Cozumel
Ticul
Peto
Campeche
Champotón
Felipe Carrillo Puerto
Chetumal

Yucatán

Ciudad Guzmán
Nevado de Colima
4240
Colima
Manzanillo
Tecomán
Uruapan
Iguala
Chilpancingo
Chilapa
Balsas
Tlapa
3550
Tlaxiaco
Oaxaca
Ciudad del Carmen
Laguna de Términos
Coatzacoalcos
San Andrés Tuxtla
Minatitlán
Villahermosa
Escárcega
Corozal
Ambergris Cay
Belize City
Turneffe Is.
BELIZE
Belmopan

Lázaro Cárdenas
Acapulco
5448
Ometepec
3397
Istmo de Tehuantepec
Tuxtla Gutiérrez
Juchitán
Palenque
San Cristóbal de las Casas
Comitán
GUATEMALA
Cobán
Gulf of Honduras
Puerto Cortés
Roatán
Dangriga
Puerto Barrios
Tela
La Ceiba

G. de Tehuantepec
Tehuantepec
3139
Salina Cruz
Tonalá
Huixtla
4093
8834
GUATEMALA
Quezaltenango
Escuintla
Santa Ana
Sonsonate
Comayagua
HONDUR
TEGUCIGA

Guatemala Trench
6662
Tapachula
SAN SALVADOR
San Vincente
San Miguel
La Union
G. de Fonseca
Choluteca
NIC
MAN

EL SALVADOR
León
Chinandega
Rivas
Pen. Nico
Nica

PACIFIC

OCEAN

I. del Coco
(Costa Rica)

JAMAICA [a]
1:3 000 000

10   0   10   20   30   40   50 km
10   0   10   20   30 miles

CARIBBEAN   SEA

Montego Bay
Lucea
Falmouth
Runaway Bay
St. Ann's Bay
Galina Point
Port Maria
Negril
South Negril Pt.
Cambridge
Wakefield
The Cockpit Country
Ocho Rios
Dry Harbour Mountains
Moneague
Annotto Bay
Port Antonio
Savanna-la-Mar
Maggotty
Mount Denham
985
Linstead
The Blue Mountains
2256
Blue Mt. Pk.
John Crow Mts.
Black River
Mandeville
Santa Cruz Mts.
Don Figuero Mts.
Spanish Town
Portmore
KINGSTON
Morant Point
JAMAICA
Great Pedro Bluff
May Pen
Alligator Pond
Portland Bight
Portland Point
Morant Bay
Port Morant

GUADELOUPE AND MARTINIQUE [G]
1:2 000 000

10   0   10   20   30   40 km
10   0   10   20   30 miles

[b]
Pte. de la Grande Vigie
61° 30'
16° 30'
Port-Louis
Grande-Terre
Pointe Allègre
Petit-Canal
Ste-Rose
La Désirade
Le Moule
Pointe des Châteaux
Pointe-Noire
Pointe-à-Pitre
Basse-Terre
Bouillante
Ste-Anne
Le Gosier
Îles de la Petite Terre
GUADELOUPE (Fr.)
Soufrière
1467
Capesterre-Belle-Eau
St-Louis
Marie-Galante
204
Basse-Terre
Trois-Rivières
Capesterre
Grand Bourg
Pte. des Basses
Îles des Saintes
Projection : Bonne

[c]
Cap St-Martin
61°
Basse-Pointe
Le Prêcheur
1397
Montagne Pelée
Ste-Marie
St-Pierre
La Trinité
Presqu'île de la Caravelle
Le Robert
Schœlcher
St-Joseph
Le François
Fort-de-France
Le Lamentin
Le St-Esprit
Rivière-Salée
MARTINIQUE (Fr.)
Rivière-Pilote
Le Marin
14° 30'
Pte. d'Enfer

m ft
0
200   600
2000   6000
4000   12 000
6000   18 000

| 6 | 7 |

PUERTO RICO **d**
1:3 000 000

ATLANTIC OCEAN

PUERTO RICO (U.S.A.)

Pta. Agujereada   Isabela   Barceloneta   **SAN JUAN**
Aguadilla   Arecibo   Manati   Vega   Bayamón   Rio Grande
Mayagüez   San Sebastian   Utuado   Baja   Carolina   Fajardo   Dewey
  Adjuntas   Córdillera Central   Caguas   Sierra de   Culebra
San German   Uroyan Mts.   C. de Punta 1338   Cayey   Humacao   Naguabo   Puerca   Vieques
  Yauco   Coamo   Esperanza
Pta. Aguila   Guanica   **Ponce**   Guayama   Yabucoa
  I. Caja de Muertos

A

VIRGIN IS. **e**
1:2 000 000

Rufling Pt.   The Settlement
Anegada   East Pt.
Virgin Islands (U.K.)
Jost Van   Great
Dyke I.   Guana I.   Camanoe
Virgin Is. (U.S.A.)   Haos   Lollik I.   Cruz   Guana I.   Virgin Gorda
  Bay   **Tortola**   Road Town   Spanish Town
Charlotte   St.   Peter I.
Amalie   St. John I.
Thomas I.

ST. LUCIA **f**
1:1 000 000

Cap Point   Pte. Hardy
Gros Islet   Esperance Bay
Castries   Marquis
  Girard
Anse la Raye   Dennery
Canaries   Millet
Soufrière   Mt. Gimie
Soufrière   750   ▲950   Trou Gras Pt.
Bay   Petit Piton   Micoud
Gros Piton Pt.   796   Vierge Pt.
Choiseul   Gros Piton
Laborie   Vieux Fort   **ST. LUCIA**
  C. Moule à Chique

B

BARBADOS
ATLANTIC OCEAN
Crab Hill   North Point
  Spring Hall
Fustic   Boscobelle
  245   Belleplaine
Speightstown   **BARBADOS**
Westmoreland   Alleynes Bay   Hillcrest   Martin's Bay
Holetown   Mt. Hillaby   Massiah
  Jackson   ▲340   Street
Black Rock   Bridgefield   Six Cross Roads
  Ellerton   The Crane
Bridgetown   Oistins   St. Martins
  Carlisle Bay   Chancery Lane
  Worthing   Oistins   South Point
  Bay

BARBADOS **g**
1:1 000 000

Map labels

Columbia   Wilmington   C. Fear
LANTA   Augusta   Long Bay
Macon   C. Romain
bus   Savannah   Charleston
assee   Jacksonville
  Altamaha
ny   Daytona Beach
ORLANDO   C. Canaveral
MPA   Melbourne
St. Petersburg   West Palm Beach   Grand Bahama
rasota   L. Okeechobee   Freeport   Abaco I.
MIAMI   Fort Lauderdale   Bimini Is.   New Providence I.   Eleuthera I.
C. Sable   Andros I.   Nassau   Cat I.
Key West   BAHAMAS   San Salvador I.
Straits of Florida   Great Exuma I.
HABANA (Havana)   Matanzas   Cárdenas   Long I.   Crooked I.
G. de   Güines   Sagua la Grande   Mayaguana I.
Batabanó   Santa Clara   Acklins I.
I. de la   Cienfuegos   Placetas   Morón
Juventud   Trinidad   Sancti Spiritus   Ciego de Ávila   Turks & Caicos Is.
C U B A   Camagüey   Cockburn   (U.K.)
  Nuevitas   Town
G r e a t e r   Great Inagua I.
  Las Tunas   Holguin   Baracoa
Cayman Is.   Banes   Puerto Plata   Monte Christi
Grand   1972   Bayamo   Port-de-Paix   Cap-Haïtien   Santiago de   San francisco
Cayman   George Town   Santiago   los Caballeros   de Macoris
(U.K.)   de Cuba   GUANTANAMO   Gonaives   La Vega
  7680   Montego Bay   BAY   3175   St-Marc   **DOMINICAN**   La Romana
Mandeville   Jérémie   **HAITI**   **REP.**   San Pedro de Macoris
JAMAICA   Spanish   Les Cayes   Jacmel   san juan   Bani   SANTO DOMINGO
  Town   **Kingston**   PORT-AU-PRINCE   Barahona
  A n   Hispaniola
  t i l l e s

Windward Passage   Puerto Rico Trench
  9200   Arecibo   **SAN JUAN**
Mayagüez   Ponce   Virgin Is.   Anguilla (U.K.)
Mona   (U.S.A.-U.K.)   St-Martin (Fr.-Neth.)
Mona   St. Croix   St-Barthélemy (Fr.)   **ST. KITTS & NEVIS**
Passage   (U.S.A.)   Basseterre   **ANTIGUA &**
PUERTO RICO (U.S.A.)   St. John's   **BARBUDA**
  Montserrat (U.K.)   **GUADELOUPE** (Fr.)
L e s s e r   Leeward   Pointe-à-Pitre
  Islands   Basse-Terre
  DOMINICA
  Roseau
  A n t i l l e s   Fort-de-France   **MARTINIQUE** (Fr.)
C A R I B B E A N   S E A   Castries   **ST. LUCIA**
  ST. VINCENT &   Kingstown   **BARBADOS**
  THE GRENADINES   Bridgetown
  W i n d w a r d
  I s l a n d s   **GRENADA**
  La Blanquilla   St. George's
  (Ven.)   Tobago

L. de Caratasca   C. Gracias a Dios
Puerto Cabezas
I. de Providencia (Colombia)
Rio Grande
Bluefields   I. de San Andrés (Colombia)
COSTA RICA   C. de Vela   Aruba (Neth.)   Curaçao   Willemstad   **NETH.**
razú   Pen. de la   Bonaire   **ANTILLES**
432   Limón   Guajira   Punto   G. de Venezuela   Pta. Gallinas
artago   G. de los Mosquitos   Fijo   La Tortuga
Volcán Barú   Colón   Riohacha   I. de Margarita   Porlamar
David   3475   Panamá   **Panamá**   Santa Marta   Coro   San   Puerto Cabello   Cumaná   Carúpano
Puerto   **P A N A M A**   Canal   Sierra Nevada   Felipe   Maiquetía   Port of Spain
muelles   Santiago   Chitré   G. del   **BARRANQUILLA**   de Santa Marta   5800   **MARACAY**   **CARACAS**   Puerto La   **TRINIDAD & TOBAGO**
I. de   Arch. de   Darién   Cartagena   Soledad   **MARACAIBO**   **VALENCIA**   Barcelona   Cruz   San Fernando
Coiba   las Perlas   La Palma   Calamar   Valledupar   Cabimas   **Barquisimeto**   2596   G. de   Maturín
Pen. de   Jaque   El Real   Sinceleto   L. de   Acarigua   Paria
Azuero   G. de Panamá   Monteria   Mompos   Maracaibo   Valera   El Tigre   Tucupita
  G. de Cupica   Antioquia   Merida   Barinas   Ciudad   Georgetown
  Quibdó   9960   Yarumal   6007   Apure   San Fernando   Orinoco   **Guayana**   Bartica
C. Corrientes   Bello   Puerto Wilches   Cúcuta   de Apure   Ciudad Bolívar   New Amsterdam   Linden
  MEDELLÍN   Barrancabermeja   San Cristóbal   Caicara   Embalse de Guri   Wismar
Manizales   Riosucio   Pamplona   **V E N E Z U E L A**   Tumereno
  Tolima   **Bucaramanga**   Puerto Carreño   Mt. Roraima   2712   **SURINAME**
Pereira   5215   Sogamoso   Angel   **G U Y A N A**
  Ibagué   **C O L O M B I A**   Tunja   Puerto Ayacucho   Falls
Armenia   **BOGOTÁ**   Sierra Pacaraima
  Girardot   Villavicencio   Serra   Boa Vista
Buenaventura   **Palmira**   Puerto Inirida   Parima
  Huila   Orinoco
I. de Malpelo   **CALI**   5750   Neiva   Guaviare
(Colombia)   Popayán   Casiquiare
  Volcán Puracé   ▲4646   **B R A Z I L**   Equator

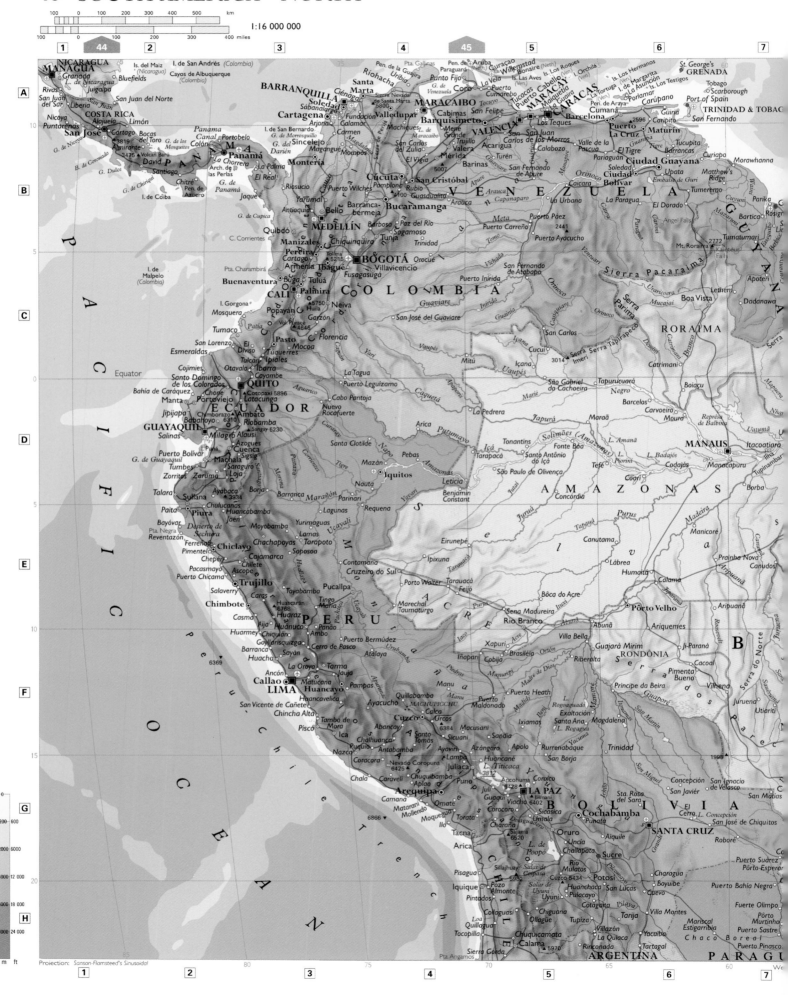

1:16 000 000

Projection: Sanson-Flamsteed's Sinusoidal

100   0   100   200   300   400   500   km
100   0   100   200   300   400   miles
1:16 000 000

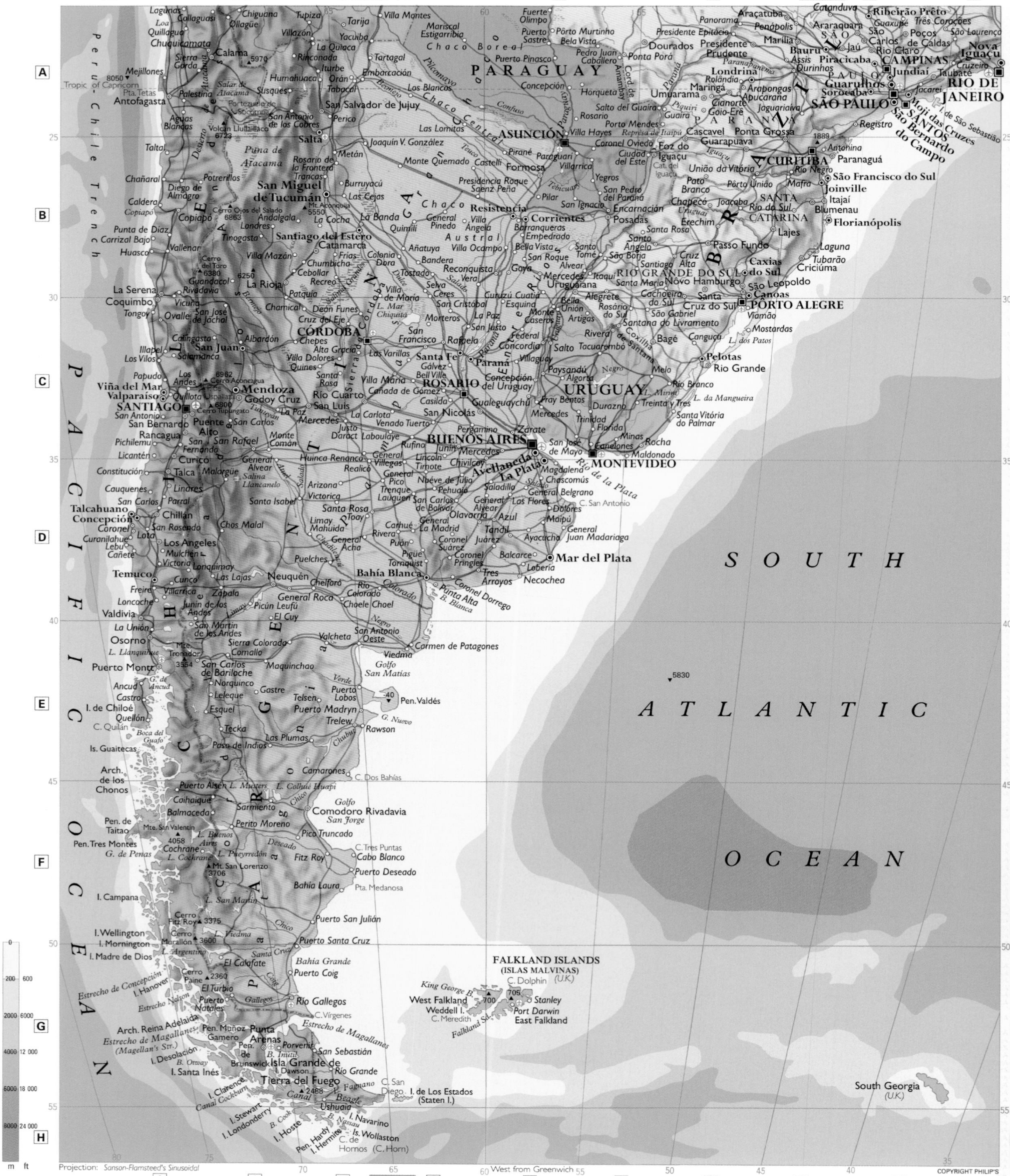

Projection: Sanson-Flamsteed's Sinusoidal

COPYRIGHT PHILIP'S

PARAGUAY

BRAZIL

ASUNCIÓN

URUGUAY

MONTEVIDEO

ARGENTINA

CÓRDOBA

San Miguel de Tucumán

BUENOS AIRES

SANTIAGO

Valparaíso

Mendoza

ROSARIO

La Plata

Mar del Plata

Bahía Blanca

Neuquén

Comodoro Rivadavia

Río Gallegos

Punta Arenas

Tierra del Fuego

SÃO PAULO

RIO DE JANEIRO

CURITIBA

PORTO ALEGRE

CAMPINAS

SANTOS

GUARULHOS

RIO GRANDE DO SUL

SANTA CATARINA

PARANÁ

Florianópolis

Antofagasta

Valdivia

Puerto Montt

Concepción

Talcahuano

Tropic of Capricorn

FALKLAND ISLANDS
(ISLAS MALVINAS)
(U.K.)

West Falkland
East Falkland
Stanley
Port Darwin

South Georgia
(U.K.)

SOUTH ATLANTIC OCEAN

PACIFIC OCEAN

Peru–Chile Trench

West from Greenwich

C. Horn

INDEX

The index contains the names of all the principal places and features shown on the maps. The alphabetical order of names composed of two or more words is governed primarily by the first word and then by the second. This is an example of the rule:

New South Wales □ **32 B4**
New York □ **42 D8**
New Zealand ■ **33 J6**
Newark, *Del., U.S.A.* **42 F8**
Newark, *N.J., U.S.A.* **42 E8**

Physical features composed of a proper name (Erie) and a description (Lake) are positioned alphabetically by the proper name. The description is positioned after the proper name and is usually abbreviated:

Erie, L. **42 D5**
Everest, Mt. **25 C7**

Where a description forms part of a settlement name or administrative name, however, it is always written in full and put in its true alphabetical position:

Lake Charles **41 K8**
Mount Isa **30 E6**

The number in bold type which follows each name in the index refers to the number of the map page where that place or feature will be found. This is usually the largest scale at which the place or feature appears.

The letter and figure which are immediately after the page number give the grid square on the map page, within which the feature is situated. The letter represents the latitude and the figure the longitude. In some cases the feature itself may fall within the specified square, while the name is outside.

Rivers are indexed to their mouths or confluences and carry the symbol → after their names. The following symbols are also used in the index: ■ country, ☑ overseas territory or dependency, □ first order administrative area, △ national park or reserve.

A

A Coruña 13 A1
Aachen 16 C3
Aalborg 7 F5
Aarau 12 C8
Aare → 12 C8
Aba 26 G7
Abaco I. 45 B9
Ābādān 24 B3
Abakan 19 D10
Abariringa 31 A16
Abbaye, Pt. 42 B1
Abbeville, *France* 12 A4
Abbeville, *Ala., U.S.A.* 43 K3
Abbeville, *La., U.S.A.* 41 L8
Abbeville, *S.C., U.S.A.* 43 H4
Abbeyfeale 11 D2
Abel Tasman △ 33 J4
Abeokuta 26 G6
Aberaeron 9 E3
Aberchirder 10 D6
Abercorn 32 A5
Aberdare 9 F4
Aberdeen, *Australia* 32 B5
Aberdeen, *China* 21 G11
Aberdeen, *U.K.* 10 D6
Aberdeen, *Ala., U.S.A.* 43 J1
Aberdeen, *Idaho, U.S.A.* 38 E7
Aberdeen, *Md., U.S.A.* 42 F7
Aberdeen, *S. Dak., U.S.A.* 40 C5
Aberdeen, *Wash., U.S.A.* 38 C2
Aberdeenshire □ 10 D6
Aberdyfi 9 E3
Aberfeldy 10 E5
Aberfoyle 10 E4
Abergavenny 9 F4
Abergele 8 D4
Abernathy 41 J4
Abert, L. 38 E3
Aberystwyth 9 E3
Abhā 24 D3
Abidjan 26 G5
Abilene, *Kans., U.S.A.* 40 F6
Abilene, *Tex., U.S.A.* 41 J5
Abingdon, *U.K.* 9 F6
Abingdon, *U.S.A.* 43 G5
Abitibi, L. 37 E12
Abminga 32 A1
Aboyne 10 D6
Absaroka Range 38 D9
Abu Dhabi = Abū Ẓāby 24 C4
Abū Ẓāby 24 C4
Abuja 26 G7
Abut Hd. 33 K3
Acadia △ 43 C11
Acaponeta 44 C3
Acapulco 44 D5
Acarigua 46 B5
Accomac 42 G8
Accra 26 G5
Accrington 8 D5
Aceh □ 23 C1
Achill Hd. 11 C1
Achill I. 11 C1
Achinsk 19 D10
Ackerman 41 J10
Acklins I. 45 C10
Aconcagua, Cerro 48 C3
Açores, Is. dos 26 A1
Acraman, L. 32 B2
Acre □ 46 E4
Ad Dammām 24 C4
Ad Dawḥah 24 C4
Ad Dīwānīyah 24 B3
Ada, *Minn., U.S.A.* 40 B6
Ada, *Okla., U.S.A.* 41 H6
Adair, C. 37 B12
Adak I. 36 D2
Adamaoua, Massif de l' 27 G8
Adaminaby 32 C4
Adams, *N.Y., U.S.A.* 42 D7
Adams, *Wis., U.S.A.* 40 D10
Adams, Mt. 38 C3
Adana 17 C5
Adare, C. 6 E15
Adavale 32 A3
Addis Abeba 28 C7
Adel 43 K4
Adelaide 32 B2
Adelaide I. 6 D3
Adelaide Pen. 36 C10
Adélie, Terre 6 D14
Aden = Al 'Adan 24 D3
Aden, G. of 24 D3
Adirondack △ 42 D8
Adirondack Mts. 42 D8
Adis Abeba = Addis Abeba 28 C7
Adjuntas 45 d
Admiralty Is. 34 H6
Adoni 25 D6
Adour → 12 E3
Adrar 26 C6
Adrian, *Mich., U.S.A.* 42 E3
Adrian, *Tex., U.S.A.* 41 H3
Adriatic Sea 14 C6
Adwa 24 D2
Ægean Sea 15 E11
Aerhtai Shan 20 B4
Afghanistan ■ 24 B5
Africa 3 D11
Afton 38 E8
Agadir 26 B4
Agalega Is. 5 E13
Agen 12 D4
Agra 25 C6
Ağrı Dağı 17 C6
Agrigento 14 F5
Agua Fria △ 39 J7
Agua Prieta 44 A3
Aguadilla 45 d
Aguascalientes 44 C4
Aguila, Punta 45 d
Agujereada, Pta. 45 d
Agulhas, C. 29 L4
Ahaggar 26 D7
Ahipara B. 33 F4
Ahmadabad 25 C6
Ahmadnagar 25 D6
Ahoskie 43 G7
Ahvāz 24 B3
Ahvenanmaa = Åland 7 E8
Aihui 21 A7
Aiken 43 J5
Ailsa Craig 10 F3
Ainsworth 40 D5
Aïr 26 E7
Air Force I. 37 C12
Airdrie, *Canada* 36 D8
Airdrie, *U.K.* 10 F5
Aire → 8 D7
Aisne → 12 B5
Aitkin 40 B8
Aitutaki 35 J12
Aix-en-Provence 12 E6
Aix-les-Bains 12 D6
Aizuwakamatsu 22 E6
Ajaccio 12 F8
Ajmer 25 C6
Ajo 39 K7
Akaroa 33 K4
Akimiski I. 37 D11
Akita 22 D7
'Akko 17 D5
Aklavik 36 C6
Akola 25 C6
Akpatok I. 37 C13
Akron, *Colo., U.S.A.* 40 E3
Akron, *Ohio, U.S.A.* 42 E5
Aksai Chin 25 B6
Aksu 20 B3
Aksum 24 D2
Akure 26 G7
Al 'Adan 24 D3
Al 'Amārah 24 B3
Al 'Aqabah 24 C2
Al 'Ayn 24 C4
Al Başrah 24 B3
Al Ḩajar al Gharbī 24 C4
Al Ḩillah 24 B3
Al Ḩudaydah 24 D3
Al Hufūf 24 C3
Al Jawf 24 C2
Al Jazirah 24 B3
Al Jubayl 24 C3
Al Khamāsīn 24 C3
Al Kūt 24 B3
Al Kuwayt 24 C3
Al Lādhiqīyah 24 B2
Al Madīnah 24 C2
Al Manāmah 24 C4
Al Mawşil 24 B3
Al Mubarraz 24 C3
Al Mukallā 24 D3
Al Mukhā 24 D3
Al Qā'im 24 B3
Al Qaţīf 24 C4
Al Qunfudhah 24 D3
Al Wajh 24 C2
Alabama □ 43 J2
Alabama → 43 K2
Alabaster 43 J2
Alachua 43 L4
Alameda 39 J10
Alamo 39 H6
Alamogordo 39 K11
Alamosa 39 H11
Åland 7 E8
Alaska □ 36 C4
Alaska, G. of 36 D5
Alaska Peninsula 36 D4
Alaska Range 36 C4
Alava, C. 38 B1
Alawoona 32 B3
Alba-Iulia 15 A10
Albacete 13 C5
Albacutya, L. 32 C3
Albanel, L. 37 D12
Albania ■ 15 D9
Albany, *Australia* 30 H2
Albany, *Ga., U.S.A.* 43 K3
Albany, *N.Y., U.S.A.* 42 D9
Albany, *Oreg., U.S.A.* 38 D2
Albany, *Tex., U.S.A.* 41 J5
Albany → 37 D11
Albemarle 43 H5
Albemarle Sd. 43 H7
Alberga → 32 A2
Albert, L., *Africa* 28 D6
Albert, L., *Australia* 32 C2
Albert Lea 40 D8
Alberta □ 36 D8
Albertville, *France* 12 D7
Albertville, *U.S.A.* 43 H2
Albi 12 E5
Albia 40 E8
Albion, *Mich., U.S.A.* 42 D3
Albion, *Nebr., U.S.A.* 40 E6
Alborz, Reshteh-ye Kūhhā-ye 24 B4
Albuquerque 39 J10
Albury 32 C4
Alcalá de Henares 13 B4
Alchevsk 17 A5
Alcova 38 E10
Aldabra Is. 5 E13
Aldan → 19 C13
Aldeburgh 9 E9
Alderney 9 H5
Aldershot 9 F7
Aledo 40 E9
Aleksandrovsk-Sakhalinskiy 19 D15
Alençon 12 B4
Alert 37 A13
Alès 12 D6
Alessándria 12 D8
Ålesund 7 E5
Aleutian Basin 34 B9
Aleutian Is. 36 D2
Aleutian Trench 34 C10
Alexander 40 B3
Alexander Arch. 36 D6
Alexander City 43 J3
Alexander I. 6 D3
Alexandra, *Australia* 32 C4
Alexandra, *N.Z.* 33 L2
Alexandria = El Iskandarîya 27 B11
Alexandria, *U.K.* 10 F4
Alexandria, *La., U.S.A.* 41 K8
Alexandria, *Minn., U.S.A.* 40 C7
Alexandria, *S. Dak., U.S.A.* 40 D6
Alexandria, *Va., U.S.A.* 42 F7
Alexandria Bay 42 C8
Alexandrina, L. 32 C2
Alford, *Aberds., U.K.* 10 D6
Alford, *Lincs., U.K.* 8 D8
Alfreton 8 D6
Algarve 13 D1
Algeciras 13 D3
Alger 26 A6
Algeria ■ 26 C6
Algiers = Alger 26 A6
Algoma 42 C2
Algona 40 D7
Alicante 13 C5
Alice 41 M5
Alice Springs 30 E5
Aliceville 43 J1
Aligarh 25 C6
Aliquippa 42 E5
Aliwal North 29 L5
Alkmaar 16 B2
All American Canal 39 K6
Allagash → 43 B11
Allahabad 25 C7
Allegheny → 42 E6
Allegheny Mts. 42 G6
Allegheny Plateau 42 E6
Allègre, Pte. 44 b
Allen, Bog of 11 C5
Allen, L. 11 B3
Allendale 43 J5
Allentown 42 E8
Alleppey 25 E6
Alleynes B. 45 g
Alliance, *Nebr., U.S.A.* 40 D3
Alliance, *Ohio, U.S.A.* 42 E5
Allier → 12 C5
Alligator Pond 44 a
Alloa 10 E5
Allora 32 A5
Alma, *Ga., U.S.A.* 43 K4
Alma, *Kans., U.S.A.* 40 F6
Alma, *Mich., U.S.A.* 42 D3
Alma, *Nebr., U.S.A.* 40 E5
Alma, *Wis., U.S.A.* 40 C9
Alma Ata = Almaty 18 E8
Almanor, L. 38 F3
Almaty 18 E8
Almelo 16 B3
Almería 13 D4
Alness 10 D4
Alnmouth 8 B6
Alnwick 8 B6
Alofi, I. 31 C15
Alor 23 D4
Alor Setar 23 C2
Alpena 42 C4
Alpine, *Ariz., U.S.A.* 39 K9
Alpine, *Tex., U.S.A.* 41 K3
Alps 12 C8
Alsace □ 12 B7
Alsask 36 D9
Alston 8 C5
Altai = Aerhtai Shan 20 B4
Altamaha → 43 K5
Altanbulag 20 A5
Altavista 42 G6
Altay 20 B3
Altiplano 46 G5
Alton, *U.K.* 9 F7
Alton, *U.S.A.* 40 F9
Altoona 42 E6
Altun Shan 20 C3
Alturas 38 F3
Altus 41 H5
Alva 41 G5
Alvarado 41 J6
Alvin 41 L7
Alvord Desert 38 E4
Alxa Zuoqi 20 C5
Alyth 10 E5
Alzada 40 C2
Amadjuak L. 37 C12
Amagasaki 22 F4
Amarillo 41 H4
Amazon = Amazonas → 47 D8
Amazonas □ 46 E6
Amazonas → 47 D8
Ambala 25 B6
Ambergris Cay 44 D7
Amberley 33 K4
Amble 8 B6
Ambleside 8 C5
Ambon 23 D4
Amboy 39 J6
Amboyna Cay 23 C3
Amchitka I. 36 D1
Ameca 44 C4
American Falls 38 E7
American Falls Res. 38 E7
American Fork 38 F8
American Highland 6 E10
American Samoa ☑ 33 B13
Americus 43 K3
Ames 40 E8
Amherst, *Canada* 37 E13
Amherst, *U.S.A.* 42 D6
Amidon 40 B3
Amiens 12 B5
Amirante Is. 5 E13
Amistad △ 41 L4
Amite 41 K9
Amlia I. 36 D2
Amlwch 8 D3
'Ammān 24 B2
Ammanford 9 F4
Ammon 38 E8
Amory 43 J1
Amos 37 E12
Amravati 25 C6
Amritsar 25 B6
Amsterdam, *Neths.* 16 B2
Amsterdam, *U.S.A.* 42 D8
Amudarya → 18 E6
Amund Ringnes I. 37 A12
Amundsen Gulf 36 B7
Amundsen Sea 6 E1
Amuntai 23 D3
Amur → 19 D15
An Nafūd 24 C3
An Najaf 24 B3
An Nāşirīyah 24 B3
An Uaimh 11 C5
Anaconda 38 C7
Anacortes 38 B2
Anadarko 41 H5
Anadolu 17 C4
Anadyr 19 C18
Anadyrskiy Zaliv 19 C19
Anaheim 39 K5
Anambas, Kepulauan 23 C2
Anamosa 40 D9
Anápolis 47 G9
Anār 24 B4
Anatolia = Anadolu 17 C4
Anchorage 36 C5
Ancohuma, Nevado 46 G5
Ancona 14 C5
Anda 21 B7
Andalucía □ 13 D3
Andalusia 43 K2
Andaman Is. 25 D8
Andaman Sea 25 D8
Andamooka 32 B2
Anderson, *Alaska, U.S.A.* 36 C5
Anderson, *Calif., U.S.A.* 38 F2
Anderson, *Ind., U.S.A.* 42 E3
Anderson, *Mo., U.S.A.* 41 G7
Anderson, *S.C., U.S.A.* 43 H4
Anderson → 36 C7
Andes, Cord. de los 46 H5
Andhra Pradesh □ 25 D6
Andijon 18 E8
Andorra ■ 12 E4
Andover 9 F6
Andreanof Is. 36 D2
Andrews, *S.C., U.S.A.* 43 J6
Andrews, *Tex., U.S.A.* 41 J3
Ándria 14 D7
Andros I. 45 C9
Anegada 45 e
Aneityum 31 E12
Angara → 19 D10
Angarsk 19 D11
Angaston 32 B2
Ånge 7 E7
Angel Falls 46 B6
Angeles 23 B4
Angels Camp 39 G3
Ångermanälven → 7 E7
Angers 12 C3
Anglesey, Isle of □ 8 D3
Angleton 41 L7
Angola 42 E3
Angola ■ 29 G3
Angoulême 12 D4
Angoumois 12 D3
Angren 18 E8
Anguilla ☑ 45 D12
Angus □ 10 E6
Anhui □ 21 C6
Animas → 39 H9
Anjou 12 C3
Ankaboa, Tanjona 29 J8
Ankang 21 C5
Ankara 17 C4
Ankeny 40 E8
Ann, C. 42 D10
Ann Arbor 42 D4
Anna 41 G10
Annaba 26 A7
Annalee → 11 B4
Annan 10 G5
Annan → 10 G5
Annapolis 42 F7
Annapurna 25 C7
Annecy 12 D7
Anning 20 D5
Anniston 43 J3
Annotto B. 44 a
Anqing 21 C6
Anse la Raye 45 f
Anshan 21 B7
Anshun 20 D5
Ansley 40 E5
Anson 41 J5
Anstruther 10 E6
Antalya = Hatay 17 C4
Antananarivo 29 H9
Antarctic Pen. 6 D4
Antarctica 6 F7
Antero, Mt. 39 G10
Anthony, *Kans., U.S.A.* 41 G5
Anthony, *N. Mex., U.S.A.* 39 K10
Anti Atlas 26 C4
Antibes 12 E7
Anticosti, Î. d' 37 E13
Antigo 40 C10
Antigonish 37 E13
Antigua & Barbuda ■ 45 D12
Antipodes Is. 34 M9
Antlers 41 H7
Antofagasta 48 A2
Anton 41 J3
Antrim 11 B5
Antrim □ 11 B5
Antrim, Mts. of 11 A5
Antsiranana 29 G9
Antwerpen 16 C2
Anxi 20 B4
Anxious B. 32 B1
Anyang 21 C6
Anzhero-Sudzhensk 18 D9
Aomori 22 C7
Aoraki Mount Cook 33 K3
Apache 41 H5
Apache Junction 39 K8
Apalachee B. 43 L4
Apalachicola 43 L3
Apalachicola → 43 L3
Apeldoorn 16 B2
Apia 33 A13
Apostle Is. 40 B9
Apostle Islands △ 40 B9
Appalachian Mts. 42 G6
Appennini 14 B4
Appleby-in-Westmorland 8 C5
Appledore 9 F3
Appleton 42 C1
Aqtöbe 18 D6
Ar Ramādī 24 B3
Ar Riyāḑ 24 C3
Ara 25 C7
Arab 43 H2
Arab, Shatt al → 24 C3
Arabia 3 C13
Arabian Gulf = Persian Gulf 24 C4
Arabian Sea 24 D5
Aracaju 47 F11
Araçatuba 47 H8
Arad 15 A9
Arafura Sea 23 D5
Aragón □ 13 B5
Araguaia → 47 E9
Arak, *Algeria* 26 C6
Arāk, *Iran* 24 B3
Arakan Yoma 25 D8
Aral 18 E7
Aral Sea 18 E7
Aran I. 11 A3
Aran Is. 11 C2
Aransas Pass 41 M6
Arapahoe 40 E5
Arapiraca 47 E11
Ar'ar 24 B3
Araraquara 47 H9
Ararat 32 C3
Ararat, Mt. = Ağrı Dağı 17 C6
Arbīl 24 B3
Arbroath 10 E6
Arbuckle 38 G2
Arcachon 12 D3
Arcadia, *Fla., U.S.A.* 43 M5
Arcadia, *La., U.S.A.* 41 J8
Arcata 38 F1
Arches △ 39 G9
Arckaringa Cr. → 32 A2
Arco 38 E7
Arctic Bay 37 B11
Arctic Ocean 6 B17
Ardabīl 24 B3
Ardara 11 B3
Ardee 11 C5
Ardenne 16 D2
Arderin 11 C4
Ardfert 11 D2
Ardglass 11 B6
Ardivachar Pt. 10 D1
Ardlethan 32 B4
Ardmore 41 H6
Ardnamurchan, Pt. of 10 E2
Ardnave Pt. 10 F2
Ardrossan, *Australia* 32 B2
Ardrossan, *U.K.* 10 F4
Ards Pen. 11 B6
Arecibo 45 d
Arena, Pt. 38 G2
Arendal 7 F5
Arequipa 46 G4
Argentan 12 B3
Argentina ■ 48 D3
Arguello, Pt. 39 J3
Argyle, L. 30 D4
Argyll △ 10 E4
Argyll & Bute □ 10 E3
Århus 7 F6
Arica 46 G4
Arima 47 K15
Arinos → 46 F7
Aripuanã → 46 E6
Arisaig 10 E3
Arizona □ 39 J8
Arkadelphia 41 H8
Arkaig, L. 10 E3
Arkansas □ 41 H8
Arkansas → 41 J9
Arkansas City 41 G6
Arkaroola 32 B2
Arkhangelsk 18 C5
Arklow 11 D5
Arles 12 E6
Arlington, *Oreg., U.S.A.* 38 D3
Arlington, *S. Dak., U.S.A.* 40 C6
Arlington, *Tex., U.S.A.* 41 J6
Arlington, *Va., U.S.A.* 42 F7
Arlington, *Wash., U.S.A.* 38 B2
Arlington Heights 42 D2
Arlon 16 D2
Armagh 11 B5
Armagh □ 11 B5
Armavir 17 A6
Armenia 46 C3
Armidale 32 B5
Armour 40 D5
Arnaud → 37 D13
Arnett 41 G5
Arnhem 16 C2
Arnhem, C. 30 C6
Arnhem Land 30 C5
Arno Bay 32 B2
Arnold 8 D6
Arorae 31 A14
Arran 10 F3
Arras 12 A5
Arrow, L. 11 B3
Arrowtown 33 L2
Arroyo Grande 39 J3
Artesia 41 J2
Arthur → 32 D3
Arthur's Pass 33 K3
Arthur's Pass △ 33 K3
Artois 12 A5
Aru, Kepulauan 23 D5
Aruba ☑ 45 E11
Arun → 9 G7
Arunachal Pradesh □ 25 C8
Arusha 28 E7
Arvada, *Colo., U.S.A.* 40 F2
Arvada, *Wyo., U.S.A.* 38 D10
Arviat 36 C10
Arxan 21 B6
As Sulaymānīyah, *Iraq* 24 B3
As Sulaymānīyah, *Si. Arabia* 24 C3
As Sulayyil 24 C3
As Suwayq 24 C4
Asahigawa 22 B8
Asansol 25 C7
Asbury Park 42 E8
Ascension I. 4 E9
Aseb 24 D3
Ash Fork 39 J7
Ash Grove 41 G8
Ash Shāriqah 24 C4
Ash Shurayf 24 C2
Ashbourne 8 D6
Ashburn 43 K4
Ashburton 33 K3
Ashdown 41 J7
Asheboro 43 H6
Asherton 41 L5
Asheville 43 H4
Ashford, *Australia* 32 A5
Ashford, *U.K.* 9 F8
Ashgabat 18 F6
Ashington 8 B6
Ashland, *Kans., U.S.A.* 41 G5
Ashland, *Ky., U.S.A.* 42 F4
Ashland, *Maine, U.S.A.* 43 B11
Ashland, *Mont., U.S.A.* 38 D10
Ashland, *Ohio, U.S.A.* 42 E4
Ashland, *Oreg., U.S.A.* 38 E2
Ashland, *Va., U.S.A.* 42 G7
Ashland, *Wis., U.S.A.* 40 B9
Ashley 40 B5
Ashtabula 42 E5
Ashton 38 D8
Ashuanipi, L. 37 D13
Asia 3 B14
'Asīr 24 D3
Asir, Ras 24 D4
Asmera 24 D2
Aspatria 8 C4
Aspen 39 G10
Aspermont 41 J4
Aspiring, Mt. 33 L2
Assam □ 25 C8
Assateague Island △ 42 F8
Assen 16 B3
Assiniboia 36 E9
Assiniboine → 36 E10
Assisi 14 C5
Assynt, L. 10 C3
Astana 18 D8
Asti 12 D8
Astoria 38 C2
Astrakhan 17 A7
Asturias □ 13 A3
Asunción 48 B5
Aswân 27 D12
Asyût 27 C12
Aţ Ţā'if 24 C3
Atacama, Desierto de 48 A3
Atafu 31 B16
Atascadero 39 J3
'Atbara 27 E12
'Atbara, Nahr → 27 E12
Atchafalaya B. 41 L9
Atchison 40 F7
Athabasca 36 D8
Athabasca → 36 D8
Athabasca, L. 36 D9
Athboy 11 C5
Athenry 11 C3
Athens = Athina 15 F10
Athens, *Ala., U.S.A.* 43 H2
Athens, *Ga., U.S.A.* 43 J4
Athens, *Ohio, U.S.A.* 42 F4
Athens, *Tenn., U.S.A.* 43 H3
Athens, *Tex., U.S.A.* 41 J7
Athina 15 F10
Athlone 11 C4
Atholl, Forest of 10 E5
Athy 11 C5
Atiu 35 J12
Atka I. 36 D2
Atkinson 40 D5
Atlanta, *Ga., U.S.A.* 43 J3
Atlanta, *Tex., U.S.A.* 41 J7
Atlantic 40 E7
Atlantic City 42 F8
Atlantic Ocean 2 D8
Atlas Mts. = Haut Atlas 26 B4
Atlin 36 D6
Atmore 43 K2
Atoka 41 H6
Attalla 43 H2
Attawapiskat 37 D11
Attawapiskat → 37 D11
Attica 42 E2
Attleboro 42 E10
Attu I. 36 D1
Atwater 39 H3
Atwood 40 F4
Atyraū 18 E6
Au Sable → 42 C4
Aube → 12 B5
Auburn, *Ala., U.S.A.* 43 J3
Auburn, *Calif., U.S.A.* 38 G3
Auburn, *Ind., U.S.A.* 42 E3
Auburn, *Maine, U.S.A.* 43 C10
Auburn, *N.Y., U.S.A.* 42 D7
Auburn, *Nebr., U.S.A.* 40 E7
Auburn Ra. 32 A5
Auburndale 43 L5
Aubusson 12 D5
Auch 12 E4
Auchterarder 10 E5
Auchtermuchty 10 E5
Auckland 33 G5
Auckland Is. 34 N8
Aude → 12 E5
Audubon 40 E7
Augathella 32 A4
Aughnacloy 11 B5
Aughrim 11 C3
Augrabies Falls 29 K4
Augsburg 16 D5
Augusta, *Australia* 30 G2
Augusta, *Ark., U.S.A.* 41 H9
Augusta, *Ga., U.S.A.* 43 J5
Augusta, *Kans., U.S.A.* 41 G6
Augusta, *Maine, U.S.A.* 43 C11
Augusta, *Mont., U.S.A.* 38 C7
Ault 40 E2
Aunis 12 C3
Aurangabad 25 C7
Aurillac 12 D5
Aurora, *Colo., U.S.A.* 40 F2
Aurora, *Ill., U.S.A.* 42 E1
Aurora, *Mo., U.S.A.* 41 G8
Aurora, *Nebr., U.S.A.* 40 E6
Austin, *Minn., U.S.A.* 40 D8
Austin, *Nev., U.S.A.* 38 G5
Austin, *Tex., U.S.A.* 41 K6
Austral Seamount Chain 35 K13
Australia ■ 30 E3
Australian Capital Territory □ 32 C4
Austria ■ 16 E7
Autun 12 C6
Auvergne □ 12 D5
Auxerre 12 C5
Ava 41 G8
Avallon 12 C5
Avellino 14 D6
Avery 38 C6
Aviemore 10 D5
Avignon 12 E6
Ávila 13 B3
Avoca →, *Australia* 32 C3
Avoca →, *Ireland* 11 D5
Avon →, *Bristol, U.K.* 9 F5
Avon →, *Dorset, U.K.* 9 G6
Avon →, *Warks., U.K.* 9 E5
Avon Park 43 M5
Avonmouth 9 F5
Avranches 12 B3
Awash 24 E3
Awatere → 33 J5
Awe, L. 10 E3
Axe → 9 F5
Axel Heiberg I. 37 B11
Axios → 15 D10
Axminster 9 G4
Ayers Rock = Uluru 30 F5
Aylesbury 9 F7
Aylmer, L. 36 C9
Ayr 10 F4
Ayr → 10 F4
Ayre, Pt. of 8 C3
Az Ẓahrān 24 C4
Azores = Açores, Is. dos 26 A1
Azov, Sea of 17 A5
Aztec 39 H10
Azuero, Pen. de 46 B2

B

Bab el Mandeb 24 D3
Babb 38 B7
Babine L. 36 D7
Bābol 24 B4
Babruysk 18 D3
Babuyan Chan. 23 B4
Babuyan Is. 23 B4
Bac Lieu 23 C2
Bacabal 47 D10
Bacău 17 A3
Back → 36 C9
Bacolod 23 B4
Bad → 40 C4
Bad Axe 42 D4
Badajoz 13 C2
Badalona 13 B7
Baden-Württemberg □ 16 D4
Badin 24 C5
Badlands 40 D3
Badlands △ 40 D3
Badu I. 30 C7
Baffin B. 37 B13
Baffin I. 37 C12
Baggs 38 F10
Baghdād 24 B3
Baghlān 25 B5
Bagley 40 B7
Baguio 23 B4
Bahamas ■ 45 C10
Bahawalpur 25 C6
Bahía = Salvador 47 F11
Bahía □ 47 F10
Bahía Blanca 48 D4
Bahrain ■ 24 C4
Baia Mare 17 A2
Baidoa 24 E3
Baie-Comeau 37 E13
Baie Verte 37 E14
Baikal, L. = Baykal, Oz. 19 D11
Bainbridge 43 K3
Baing 23 E4
Bairnsdale 32 C4
Baiyin 20 C5
Baja, Pta. 44 B1
Baja California 44 A1
Bajimba, Mt. 32 A5
Baker, *Calif., U.S.A.* 39 J5
Baker, *Mont., U.S.A.* 40 B2
Baker, L. 36 C10
Baker, Mt. 38 B3
Baker City 38 D5
Baker I. 31 A15
Baker Lake 36 C10
Bakers Dozen Is. 37 D12
Bakersfield 39 J4
Bākhtarān = Kermānshāh 24 B3
Bakı 17 B7
Bakony 16 E8
Baku = Bakı 17 B7
Bala 8 E4
Bala, L. 8 E4
Balabac I. 23 C3
Balabac Str. 23 C3
Balakovo 18 D5
Balaton 16 E8
Balbi, Mt. 31 B10
Balbriggan 11 C5
Balclutha 33 M2
Balcones Escarpment 41 L5
Bald Knob 41 H9
Baldwin 42 D3
Baldy Peak 39 K9
Baleares, Is. 13 C7
Baleshare 10 D1
Bali 23 D3
Balıkeşir 15 E12
Balikpapan 23 D3
Balkan Mts. = Stara Planina 15 C10
Ballachulish 10 E3
Ballaghaderreen 11 C3
Ballarat 32 C3
Ballater 10 D5
Ballenas, B. de 44 B2
Ballina, *Australia* 32 A5
Ballina, *Ireland* 11 B2
Ballinasloe 11 C3
Ballinger 41 K5
Ballinrobe 11 C2
Ballinskelligs B. 11 E1
Ballyboghil 11 C5
Ballybunion 11 D2
Ballycanew 11 D5
Ballycastle 11 A5
Ballyclare 11 B5
Ballydehob 11 E2
Ballygawley 11 B4
Ballyhaunis 11 C3
Ballyheige 11 D2
Ballymena 11 B5
Ballymoney 11 A5
Ballymote 11 B3
Ballynahinch 11 B6
Ballyquintin Pt. 11 B6
Ballyshannon 11 B3
Balmoral 32 C3
Balmorhea 41 K3
Balonne → 32 A4
Balqash 18 E8
Balqash Köl 18 E8
Balranald 32 B3
Balsas → 44 D4
Bălţi 17 A3
Baltic Sea 7 F7
Baltimore, *Ireland* 11 E2
Baltimore, *U.S.A.* 42 F7
Baltinglass 11 D5
Baluchistan □ 24 C5
Bam 24 C4
Bamako 26 F4
Bamberg, *Germany* 16 D5
Bamberg, *U.S.A.* 43 J5
Bamburgh 8 B6
Bamenda 28 C2
Banaba 34 H8
Banbridge 11 B5
Banbury 9 E6
Banchory 10 D6
Banda, Kepulauan 23 D4
Banda Aceh 23 C1
Banda Banda, Mt. 32 B5
Banda Sea 23 D5
Bandar-e Abbās 24 C4
Bandar-e Emām Khomeynı 24 B3
Bandar Seri Begawan 23 C3
Bandon 11 E3
Bandon → 11 E3
Bandundu 28 E3
Bandung 23 D2
Banes 45 C9
Banff, *Canada* 36 D8
Banff, *U.K.* 10 D6
Bangalore 25 D6
Banggai, Kepulauan 23 D4
Banggi, Pulau 23 C3
Banghāzī 27 B10
Bangka 23 D2
Bangka, Selat 23 D2
Bangkok 23 B2
Bangladesh ■ 25 C8
Bangor, *Down, U.K.* 11 B6
Bangor, *Gwynedd, U.K.* 8 D3
Bangor, *U.S.A.* 43 C11
Bangui 28 D3
Bangweulu, L. 28 G6
Baní 45 D10
Banja Luka 14 B7
Banjarmasin 23 D3
Banjul 26 F2
Banks I. 36 B7
Banks Is. 31 C12
Banks Pen. 33 K4
Banks Str. 32 D4
Bann →, *Armagh, U.K.* 11 B5
Bann →, *L'derry., U.K.* 11 A5
Banning 39 K5
Bannockburn 10 E5
Banská Bystrica 16 D9
Bantry 11 E2
Bantry B. 11 E2
Banyak, Kepulauan 23 C1
Banyuwangi 23 D3
Baoding 21 C6
Baoji 20 C5
Baoshan 20 D4
Baotou 21 B6
Bar Harbor 43 C11
Bar-le-Duc 12 B6
Baraboo 40 D10
Baracoa 45 C10
Baraga 40 B10
Barahona 45 D10
Barakaldo 13 A4
Baranavichy 18 D3
Baranof I. 36 D6
Barataria B. 41 L10
Barbados ■ 45 g
Barberton 42 E5
Barbourville 43 G4
Barcelona 13 B7
Barceloneta 45 d
Bardera 24 E3
Bardsey I. 8 E3
Bardstown 42 G3
Bareilly 25 C6
Barents Sea 6 B8
Bari 14 D7
Baring, C. 36 C8
Barisal 25 C8
Barisan, Bukit 23 D2
Barito → 23 D3
Barkley, L. 43 G2
Barkly Tableland 30 D6
Barkol Kazak Zizhixian 20 B4
Barlee, L. 30 F2
Barletta 14 D7
Barmedman 32 B4
Barmera 32 B3
Barmouth 8 E3
Barnard Castle 8 C6
Barnaul 18 D9
Barnesville, *Ga., U.S.A.* 43 J3
Barnesville, *Minn., U.S.A.* 40 B6
Barnet □ 9 F7
Barnhart 41 K4
Barnsley 8 D6
Barnstaple 9 F3
Barnwell 43 J5
Barques, Pt. Aux 42 C4
Barquisimeto 46 A5
Barra 10 E1
Barra, Sd. of 10 D1
Barra Hd. 10 E1
Barraba 32 B5
Barrancabermeja 46 B4
Barranquilla 46 A4
Barre 42 C9
Barrie 37 E12
Barrier Ra. 32 B3
Barrington Tops 32 B5
Barringun 32 A4
Barron 40 C9
Barrow 36 B4
Barrow → 11 D5
Barrow-in-Furness 8 C4
Barry 9 F4
Barstow 39 J5
Bartlesville 41 G7
Bartlett 41 H10
Barton upon Humber 8 D7
Bartow 43 M5
Barysaw 7 C9
Basel 12 C7
Bashi Channel 23 A4
Basilan I. 23 C4
Basildon 9 F8
Basin 38 D9
Basingstoke 9 F6
Basle = Basel 12 C7
Basque Provinces = País Vasco □ 13 A4
Basra = Al Başrah 24 B3
Bass Str. 32 C4
Basse-Pointe 44 c
Basse-Terre 44 b
Bassein 25 D8
Basses, Pte. des 44 b
Basseterre 45 D12
Bassett 40 D5
Bastia 12 E8
Bastrop, *La., U.S.A.* 41 J9
Bastrop, *Tex., U.S.A.* 41 K6
Bata 28 D1
Batabanó, G. de 45 C8
Batan I. 23 A4
Batangas 23 B4
Batavia 42 D6
Batdambang 23 B2
Batemans B. 32 C5
Batemans Bay 32 C5
Batesburg-Leesville 43 J5
Batesville, *Ark., U.S.A.* 41 H9
Batesville, *Miss., U.S.A.* 41 H10
Batesville, *Tex., U.S.A.* 41 L5
Bath, *U.K.* 9 F5
Bath, *Maine, U.S.A.* 43 D11
Bath, *N.Y., U.S.A.* 42 D7
Bathsheba 45 g
Bathurst, *Australia* 32 B4
Bathurst, *Canada* 37 E13
Bathurst, C. 36 B7
Bathurst Harb. 32 D4
Bathurst I. 37 B11
Bathurst Inlet 36 C9
Batlow 32 C4
Batna 26 A7
Baton Rouge 41 K9
Batticaloa 25 E7
Battle 9 G8
Battle → 36 D9
Battle Creek 42 D3
Battle Ground 38 D2
Battle Lake 40 B7
Battle Mountain 38 F5
Batu, Kepulauan 23 D1
Batu Pahat 23 C2
Batumi 17 B6
Baudette 40 A7
Bauer, C. 32 B1
Bauld, C. 37 D14
Bauru 47 H9
Bavaria = Bayern □ 16 D6
Bawean 23 D3
Baxley 43 K4
Baxter 40 B7
Baxter Springs 41 G7
Baxter State △ 43 B11
Bay City, *Mich., U.S.A.* 42 D4
Bay City, *Tex., U.S.A.* 41 L7
Bay Minette 43 K2
Bay St. Louis 41 K10
Bay Springs 41 K10
Bay View 33 H6
Bayamo 45 C9
Bayamón 45 d
Bayan Har Shan 20 C4
Bayanhongor 20 B5
Bayard, *N. Mex., U.S.A.* 39 K9
Bayard, *Nebr., U.S.A.* 40 E3
Bayern □ 16 D6
Bayeux 12 B3
Bayfield 40 B9
Baykal, Oz. 19 D11
Bayonne 12 E3
Bayramaly 24 B5
Bayrūt 17 D5
Baytown 41 L7
Beach 40 B3
Beachport 32 C3
Beachy Hd. 9 G8
Beacon 42 E9
Beaconsfield 32 D4
Beagle, Canal 48 H3
Beals Cr. → 41 J4
Bear I. 11 E2
Bear L. 38 F8
Beardmore Glacier 6 F15
Beardstown 40 F9
Béarn 12 E3
Bearpaw Mts. 38 B9
Beatrice 40 E6
Beatty 39 H5
Beauce, Plaine de la 12 B4
Beaudesert 32 A5
Beaufort, *N.C., U.S.A.* 43 H7
Beaufort, *S.C., U.S.A.* 43 J5
Beaufort Sea 6 B18
Beaufort West 29 L4
Beauly 10 D4
Beauly → 10 D4
Beaumaris 8 D3
Beaumont 41 K7
Beaune 12 C6
Beauvais 12 B5
Beaver, *Okla., U.S.A.* 41 G4
Beaver, *Utah, U.S.A.* 39 G7
Beaver →, *Canada* 36 D9
Beaver →, *U.S.A.* 41 G5
Beaver City 40 E5
Beaver Creek 36 C5
Beaver Dam 40 D10
Beaver Falls 42 E5
Beaver I. 42 C3
Beavercreek 42 F3
Beaverton 38 D2
Beawar 25 C6
Bécancour 42 B9
Beccles 9 E9
Béchar 26 B5
Beckley 42 G5
Bedford, *U.K.* 9 E7
Bedford, *Ind., U.S.A.* 42 F2
Bedford, *Iowa, U.S.A.* 40 E7
Bedford, *Va., U.S.A.* 42 G6
Bedfordshire □ 9 E7
Beef I. 45 e
Beenleigh 32 A5
Beeston 8 E6
Beeville 41 L6
Bega 32 C4
Bei Jiang → 21 D6
Bei'an 21 B7
Beihai 21 D5
Beijing 21 C6
Beilpajah 32 B3
Beira 29 H6
Beirut = Bayrūt 17 D5
Bejaïa 26 A7
Bela 24 C5
Belarus ■ 18 D3
Belau = Palau ■ 23 C5
Belawan 23 C1
Belcher Chan. 37 B11
Belcher Is. 37 D12
Belém 47 D9
Belen 39 J10
Belep, Îs. 31 D11
Belet Uen 24 E3
Belfast, *U.K.* 11 B6
Belfast, *U.S.A.* 43 C11
Belfast L. 11 B6
Belfield 40 B3
Belfort 12 C7
Belfry 38 D9
Belgaum 25 D6
Belgium ■ 16 C2
Belgorod 18 D4
Belgrade = Beograd 15 B9
Belgrade 38 D8
Belhaven 43 H7
Belitung 23 D2
Belize ■ 44 D7
Belize City 44 D7
Bell Peninsula 37 C11
Bella Coola 36 D7
Bellaire 42 E5
Bellary 25 D6
Bellata 32 A4
Belle Fourche 40 C3
Belle Fourche → 40 C3
Belle Glade 43 M5
Belle-Île 12 C2
Belle Isle 37 D14
Belle Isle, Str. of 37 D14
Belle Plaine 40 E8
Bellefontaine 42 E4
Bellefonte 42 E7
Belleplaine 45 g
Belleville, *Canada* 37 E12
Belleville, *Ill., U.S.A.* 40 F10
Belleville, *Kans., U.S.A.* 40 F6
Bellevue, *Idaho, U.S.A.* 38 E6
Bellevue, *Nebr., U.S.A.* 40 E7
Bellevue, *Wash., U.S.A.* 38 C2
Bellingen 32 B5
Bellingham 38 B2
Bellingshausen Sea 6 D3
Bellinzona 12 C8
Bello 46 B3
Bellona 31 C10
Bellows Falls 42 D9
Belmopan 44 D7
Belmullet 11 B2
Belo Horizonte 47 G10
Beloit, *Kans., U.S.A.* 40 F5
Beloit, *Wis., U.S.A.* 40 D10
Belorussia = Belarus ■ 18 D3
Belovo 18 D9
Beloye More 7 D11
Belpre 42 F5
Belt 38 C8
Beltana 32 B2
Belton 41 K6
Belton L. 41 K6
Belturbet 11 B4
Belukha 18 E9
Belvidere 40 D10
Belzoni 41 J9
Bemidji 40 B7
Ben Cruachan 10 E3
Ben Dearg 10 D4
Ben Hope 10 C4
Ben Lawers 10 E4
Ben Lomond, *N.S.W., Australia* 32 B5
Ben Lomond, *Tas., Australia* 32 D4
Ben Lomond, *U.K.* 10 E4
Ben Lomond △ 32 D4
Ben Macdhui 10 D5
Ben Mhor 10 D1
Ben More, *Argyll & Bute, U.K.* 10 E2
Ben More, *Stirling, U.K.* 10 E4
Ben More Assynt 10 C4
Ben Nevis 10 E3
Ben Vorlich 10 E4
Ben Wyvis 10 D4
Benalla 32 C4
Benares = Varanasi 25 C7
Benavides 41 M5
Benbecula 10 D1
Benbonyathe Hill 32 B2
Bend 38 D3
Bender Beila 24 E4
Bendigo 32 C3
Benevento 14 D6
Bengal, Bay of 25 D7
Bengbu 21 C6
Benghazi = Banghāzī 27 B10
Bengkulu 23 D2
Beni Mellal 26 B4
Beni Suef 27 C12
Benidorm 13 C5
Benin ■ 26 G6
Benin, Bight of 26 H6
Benin City 26 G7
Benkelman 40 E4
Bennettsville 43 H6
Bennington 42 D9
Benoni 29 K5
Benson, *Ariz., U.S.A.* 39 L8
Benson, *Minn., U.S.A.* 40 C7
Benton, *Ark., U.S.A.* 41 H8
Benton, *Ill., U.S.A.* 40 G10
Benton Harbor 42 D2
Bentonville 41 G7
Benue → 26 G7
Benxi 21 B7
Beograd 15 B9
Beppu 22 G2
Berau, Teluk 23 D5
Berbera 24 D3
Berbérati 28 D3
Berdyansk 17 A5
Berea 42 G3
Bereda 24 D4
Berens → 36 D10
Beresford 40 D6
Berezniki 18 D6
Bérgamo 12 D8
Bergen 7 E5
Bergerac 12 D4
Berhala, Selat 23 D2
Bering Sea 36 D2
Bering Strait 36 C3
Berkeley 38 H2
Berkner I. 6 E4
Berkshire Downs 9 F6
Berlin, *Germany* 16 B6
Berlin, *Md., U.S.A.* 42 F8
Berlin, *N.H., U.S.A.* 42 C10
Berlin, *Wis., U.S.A.* 42 D1
Bermuda ☑ 4 C6
Bern 12 C7
Bernalillo 39 J10
Berneray 10 D1
Berri 32 B3
Berry, *Australia* 32 B5
Berry, *France* 12 C5
Berryville 41 G8
Berthold 40 A4
Berthoud 40 E2
Bertraghboy B. 11 C2
Beru 31 A14
Berwick 42 E7
Berwick-upon-Tweed 8 B6
Berwyn Mts. 8 E4
Besançon 12 C7
Besar 23 D3
Bessemer, *Ala., U.S.A.* 43 J2
Bessemer, *Mich., U.S.A.* 40 B9
Bethany, *Mo., U.S.A.* 40 E7
Bethany, *Okla., U.S.A.* 41 H6
Bethel 36 C3
Bethlehem, *S. Africa* 29 K5
Bethlehem, *U.S.A.* 42 E8
Béthune 12 A5
Bettendorf 40 E9
Betws-y-Coed 8 D4
Beulah, *Mich., U.S.A.* 42 C2
Beulah, *N. Dak., U.S.A.* 40 B4
Beverley 8 D7
Beverly Hills, *Calif., U.S.A.* 39 J4
Beverly Hills, *Fla., U.S.A.* 43 L4
Bexhill 9 G8
Béziers 12 E5
Bhagalpur 25 C7
Bharuch 25 C6
Bhavnagar 25 C6
Bhilainagar-Durg 25 C7
Bhima → 25 D6
Bhopal 25 C6
Bhubaneshwar 25 C7
Bhuj 25 C5
Bhutan ■ 25 C8
Biak 23 D5
Białystok 7 G8
Biarritz 12 E3
Bicester 9 F6
Bicheno 32 D4
Biddeford 43 D10
Bideford 9 F3
Bideford Bay 9 F3
Bié, Planalto de 29 G3
Bieber 38 F3
Biel 12 C7
Bielefeld 16 B4
Bielsko-Biała 16 D9
Bien Hoa 23 B2
Bienville, L. 37 D12
Big Belt Mts. 38 C8
Big Bend △ 41 L3
Big Black → 41 K9
Big Blue → 40 F6
Big Cypress △ 43 M5
Big Falls 40 A8
Big Fork → 40 A8
Big Lake 41 K4
Big Muddy Cr. → 40 A2
Big Pine 39 H4
Big Piney 38 E8
Big Rapids 42 D3
Big Sable Pt. 42 C2
Big Sandy 38 B8
Big Sandy → 42 F4
Big Sandy Cr. → 40 F3
Big Sioux → 40 D6
Big South Fork △ 43 G3
Big Spring 41 J4
Big Stone City 40 C6
Big Stone Gap 43 G4
Big Stone L. 40 C6
Big Timber 38 D9
Big Trout L. 37 D11
Biggar, *Canada* 36 D9
Biggar, *U.K.* 10 F5
Biggenden 32 A5
Biggleswade 9 E7
Bighorn 38 C10
Bighorn → 38 C10
Bighorn Canyon △ 38 D9
Bighorn L. 38 D9
Bighorn Mts. 38 D10
Bihar □ 25 C7
Bijapur 25 D6
Bikaner 25 C6
Bikini Atoll 34 F8
Bilaspur 25 C7
Bilauk Taungdan 25 D8
Bilbao 13 A4
Billings 38 D9
Bilma 27 E8
Biloxi 41 K10
Bimini Is. 45 B9
Binalong 32 B4
Bingara 32 A5

Gagnon

Coonamble 32 B4
Cooninnie, L. 32 A2
Cooper 41 J7
Cooper Cr. → 32 A2
Cooper Ridge 35 F12
Cooperstown, N. Dak., U.S.A. 40 B5
Cooperstown, N.Y., U.S.A. 42 D8
Coorong, The 32 C2
Cooroy 32 A5
Coos Bay 38 E1
Coosa → 43 J2
Cootamundra 32 B4
Cootehill 11 B4
Cope 40 F3
Copenhagen = København 7 F6
Copper Harbor 42 B2
Copperas Cove 41 K6
Coppermine → 36 C8
Coquet → 8 B6
Coquille 38 E1
Coraki 32 A5
Coral Gables 43 N5
Coral Harbour 37 C11
Coral Sea 30 C9
Coral Sea Basin 34 J7
Coral Sea Islands Terr. □ 30 D9
Coral Springs 43 M5
Corbin 42 G3
Corby 9 E7
Corcoran 39 H4
Cordele 43 K4
Cordell 41 H5
Córdoba, Argentina 48 C4
Córdoba, Mexico 44 D5
Córdoba, Spain 13 D3
Córdoba, Sierra de 48 C4
Cordova 36 C5
Corfu = Kerkyra 15 E8
Corinth 43 H1
Corinth, G. of = Korinthiakos Kolpos 15 E10
Cork 11 E3
Cork □ 11 E3
Cork Harbour 11 E3
Corner Brook 37 E14
Corning, Ark., U.S.A. 41 G9
Corning, Calif., U.S.A. 38 G2
Corning, Iowa, U.S.A. 40 E7
Corning, N.Y., U.S.A. 42 D7
Cornwall 37 E12
Cornwall □ 9 G3
Cornwall I. 37 A11
Cornwallis I. 37 B10
Corny Pt. 32 B2
Coro 46 A5
Coromandel 33 G5
Coromandel Coast 25 D7
Corona, Calif., U.S.A. 39 K5
Corona, N. Mex., U.S.A. 39 J11
Coronation Gulf 36 C9
Corowa 32 C4
Corpus Christi 41 M6
Corpus Christi, L. 41 L6
Corraun Pen. 11 C2
Corrib, L. 11 C2
Corrientes 48 B5
Corrientes, C. 44 C3
Corrigan 41 K7
Corry 42 E6
Corse □ 12 F8
Corse, C. 12 E8
Corsica = Corse □ 12 F8
Corsicana 41 J6
Corte 12 E8
Cortez 39 H9
Cortland 42 D7
Corumbá 46 G7
Corunna = A Coruña 13 A1
Corvallis 38 D2
Corydon 40 E8
Cosenza 14 E7
Coshocton 42 E5
Costa Blanca 13 C5
Costa Brava 13 B7
Costa del Sol 13 D3
Costa Dorada 13 B6
Costa Rica ■ 45 F8
Cotabato 23 C4
Côte d'Azur 12 E7
Côte-d'Ivoire = Ivory Coast ■ 26 G4
Coteau des Prairies 40 C6
Coteau du Missouri 40 B4
Cotentin 12 B3
Cotonou 26 G6
Cotopaxi 46 D3
Cotswold Hills 9 F5
Cottage Grove 38 E2
Cottbus 16 C7
Cottonwood 39 J7
Cotulla 41 L5
Coudersport 42 E6
Couedic, C. du 32 C2
Coulee City 38 C4
Council 38 D5
Council Bluffs 40 E7
Council Grove 40 F6
Courantyne → 46 B7
Courtenay 36 E7
Coushatta 41 J8
Coutts Crossing 32 A5
Coventry 9 E6
Covington, Ga., U.S.A. 43 J4
Covington, Ky., U.S.A. 42 F3
Covington, Tenn., U.S.A. 41 H10
Covington, Va., U.S.A. 42 G5
Cowal, L. 32 B4
Cowangie 32 C3
Coward Springs 32 A2
Cowdenbeath 10 E5
Cowell 32 B2
Cowes 9 G6
Cowra 32 B4
Cozad 40 E5
Cozumel, Isla 44 C7
Crab Hill 45 g
Cracow 32 A5
Cradle Mt.-Lake St. Clair △ 32 D4
Cradock, Australia 32 B2
Cradock, S. Africa 29 L5
Craig 38 F10
Craigavon 11 B5
Craiova 15 B10
Cranbrook 36 E8
Crandon 40 C10
Crane, Oreg., U.S.A. 38 E4
Crane, Tex., U.S.A. 41 K3
Crane, The 45 g
Crater L. 38 E2
Crater Lake △ 38 E2
Craters of the Moon △ 38 E7
Crawford 40 D3
Crawfordsville 42 E2
Crawley 9 F7
Crazy Mts. 38 C8
Crediton 9 G4
Cree →, Canada 36 D9
Cree →, U.K. 10 G4
Cree L. 36 D9
Creede 39 H10
Creighton 40 D6
Cremona 12 D9
Crescent City 38 F1
Creston 40 E7
Crestview 43 K2
Crete = Kriti 15 G11
Crete 40 E6
Creuse → 12 C4
Crewe 8 D5
Crewkerne 9 G5
Crianlarich 10 E4
Crieff 10 E5
Crimean Pen. = Krymskyy Pivostriv 17 B4
Croagh Patrick 11 C2
Croatia ■ 14 B7
Crockett 41 K7
Crohy Hd. 11 B3
Croker, C. 30 C5
Cromarty 10 D4
Cromer 8 E9
Cromwell 33 L2
Crook 8 C6
Crooked → 38 D3
Crooked I. 45 C10
Crookston, Minn., U.S.A. 40 B6
Crookston, Nebr., U.S.A. 40 D4
Crookwell 32 B4
Crosby, U.K. 8 D4
Crosby, U.S.A. 40 A3
Crosbyton 41 J4
Cross City 43 L4
Cross Fell 8 C5
Cross Sound 36 D6
Crossett 41 J9
Crosshaven 11 E3
Crossmaglen 11 B5
Crossmolina 11 B2
Crossville 43 G3
Crow Agency 38 D10
Crow Hd. 11 E1
Crowell 41 J5
Crowley 41 K8
Crown Point 42 E2
Crownpoint 39 J9
Crows Nest 32 A5
Crowsnest Pass 36 E8
Croydon □ 9 F7
Crozet, Is. 5 G13
Crusheen 11 D3
Cruz Bay 45 e
Cruzeiro do Sul 46 E4
Crystal Brook 32 B2
Crystal City 41 L5
Crystal Falls 42 B1
Crystal River 43 L4
Crystal Springs 41 K9
Cuando → 29 H4
Cuanza → 28 F2
Cuauhtémoc 44 B3
Cuba 39 J10
Cuba ■ 45 C9
Cubango → 29 H4
Cuckfield 9 F7
Cúcuta 46 B4
Cuenca, Ecuador 46 D3
Cuenca, Spain 13 B4
Cuernavaca 44 D5
Cuero 41 L6
Cuiabá 47 G7
Cuihangcun 21 G10
Cuillin Hills 10 D2
Cuillin Sd. 10 D2
Culbertson 40 A2
Culcairn 32 C4
Culebra 45 d
Culgoa → 32 A4
Culgoa Flood Plain △ 32 A4
Culiacán 44 C3
Cullarin Ra. 32 B4
Cullen 10 D6
Cullman 43 H2
Cullompton 9 G4
Culpeper 42 F7
Culverden 33 K4
Cumaná 46 A6
Cumberland 42 F6
Cumberland → 43 G2
Cumberland, L. 43 G3
Cumberland Gap △ 43 G4
Cumberland I. 43 K5
Cumberland Island △ 43 K5
Cumberland Pen. 37 C13
Cumberland Plateau 43 H3
Cumberland Sd. 37 C13
Cumbernauld 10 F5
Cumborah 32 A4
Cumbria □ 8 C5
Cumbrian Mts. 8 C5
Cummins 32 B2
Cumnock, Australia 32 B4
Cumnock, U.K. 10 F4
Cunene → 29 H2
Cúneo 12 D7
Cunnamulla 32 A4
Cupar 10 E5
Curaçao 45 E11
Curitiba 48 B7
Currabubula 32 B5
Currane, L. 11 E1
Currant 38 G6
Currawinya △ 32 A3
Current → 41 G9
Currie, Australia 32 C3
Currie, U.S.A. 38 F6
Curtis 40 E4
Curtis Group 32 C4
Curtis I. 31 G15
Cushendall 11 A5
Cushing 41 H6
Custer 40 D3
Cut Bank 38 B7
Cuthbert 43 K3
Cuttaburra → 32 A3
Cuttack 25 C7
Cuvier I. 33 G5
Cuxhaven 16 B4
Cuyahoga Falls 42 E5
Cuzco 46 F4
Cwmbran 9 F4
Cyclades 15 F11
Cygnet 32 D4
Cynthiana 42 F3
Cyprus ■ 17 D4
Cyrenaica 27 C10
Czech Rep. ■ 16 D7
Częstochowa 16 C9

D

Da Hinggan Ling 21 B7
Da Lat 23 B2
Da Nang 23 B2
Da Qaidam 20 C4
Daba Shan 21 C5
Dacca = Dhaka 25 C8
Dade City 43 L4
Daegu 21 C7
Daejeon 21 C7
Dagupan 23 B4
Dahlak Kebir 24 D3
Dahlonega 43 H4
Daingean 11 C4
Dajarra 30 E6
Dakar 26 F2
Dakhla 26 D2
Dakota City 40 D6
Dalandzadgad 20 B5
Dalap-Uliga-Darrit 34 G9
Dalbeattie 10 G5
Dalby 32 A5
Dale City 42 F7
Dale Hollow L. 43 G3
Dalhart 41 G3
Dali 20 D5
Dalian 21 C7
Daliang Shan 20 D5
Dalkeith 10 F5
Dallas, Oreg., U.S.A. 38 D2
Dallas, Tex., U.S.A. 41 J6
Dalles, The 38 D3
Dalmacija 14 C7
Dalmatia = Dalmacija 14 C7
Dalmellington 10 F4
Daloa 26 G4
Dalry 10 F4
Dalrymple, L. 30 E8
Dalton, Ga., U.S.A. 43 H3
Dalton, Nebr., U.S.A. 40 E3
Dalton-in-Furness 8 C4
Daly Waters 30 D5
Damanhûr 27 B12
Damaraland 29 H2
Damascus = Dimashq 24 B2
Damāvand, Qolleh-ye 24 B4
Dampier 30 E2
Danbury 42 E9
Danby L. 39 J6
Dandenong 32 C4
Dandong 21 B7
Daniel 38 E8
Dannemora 42 C9
Dannevirke 33 J6
Dansville 42 D7
Danube = Dunărea → 15 B13
Danville, Ill., U.S.A. 42 E2
Danville, Ky., U.S.A. 42 G3
Danville, Va., U.S.A. 43 G6
Danzig = Gdańsk 16 A9
Dar es Salaam 28 F7
Darbhanga 25 C7
Dardanelle 41 H8
Dardanelles = Çanakkale Boğazı 15 D12
Dargaville 33 F4
Darhan 20 B5
Darién, G. del 46 B3
Darjiling 25 C7
Darling → 32 B3
Darling Downs 32 A5
Darling Ra. 30 G2
Darlington, U.K. 8 C6
Darlington, U.S.A. 43 H6
Darmstadt 16 D4
Darnley, C. 6 D10
Darnley B. 36 C7
Darrington 38 B3
Dart → 9 G4
Dartford 9 F8
Dartmoor 9 G4
Dartmoor △ 9 G4
Dartmouth, Canada 37 E13
Dartmouth, U.K. 9 G4
Dartmouth Res. 32 A4
Darwen 8 D5
Darwin 30 C5
Dashen, Ras 28 B7
Dashoguz 24 A4
Dasht → 24 C5
Dasht-i-Tahlab 24 C5
Datong 21 B6
Daugavpils 18 D3
Dauphin 36 D9
Dauphiné 12 D6
Davangere 25 D6
Davao 23 C4
Davao G. 23 C4
Davenport, Iowa, U.S.A. 40 E9
Davenport, Wash., U.S.A. 38 C4
Daventry 9 E6
David 46 B2
David City 40 E6
Davis 38 G3
Davis Dam 39 J6
Davis Mts. 41 K2
Davis Str. 6 C4
Dawlish 9 G4
Dawros Hd. 11 B3
Dawson, Canada 36 C6
Dawson, U.S.A. 43 K3
Dawson Creek 36 D7
Dax 12 E3
Daxian 20 C5
Daxue Shan 20 C5
Daylesford 32 C3
Dayr az Zawr 24 B3
Dayton, Ohio, U.S.A. 42 F3
Dayton, Tenn., U.S.A. 43 H3
Dayton, Wash., U.S.A. 38 C4
Dayton, Wyo., U.S.A. 38 D10
Daytona Beach 43 L5
Dayville 38 D4
De Aar 29 L4
De Funiak Springs 43 K2
De Land 43 L5
De Leon 41 J5
De Pere 42 C1
De Queen 41 H7
De Quincy 41 K8
De Smet 40 C6
De Soto 40 F9
De Tour Village 42 C4
De Witt 41 H9
Dead Sea 17 D5
Deadwood 40 C3
Deal 9 F9
Deal I. 32 C4
Dean, Forest of 9 F5
Dease → 36 D7
Dease Lake 36 D6
Death Valley 39 H5
Death Valley △ 39 H5
Death Valley Junction 39 H5
Debrecen 17 A2
Decatur, Ala., U.S.A. 43 H2
Decatur, Ga., U.S.A. 43 J3
Decatur, Ill., U.S.A. 40 F10
Decatur, Ind., U.S.A. 42 E3
Decatur, Tex., U.S.A. 41 J6
Deccan 25 D6
Deception Bay 32 A5
Decorah 40 D9
Dee →, Aberds., U.K. 10 D6
Dee →, Dumf. & Gall., U.K. 10 G4
Dee →, Wales, U.K. 8 D4
Deepwater 32 A5
Deer Lake 37 E14
Deer Lodge 38 C7
Deer Park 38 C5
Deer River 40 B8
Defiance 42 E3
Dehiwala 25 E6
Dehra Dun 25 B6
DeKalb 40 E10
Del Norte 39 H10
Del Rio 41 L4
Delano 39 J4
Delano Peak 39 G7
Delavan 40 D10
Delaware 42 E4
Delaware □ 42 F8
Delaware B. 42 F8
Delegate 32 C4
Delgado, C. 28 G8
Delhi, India 25 C6
Delhi, U.S.A. 41 J9
Delicias 44 B3
Déline 36 C7
Dell City 39 L11
Dell Rapids 40 D6
Deloraine 32 D4
Delphi 42 E2
Delphos 42 E3
Delray Beach 43 M5
Delta, Colo., U.S.A. 39 G9
Delta, Utah, U.S.A. 38 G7
Delta Junction 36 C5
Deltona 43 L5
Delungra 32 A5
Deming 39 K10
Demopolis 43 J2
Den Haag = 's-Gravenhage 16 B2
Den Helder 16 B2
Denali = McKinley, Mt. 36 C4
Denbigh 8 D4
Denbighshire □ 8 D4
Denham, Mt. 44 a
Denial B. 32 B1
Deniliquin 32 C3
Denison, Iowa, U.S.A. 40 E7
Denison, Tex., U.S.A. 41 J6
Denizli 17 C3
Denmark ■ 7 F6
Denmark Str. 6 C5
Dennery 45 f
Denny 10 E5
Denpasar 23 D3
Denton, Mont., U.S.A. 38 C9
Denton, Tex., U.S.A. 41 J6
D'Entrecasteaux, Pt. 31 D11
D'Entrecasteaux Is. 30 B9
Denver 40 F2
Denver City 41 J3
Dera Ismail Khan 25 B6
Derby, Australia 30 D3
Derby, U.K. 8 E6
Derby, U.S.A. 41 G6
Derbyshire □ 8 D6
Dereham 9 E8
Derg → 11 B4
Derg, L. 11 D3
Deridder 41 K8
Dermott 41 J9
Derry = Londonderry 11 B4
Derryveagh Mts. 11 B3
Derwent →, Cumb., U.K. 8 C4
Derwent →, Derby, U.K. 8 E6
Derwent →, N. Yorks., U.K. 8 D7
Derwent Water 8 C4
Des Moines, Iowa, U.S.A. 40 E8
Des Moines, N. Mex., U.S.A. 41 G3
Des Moines → 40 E9
Deschutes → 38 D3
Dese 24 D2
Desert Center 39 K6
Dessau 16 C6
D'Estrees B. 32 C2
Detour, Pt. 42 C2
Detroit 42 D4
Detroit Lakes 40 B7
Deutsche Bucht 16 A4
Deventer 16 B3
Deveron → 10 D6
Devils Lake 40 A5
Devils Tower 40 C2
Devils Tower △ 40 C2
Devine 41 L5
Devizes 9 F6
Devon □ 9 G4
Devon I. 37 B10
Devonport, Australia 32 D4
Devonport, N.Z. 33 G5
Dewey 45 d
Dexter, Maine, U.S.A. 43 C11
Dexter, Mo., U.S.A. 41 G10
Dexter, N. Mex., U.S.A. 41 J2
Dezfūl 24 B3
Dezhneva, Mys 19 C19
Dhahran = Az Ẓahrān 24 C4
Dhaka 25 C8
Dhamār 24 D3
Dhanbad 25 C7
Dharwad 25 D6
Dhaulagiri 25 C7
Dhule 25 C6
Diamantina → 32 A2
Diamond Mts. 38 G6
Dibrugarh 25 C8
Dickens 41 J4
Dickinson 40 B3
Dickson 43 G2
Diefenbaker, L. 36 D9
Dieppe 12 B4
Dierks 41 H8
Digby 37 E13
Dighton 40 F4
Digne-les-Bains 12 D7
Dijlah, Nahr → 24 B3
Dijon 12 C6
Dili 23 D4
Dilley 41 L5
Dillingham 36 D4
Dillon, Mont., U.S.A. 38 D7
Dillon, S.C., U.S.A. 43 H6
Dimashq 24 B2
Dimboola 32 C3
Dimitrovgrad 15 C11
Dimmitt 41 H3
Dinan 12 B2
Dinant 16 C2
Dinara Planina 14 C7
Dingle 11 D1
Dingle B. 11 D1
Dingwall 10 D4
Dinin → 11 D4
Dinosaur △ 38 F9
Dinuba 39 H4
Dipolog 23 C4
Dire Dawa 24 E3
Dirranbandi 32 A4
Disappointment, C. 38 C2
Disappointment, L. 30 E3
Disaster B. 32 C4
Discovery B., Australia 32 C3
Discovery B., China 21 G11
Diss 9 E9
District of Columbia □ 42 F7
Divide 38 D7
Dixon 40 E10
Dixon Entrance 36 D6
Diyarbakır 17 C6
Djakarta = Jakarta 23 D2
Djerid, Chott 26 B7
Djibouti 24 D3
Djibouti ■ 24 D3
Dnepr = Dnipro → 17 A4
Dnestr = Dnister → 18 E4
Dnipro → 17 A4
Dniprodzerzhynsk 17 A4
Dnipropetrovsk 17 A5
Dnister → 18 E4
Doberai, Jazirah 23 D5
Dobrich 15 C12
Dodecanese 15 F12
Dodge City 41 G5
Dodgeville 40 D9
Dodoma 28 F7
Dodson 38 B9
Doha = Ad Dawḥah 24 C4
Dolbeau-Mistassini 37 E12
Dole 12 C6
Dolgellau 8 E4
Dolo 24 E3
Dolomiti 14 A4
Dolores 39 H9
Dolores → 39 G9
Dolphin and Union Str. 36 C8
Dominica ■ 45 D12
Dominican Rep. ■ 45 D10
Domville, Mt. 32 A5
Don →, Russia 18 E4
Don →, Aberds., U.K. 10 D6
Don →, S. Yorks., U.K. 8 D7
Don Figuerero Mts. 44 a
Donaghadee 11 B6
Donaghmore 11 D4
Donald 32 C3
Donaldsonville 41 K9
Donalsonville 43 K3
Doncaster 8 D6
Dondra Head 25 E7
Donegal 11 B3
Donegal □ 11 B4
Donegal B. 11 B3
Donetsk 17 A5
Dong Hoi 23 B2
Dongbei 21 B7
Dongchuan 20 D5
Dongting Hu 21 D6
Donington, C. 32 B2
Doniphan 41 G9
Donna 41 M5
Donnelly's Crossing 33 F4
Donostia-San Sebastián 13 A5
Doon → 10 F4
Dorchester 9 G5
Dorchester, C. 37 C12
Dordogne → 12 D3
Dordrecht 16 C2
Dorking 9 F7
Dornie 10 D3
Dornoch 10 D4
Dornoch Firth 10 D4
Döröö Nuur 20 B4
Dorrigo 32 B5
Dorris 38 F3
Dorset □ 9 G5
Dortmund 16 C3
Dothan 43 K3
Douai 12 A5
Douala 28 D1
Double Island Pt. 32 A5
Double Mountain Fork → 41 J4
Doubs → 12 C6
Doubtful Sd. 33 L1
Doubtless B. 33 F4
Douglas, I. of Man 8 C3
Douglas, Ariz., U.S.A. 39 L9
Douglas, Ga., U.S.A. 43 K4
Douglas, Wyo., U.S.A. 40 D2
Douglas Apsley △ 32 D4
Douglasville 43 J3
Dounreay 10 C5
Dourados 47 H8
Douro → 13 B1
Dove → 8 E6
Dove Creek 39 H9
Dover, Australia 32 D4
Dover, U.K. 9 F9
Dover, Del., U.S.A. 42 F8
Dover, N.H., U.S.A. 42 D10
Dover, Ohio, U.S.A. 42 E5
Dover, Str. of 9 G9
Dover-Foxcroft 43 C11
Dovrefjell 7 E5
Dowagiac 42 E2
Down □ 11 B5
Downey 38 E7
Downham Market 9 E8
Downieville 38 G3
Downpatrick 11 B6
Downpatrick Hd. 11 B2
Draguignan 12 E7
Drain 38 E2
Drake 40 B4
Drake Passage 6 B
Drakensberg 29 L5
Drammen 7 F6
Drava → 15 B8
Dresden 16 C6
Dreux 12 B4
Driffield 8 C7
Driggs 38 E8
Drina → 15 B8
Drobeta-Turnu Severin 15 B10
Drogheda 11 C5
Droichead Nua 11 C5
Droitwich 9 E5
Dromedary, C. 32 C5
Dromore 11 B4
Dromore West 11 B3
Dronfield 8 D6
Dronning Maud Land 6 E7
Drumcliff 11 B3
Drumheller 36 D8
Drummond 38 C7
Drummond I. 42 C4
Drummond Pt. 32 B2
Drumright 41 H6
Dry Harbour Mts. 44 a
Dryden 36 E10
Drygalski I. 6 D11
Du Quoin 40 G10
Dubai = Dubayy 24 C4
Dubawnt → 36 C9
Dubawnt L. 36 C9
Dubayy 24 C4
Dubbo 32 B4
Dublin, Ireland 11 C5
Dublin, Ga., U.S.A. 43 J4
Dublin, Tex., U.S.A. 41 J5
Dublin □ 11 C5
Dublin (DUB) 11 C5
Dubois, Idaho, U.S.A. 38 D7
Dubois, Pa., U.S.A. 42 E6
Dubrovnik 15 C8
Dubuque 40 D9
Duchesne 38 F8
Ducie I. 35 K15
Duck → 43 G2
Dudinka 19 C9
Dudley 9 E5
Duff Is. 31 B12
Dufftown 10 D5
Duisburg 16 C3
Dulce 39 H10
Duluth 40 B8
Dumaguete 23 C4
Dumas, Ark., U.S.A. 41 J9
Dumas, Tex., U.S.A. 41 H4
Dumbarton 10 F4
Dumfries 10 F5
Dumfries & Galloway □ 10 F5
Dumyât 27 B12
Dún Laoghaire 11 C5
Dunărea → 15 B13
Dunback 33 L3
Dunbar 10 E6
Dunblane 10 E5
Duncan, Ariz., U.S.A. 39 K9
Duncan, Okla., U.S.A. 41 H6
Duncansby Head 10 C5
Dundalk, Ireland 11 B5
Dundalk, U.S.A. 42 F7
Dundalk Bay 11 C5
Dundas 42 D6
Dundee 10 E6
Dundrum 11 B6
Dundrum B. 11 B6
Dunedin, N.Z. 33 L3
Dunedin, U.S.A. 43 L4
Dunfanaghy 11 A4
Dunfermline 10 E5
Dungannon 11 B5
Dungarvan 11 D4
Dungarvan Harbour 11 D4
Dungeness 9 G8
Dunglow 11 B3
Dungog 32 B5
Dunhuang 20 B4
Dunkeld, Australia 32 B4
Dunkeld, U.K. 10 E5
Dunkerque 12 A5
Dunkery Beacon 9 F4
Dunkirk = Dunkerque 12 A5
Dunkirk 42 D6
Dunleer 11 C5
Dunmanus B. 11 E2
Dunmanway 11 E2
Dunmore 42 E8
Dunmore East 11 D5
Dunmore Hd. 11 D1
Dunn 43 H6
Dunnellon 43 L4
Dunnet Hd. 10 C5
Dunning 40 E4
Dunolly 32 C3
Dunoon 10 F4
Duns 10 F6
Dunseith 40 A4
Dunshaughlin 11 C5
Dunsmuir 38 F2
Dunstable 9 F7
Dunstan Mts. 33 L2
Dunvegan 10 D2
Dupree 40 C4
Dupuyer 38 B7
Durance → 12 E6
Durand 40 C9
Durango, Mexico 44 C4
Durango, U.S.A. 39 H10
Durant, Miss., U.S.A. 41 J10
Durant, Okla., U.S.A. 41 J6
Durban 29 K6
Düren 16 C3
Durham, U.K. 8 C6
Durham, U.S.A. 43 H6
Durham □ 8 C6
Durness 10 C4
Durrës 15 D8
Durrow 11 D4
Dursey I. 11 E1
Dursley 9 F5
D'Urville I. 33 J4
Dushanbe 18 F7
Dusky Sd. 33 L1
Düsseldorf 16 C3
Dutch Harbor 36 D3
Duyun 20 D5
Dvina, Severnaya → 18 C5
Dwight 42 E1
Dyce 10 D6
Dyer, C. 37 C13
Dyersburg 41 G10
Dyfi → 9 E3
Dzhugdzur, Khrebet 19 D14
Dzungarian Gate 20 B3
Dzuumod 20 B5

E

Eads 40 F3
Eagar 39 J9
Eagle, Alaska, U.S.A. 36 C5
Eagle, Colo., U.S.A. 38 G10
Eagle Butte 40 C4
Eagle Grove 40 D8
Eagle L., Calif., U.S.A. 38 F3
Eagle L., Maine, U.S.A. 43 B11
Eagle Lake, Maine, U.S.A. 43 B11
Eagle Lake, Tex., U.S.A. 41 L6
Eagle Nest 39 H11
Eagle Pass 41 L4
Eagle River, Mich., U.S.A. 42 B1
Eagle River, Wis., U.S.A. 40 C10
Eaglehawk 32 C3
Ealing □ 9 F7
Earle 41 H9
Earlimart 39 J4
Earn → 10 E5
Earn, L. 10 E4
Earnslaw, Mt. 33 L2
Earth 41 H3
Easley 43 H4
East Anglia 8 E9
East Ayrshire □ 10 F4
East C. 33 G7
East Caroline Basin 34 G6
East Chicago 42 E2
East China Sea 21 D7
East Dunbartonshire □ 10 F4
East Falkland 48 G5
East Grand Forks 40 B6
East Grinstead 9 F8
East Helena 38 C8
East Kilbride 10 F4
East Lamma Channel 21 G11
East Lansing 42 D3
East Liverpool 42 E5
East London 29 L5
East Lothian □ 10 F6
East Mariana Basin 34 F7
East Orange 42 E8
East Pacific Rise 35 J17
East Point 43 J3
East Pt. 45 e
East Renfrewshire □ 10 F4
East Riding of Yorkshire □ 8 D7
East St. Louis 40 F9
East Sea = Japan, Sea of 22 D4
East Siberian Sea 19 B17
East Stroudsburg 42 E8
East Sussex □ 9 G8
East Tasman Plateau 34 M7
East Tawas 42 C4
East Timor ■ 23 D4
East Toorale 32 B4
Eastbourne, N.Z. 33 J5
Eastbourne, U.K. 9 G8
Easter Fracture Zone 35 K16
Easter I. = Pascua, I. de 35 K17
Eastern Ghats 25 D6
Eastland 41 J5
Eastleigh 9 G6
Eastmain 37 D12
Eastmain → 37 D12
Eastman 43 J4
Easton, Md., U.S.A. 42 F7
Easton, Pa., U.S.A. 42 E8
Eastport 43 C12
Eaton 40 E2
Eatonton 43 J4
Eau Claire 40 C9
Eau Claire, L. à l' 37 D12
Eauripik Rise 34 G6
Ebbw Vale 9 F4
Ebro → 13 B6
Ech Chéliff 26 A6
Echo Bay 36 C8
Eclipse Sd. 37 B12
Ecuador ■ 46 D3
Eday 10 B6
Eddrachillis B. 10 C3
Eddystone 9 G3
Eddystone Pt. 32 D4
Eden, Australia 32 C4
Eden, N.C., U.S.A. 43 G6
Eden, Tex., U.S.A. 41 K5
Eden → 8 C4
Edenderry 11 C4
Edenton 43 G7
Edgar 40 E6
Edge Hill 9 E6
Edgefield 43 J5
Edgeley 40 B5
Edgemont 40 D3
Edievale 33 L2
Edina 40 E8
Edinburg 41 M5
Edinburgh 10 F5
Edinburgh (EDI) 10 F5
Edithburgh 32 C2
Edmond 41 H6
Edmonds 38 C2
Edmonton 36 D8
Edmundston 37 E13
Edna 41 L6
Edson 36 D8
Edward → 32 C3
Edward, L. 28 E5
Edward VII Land 6 F17
Edwards Plateau 41 K4
Efate, I. 31 D12
Effigy Mounds △ 40 D9
Effingham 42 F1
Egan Range 38 G6
Eglinton I. 37 A10
Egmont △ 33 H5
Egmont, C. 33 H4
Egypt ■ 27 C12
Eidsvold 32 A5
Eifel 16 C3
Eigg 10 E2
Eil 24 E3
Eil, L. 10 E3
Eildon, L. 32 C4
Eindhoven 16 C2
Eire = Ireland ■ 11 C4
Eivissa 13 C6
Ekalaka 40 C2
Eketahuna 33 J5
El Aaiún 26 C3
El Cajon 39 K5
El Campo 41 L6
El Centro 39 K6
El Djouf 26 D4
El Dorado, Ark., U.S.A. 41 J8
El Dorado, Kans., U.S.A. 41 G6
El Dorado Springs 41 G8
El Faiyûm 27 C12
El Fâsher 27 F11
El Fuerte 44 B3
El Gîza 27 C12
El Iskandarîya 27 B11
El Jadida 26 B4
El Khârga 27 C12
El Khartûm 27 E12
El Khartûm Bahrî 27 E12
El Mahalla el Kubra 27 B12
El Malpais △ 39 J10
El Mansûra 27 B12
El Minyâ 27 C12
El Obeid 27 F12
El Paso 39 L10
El Qâhira 27 B12
El Salvador ■ 44 E7
El Suweis 27 C12
Elâzığ 17 C5
Elba, Italy 14 C4
Elba, U.S.A. 43 K2
Elbasan 15 D9
Elbe → 16 B4
Elbert, Mt. 39 G10
Elberton 43 H4
Elbeuf 12 B4
Elbląg 16 A9
Elbrus 18 E5
Elche 13 C5
Eldon 40 F8
Eldora 40 D8
Eldorado, Ill., U.S.A. 42 G1
Eldorado, Tex., U.S.A. 41 K4
Eldoret 28 D7
Elefantes → 29 J6
Elephant Butte Res. 39 K10
Elephant I. 6 D4
Eleuthera 45 C9
Elgin, U.K. 10 D5
Elgin, Ill., U.S.A. 42 D1
Elgin, N. Dak., U.S.A. 40 B4
Elgin, Oreg., U.S.A. 38 D5
Elgin, Tex., U.S.A. 41 K6
Elgon, Mt. 28 D6
Elizabeth, Australia 32 B2
Elizabeth, U.S.A. 42 E8
Elizabeth City 43 G7
Elizabethton 43 G4
Elizabethtown 42 G3
Elk → 43 H2
Elk City 41 H5
Elk River, Idaho, U.S.A. 38 C5
Elk River, Minn., U.S.A. 40 C8
Elkhart, Ind., U.S.A. 42 E3
Elkhart, Kans., U.S.A. 41 G4
Elkhorn → 40 E6
Elkin 43 G5
Elkins 42 F6
Elko 38 F6
Ellef Ringnes I. 37 B10
Ellendale 40 B5
Ellensburg 38 C3
Ellenville 42 E8
Ellerton 45 g
Ellery, Mt. 32 C4
Ellesmere, L. 33 M4
Ellesmere I. 37 B10
Ellesmere Port 8 D5
Ellice Is. = Tuvalu ■ 31 B14
Elliot Lake 37 E11
Ellis 40 F5
Elliston 32 B1
Ellisville 41 K10
Ellon 10 D6
Ellsworth, Kans., U.S.A. 40 F5
Ellsworth, Maine, U.S.A. 43 C11
Ellsworth Land 6 E2
Elma 38 C2
Elmhurst 42 E2
Elmira 42 D7
Elmore 32 C3
Eloy 39 K8
Eltham 33 H5
Eluru 25 D7
Elwood, Ind., U.S.A. 42 E3
Elwood, Nebr., U.S.A. 40 E5
Ely, U.K. 9 E8
Ely, Minn., U.S.A. 40 B9
Ely, Nev., U.S.A. 38 G6
Elyria 42 E4
Emāmrūd 24 B4
Emden 16 B3
Emerald 30 E8
Emmen 16 B3
Emmetsburg 40 D7
Emmett 38 E5
Emmonak 36 C3
Empalme 44 B2
Empangeni 29 K6
Emperor Seamount Chain 34 D9
Emperor Trough 34 C9
Emporia, Kans., U.S.A. 40 F6
Emporia, Va., U.S.A. 43 G7
Emporium 42 E6
Ems → 16 B3
Enard B. 10 C3
Encampment 38 F10
Encino 39 J11
Encounter B. 32 C2
Ende 23 D4
Enderbury I. 31 A16
Enderby Land 6 D9
Enderlin 40 B6
Endicott 42 D7
Enewetak Atoll 34 F8
Enfer, Pte. d' 44 c
Enfield 43 G7
Engadin 12 C9
Engels 18 D5
Enggano 23 D2
England 41 H9
England □ 9 E5
Englewood 40 F2
English → 36 D10
English Channel 9 G6
Enid 41 G6
Ennadai L. 36 C9
Enngonia 32 A4
Ennis, Ireland 11 D3
Ennis, Mont., U.S.A. 38 D8
Ennis, Tex., U.S.A. 41 J6
Enniscorthy 11 D5
Enniskillen 11 B4
Ennistimon 11 D2
Enns → 16 D7
Enschede 16 B3
Ensenada 44 A1
Entebbe 28 D6
Enterprise, Ala., U.S.A. 43 K3
Enterprise, Oreg., U.S.A. 38 D5
Enugu 26 G7
Enumclaw 38 C3
Épernay 12 B5
Ephraim 38 G8
Ephrata 38 C4
Epi 31 D12
Épinal 12 B7
Epsom 9 F7
Equatorial Guinea ■ 28 D1
Erdenet 20 B5
Erebus, Mt. 6 E15
Erfurt 16 C5
Eriboll, L. 10 C4
Erie 42 D5
Erie, L. 42 D5
Erigavo 24 D3
Eriskay 10 D1
Eritrea ■ 24 D2
Erlangen 16 D5
Erne → 11 B3
Erne, Lower L. 11 B4
Erne, Upper L. 11 B4
Eromanga 32 A3
Errigal 11 A3
Erris Hd. 11 B1
Erromango 31 D12
Erskine 40 B7
Erwin 43 G4
Erzgebirge 16 C6
Erzurum 17 C6
Es Sahrâ' Esh Sharqîya 27 C12
Esbjerg 7 F5
Escalante 39 H8
Escalante → 39 H8
Escambia → 43 K2
Escanaba 42 C2
Esch-sur-Alzette 12 B6
Escondido 39 K5
Escuinapa de Hidalgo 44 C3
Escuintla 44 E6
Eşfahān 24 B4
Esha Ness 10 A7
Esher 9 F7
Esk →, Cumb., U.K. 10 G5
Esk →, N. Yorks., U.K. 8 C7
Esker 37 D13
Eskilstuna 7 F7
Eskişehir 17 C4
Esmeraldas 46 C3
Espanola 39 H10
Esperance 30 G3
Esperance Harbour 45 f
Esperanza 45 d
Espinhaço, Serra do 47 G10
Espíritu Santo 31 D12
Espoo 7 E8
Essen 16 C3
Essequibo → 46 B7
Essex □ 9 F8
Estancia 39 J10
Estevan 36 E9
Estherville 40 D7
Estrela, Serra da 13 B2
Etawah 25 C6
eThekwini = Durban 29 K6
Ethiopia ■ 28 B7
Ethiopian Highlands 3 D12
Etive, L. 10 E3
Etna 14 F6
Etowah 43 H3
Etrek 24 B4
Ettrick Water → 10 F6
Eua 31 E16
Euclid 42 E5
Eucumbene, L. 32 C4
Eudora 41 J9
Eufaula, Ala., U.S.A. 43 K3
Eufaula, Okla., U.S.A. 41 H7
Eufaula L. 41 H7
Eugene 38 E2
Eugowra 32 B4
Eulo 32 A4
Eunice, La., U.S.A. 41 K8
Eunice, N. Mex., U.S.A. 41 J3
Euphrates = Furāt, Nahr al → 24 B3
Eureka, Canada 37 B10
Eureka, Calif., U.S.A. 38 F1
Eureka, Kans., U.S.A. 41 G6
Eureka, Mont., U.S.A. 38 B6
Eureka, Nev., U.S.A. 38 G5
Eureka, S. Dak., U.S.A. 40 C5
Euroa 32 C4
Europe 3 B11
Eustis 43 L5
Evans 40 E2
Evans Head 32 A5
Evanston, Ill., U.S.A. 42 E2
Evanston, Wyo., U.S.A. 38 F8
Evansville 42 G2
Eveleth 40 B8
Everard, L. 32 B2
Everest, Mt. 25 C7
Everett 38 C2
Everglades △ 43 N5
Everglades, The 43 N5
Everglades City 43 N5
Evergreen, Ala., U.S.A. 43 K2
Evergreen, Mont., U.S.A. 38 B6
Evesham 9 E6
Evia 15 E11
Évora 13 C2
Évreux 12 B4
Ewe, L. 10 D3
Ewing 40 D5
Excelsior Springs 40 F7
Exe → 9 G4
Exeter, U.K. 9 G4
Exeter, U.S.A. 39 H4
Exmoor 9 F4
Exmoor △ 9 F4
Exmouth 9 G4
Exmouth Plateau 34 J3
Expedition △ 32 A4
Extremadura □ 13 C2
Eye Pen. 10 C2
Eyemouth 10 F6
Eyre (North), L. 32 A2
Eyre (South), L. 32 A2
Eyre, L. 30 F6
Eyre Mts. 33 L2
Eyre Pen. 32 B2

F

F.Y.R.O.M. = Macedonia ■ 15 D9
Fabens 39 L10
Færoe Is. = Føroyar ⊠ 4 A9
Fair Haven 42 D9
Fair Hd. 11 A5
Fairbanks 36 C5
Fairbury 40 E6
Fairfield, Ala., U.S.A. 43 J2
Fairfield, Calif., U.S.A. 38 G2
Fairfield, Idaho, U.S.A. 38 E6
Fairfield, Ill., U.S.A. 42 F1
Fairfield, Iowa, U.S.A. 40 E9
Fairfield, Tex., U.S.A. 41 K7
Fairhope 43 K2
Fairlie 33 L3
Fairmont, Minn., U.S.A. 40 D7
Fairmont, W. Va., U.S.A. 42 F5
Fairmount 42 D7
Fairplay 39 G11
Fairport 42 D7
Fairview, Mont., U.S.A. 40 B2
Fairview, Okla., U.S.A. 41 G5
Fairweather, Mt. 36 D6
Faisalabad 25 B6
Faith 40 C3
Fajardo 45 d
Fakaofo 31 B16
Fakenham 8 E8
Fakfak 23 D5
Falcon Res. 41 M5
Falfurrias 41 M5
Falkirk 10 F5
Falkland 10 E5
Falkland Is. ⊠ 48 G5
Fall River 42 E10
Fallon 38 G4
Falls City 40 E7
Falmouth, Jamaica 44 a
Falmouth, U.K. 9 G2
Falun 7 E7
Fanad Hd. 11 A4
Fanling 21 F11
Fannich, L. 10 D4
Farāh 24 B5
Farāh → 24 B5
Farasān, Jazā'ir 24 D3
Fareham 9 G6
Farewell, C. 33 J4
Farghona 18 E8
Fargo 40 B6
Faribault 40 C8
Faridabad 25 C6
Farina 32 B2
Farmerville 41 J8
Farmington, Maine, U.S.A. 43 C10
Farmington, Mo., U.S.A. 41 G9
Farmington, N. Mex., U.S.A. 39 H9
Farmington, Utah, U.S.A. 38 F8
Farmville 42 G6
Farne Is. 8 B6
Faro 36 C6
Farson 38 E9
Fartak, Ra's 24 D4
Farwell 41 H3
Fastnet Rock 11 E2
Fataka 31 C12
Faulkton 40 C5
Fayette, Ala., U.S.A. 43 J2
Fayette, Mo., U.S.A. 40 F8
Fayetteville, Ark., U.S.A. 41 G7
Fayetteville, N.C., U.S.A. 43 H6
Fayetteville, Tenn., U.S.A. 43 H2
Fdérik 26 D3
Feakle 11 D3
Feale → 11 D2
Fear, C. 43 J7
Feather → 38 G3
Featherston 33 J5
Fécamp 12 B4
Feilding 33 J5
Feira de Santana 47 F11
Felipe Carrillo Puerto 44 D7
Felixstowe 9 F9
Fens, The 8 E7
Fenton 42 D4
Fenyang 21 C6
Ferbane 11 C4
Fergus 42 D5
Fergus Falls 40 B6
Fermanagh □ 11 B4
Fermont 37 D13
Fermoy 11 D3
Fernandina Beach 43 K5
Fernando Póo = Bioko 28 D1
Ferndale 38 B2
Fernley 38 G4
Ferrara 14 B4
Ferret, C. 12 D3
Ferriday 41 K9
Ferron 39 G8
Fertile 40 B6
Fès 26 B5
Fessenden 40 B5
Festus 40 F9
Fetlar 10 A8
Feuilles → 37 D12
Feyzābād 25 B6
Fez = Fès 26 B5
Fezzan 27 C8
Fianarantsoa 29 J9
Fife △, U.K. 10 E5
Fife □, U.K. 10 E5
Fife Ness 10 E6
Figeac 12 D5
Fiji ■ 33 C8
Filey 8 C7
Filey B. 8 C7
Fillmore 39 G7
Findhorn → 10 D5
Findlay 42 E4
Finisterre, C. = Fisterra, C. 13 A1
Finland ■ 7 E9
Finland, G. of 7 F9
Finlay → 36 D7
Finley, Australia 32 C4
Finley, U.S.A. 40 B6
Finn → 11 B4
Finniss, C. 32 B1
Fiordland △ 33 L1
Firenze 14 C4
Fish → 29 K3
Fishguard 9 E3
Fisterra, C. 13 A1
Fitchburg, Mass., U.S.A. 42 D10
Fitchburg, Wis., U.S.A. 40 D10
Fitzgerald 43 K4
Flagstaff 39 J8
Flagstaff L. 43 C10
Flambeau → 40 C9
Flamborough Hd. 8 C7
Flaming Gorge △ 38 F9
Flaming Gorge Res. 38 F9
Flandre 12 A5
Flandreau 40 C6
Flannan Is. 10 C1
Flathead L. 38 C7
Flattery, C. 38 B1
Flatwoods 42 F4
Fleetwood 8 D4
Flensburg 16 A4
Flers 12 B3
Fleurieu Pen. 32 C2
Flin Flon 36 D9
Flinders → 30 D7
Flinders I., S. Austral., Australia 32 B1
Flinders I., Tas., Australia 32 D4
Flinders Ranges 32 B2
Flint, U.K. 8 D4
Flint, U.S.A. 42 D4
Flint → 43 K3
Flint I. 35 J12
Flintshire □ 8 D4
Flodden 8 B5
Floodwood 40 B8
Flora 42 F1
Florala 43 K2
Florence = Firenze 14 C4
Florence, Ala., U.S.A. 43 H2
Florence, Ariz., U.S.A. 39 K8
Florence, Colo., U.S.A. 40 F2
Florence, Oreg., U.S.A. 38 E1
Florence, S.C., U.S.A. 43 H6
Florence, L. 32 A2
Flores 23 D4
Flores Sea 23 D4
Floresville 41 L5
Florianópolis 48 B7
Florida □ 43 L5
Florida, Straits of 45 C9
Florida Is. 31 B11
Florida Keys 43 N5
Florissant 40 F9
Florø 7 E5
Floydada 41 J4
Fly → 30 B7
Fochabers 10 D5
Focşani 15 B12
Fóggia 14 D6
Foix 12 E4
Foley 43 K2
Folkestone 9 F9
Folkston 43 K5
Fond-du-Lac, Canada 36 D9
Fond du Lac, U.S.A. 40 D10
Fongafale 31 B14
Fontainebleau 12 B5
Fontenay-le-Comte 12 C3
Fontenelle Res. 38 E8
Forbes 32 B4
Fords Bridge 32 A4
Fordyce 41 J8
Forel, Mt. 6 C5
Forest 41 J10
Forest City, Iowa, U.S.A. 40 D8
Forest City, N.C., U.S.A. 43 H5
Forest Grove 38 D2
Forestier Pen. 32 D4
Forfar 10 E6
Forks 38 C1
Forlì 14 B5
Forman 40 B6
Formby Pt. 8 D4
Føroyar ⊠ 4 A9
Forres 10 D5
Forrest City 41 H9
Forsayth 30 D7
Forsyth 38 C10
Fort Albany 37 D11
Fort Augustus 10 D4
Fort Beaufort 29 L5
Fort Benton 38 C8
Fort Bragg 38 G2
Fort Bridger 38 F8
Fort Chipewyan 36 D8
Fort Collins 40 E2
Fort Davis 41 K3
Fort-de-France 44 c
Fort Defiance 39 J9
Fort Dodge 40 D7
Fort Fairfield 43 B12
Fort Garland 39 H11
Fort Good Hope 36 C7
Fort Hancock 39 L11
Fort Kent 43 B11
Fort Klamath 38 E3
Fort Laramie 40 D2
Fort Lauderdale 43 M5
Fort Liard 36 C7
Fort Lupton 40 E2
Fort MacKay 36 D8
Fort Macleod 36 E8
Fort McMurray 36 D8
Fort McPherson 36 C6
Fort Madison 40 E9
Fort Meade 43 M5
Fort Morgan 40 E3
Fort Myers 43 M5
Fort Nelson 36 D7
Fort Nelson → 36 D7
Fort Payne 43 H3
Fort Peck 38 B10
Fort Peck Dam 38 C10
Fort Peck L. 38 C10
Fort Pierce 43 M5
Fort Pierre 40 C4
Fort Providence 36 C8
Fort Resolution 36 C8
Fort St. John 36 D7
Fort Scott 41 G7
Fort Simpson 36 C7
Fort Smith, Canada 36 D8
Fort Smith, U.S.A. 41 H7
Fort Stockton 41 K3
Fort Sumner 41 H2
Fort Thompson 40 C5
Fort Union △ 41 H2
Fort Valley 43 J4
Fort Walton Beach 43 K2
Fort Wayne 42 E3
Fort William 10 E3
Fort Worth 41 J6
Fort Yates 40 B4
Fort Yukon 36 C5
Fortaleza 47 D11
Forth → 10 E5
Forth, Firth of 10 E6
Fortrose 10 D4
Fortuna, Calif., U.S.A. 38 F1
Fortuna, N. Dak., U.S.A. 40 A3
Foshan 21 D6
Fossil 38 D3
Fossil Butte △ 38 F8
Fostoria 42 E4
Fougères 12 B3
Foula 10 A6
Foulness I. 9 F8
Fountain 40 F2
Fountain Hills 39 K8
Fouta Djallon 26 F3
Foveaux Str. 33 M2
Fowey 9 G3
Fowler 40 F3
Foxe Basin 37 C12
Foxe Chan. 37 C12
Foxe Pen. 37 C12
Foxford 11 C2
Foxton 33 J5
Foyle, Lough 11 A4
Foynes 11 D2
Franca 47 H9
France ■ 12 C5
Frances 32 C3
Franche-Comté □ 12 C6
Francis Case, L. 40 D5
Francistown 29 J5
François L. 36 D7
Francs Pk. 38 E9
Frankfort, Ind., U.S.A. 42 E2
Frankfort, Kans., U.S.A. 40 F6
Frankfort, Ky., U.S.A. 42 F3
Frankfurt, Brandenburg, Germany 16 B7
Frankfurt, Hessen, Germany 16 C4
Franklin, Ky., U.S.A. 43 G2
Franklin, La., U.S.A. 41 L9
Franklin, N.H., U.S.A. 42 D10
Franklin, Nebr., U.S.A. 40 E5
Franklin, Pa., U.S.A. 42 E6
Franklin, Va., U.S.A. 43 G7
Franklin, W. Va., U.S.A. 42 F6
Franklin B. 36 C7
Franklin D. Roosevelt L. 38 B4
Franklin-Gordon Wild Rivers △ 32 D4
Franklin L. 38 F6
Franklin Mts. 36 C7
Franklin Str. 36 B10
Franklinton 41 K9
Frankston 32 C4
Frantsa Iosifa, Zemlya 18 A6
Fraser → 36 E7
Fraser I. 32 A5
Fraserburgh 10 D6
Frederick, Md., U.S.A. 42 F7
Frederick, Okla., U.S.A. 41 H5
Frederick, S. Dak., U.S.A. 40 C5
Fredericksburg, Tex., U.S.A. 41 K5
Fredericksburg, Va., U.S.A. 42 F7
Fredericktown 41 G9
Fredericton 37 E13
Frederikshavn 7 F6
Fredonia, Ariz., U.S.A. 39 H7
Fredonia, Kans., U.S.A. 41 G7
Fredonia, N.Y., U.S.A. 42 D6
Fredrikstad 7 F6
Free State □ 29 K5
Freeman 40 D6
Freeport, Bahamas 45 B9
Freeport, Ill., U.S.A. 40 D10
Freeport, N.Y., U.S.A. 42 E9
Freeport, Tex., U.S.A. 41 L7
Freetown 26 G3
Freiburg 16 E3
Fremont, Calif., U.S.A. 39 H2
Fremont, Mich., U.S.A. 42 D3
Fremont, Nebr., U.S.A. 40 E6
Fremont, Ohio, U.S.A. 42 E4
Fremont → 39 G8
French Guiana ⊠ 47 C8
French Polynesia ⊠ 35 K13
Frenchman Cr. →, N. Amer. 38 B10
Frenchman Cr. →, U.S.A. 40 E4
Fresnillo 44 C4
Fresno 39 H4
Fresno Res. 38 B9
Freycinet △ 32 D4
Freycinet Pen. 32 D4
Fria, C. 29 H2
Frio → 41 L5
Friona 41 H3
Fritch 41 H4
Frobisher B. 37 C13
Frobisher L. 36 D9
Frome 9 F5
Frome →, Australia 32 A2
Frome →, U.K. 9 G5
Frome, L. 32 B2
Front Royal 42 F6
Frostburg 42 F6
Frýdek-Místek 16 D9
Fuchū 22 F3
Fuerte → 44 B3
Fuhai 20 B3
Fuji 22 F6
Fuji-San 22 F6
Fujian □ 21 D6
Fukui 22 E5
Fukuoka 22 G2
Fukushima 22 E7
Fukuyama 22 F3
Fulda 16 C4
Fulda → 16 C4
Fullerton 40 E6
Fulton, Mo., U.S.A. 40 F9
Fulton, N.Y., U.S.A. 42 D7
Funabashi 22 F7
Funafuti 31 B14
Fundy, B. of 37 E13
Furāt, Nahr al → 24 B3
Furneaux Group 32 D4
Fürth 16 D5
Fury and Hecla Str. 37 C11
Fushun 21 B7
Fustic 45 g
Futian 21 F11
Futuna 33 B8
Fuxin 21 B7
Fuyong 21 F10
Fuyu 21 B7
Fuzhou 21 D6
Fylde 8 D5
Fyn 7 F6
Fyne, L. 10 F3

G

Gabès, G. de 27 B8
Gabon ■ 28 E2
Gaborone 29 J5
Gābrīk 24 C4
Gabrovo 15 C11
Gadag 25 D6
Gadsden 43 H3
Gaffney 43 H5
Gagnon 37 D13

Gail 41 J4
Gainesville, *Fla., U.S.A.* 43 L4
Gainesville, *Ga., U.S.A.* 43 H4
Gainesville, *Mo., U.S.A.* 41 G8
Gainesville, *Tex., U.S.A.* 41 J6
Gainsborough 8 D7
Gairdner, L. 32 B2
Gairloch 10 D3
Gairloch, L. 10 D3
Galápagos = Colón, Arch. de 35 H18
Galapagos Fracture Zone 35 G17
Galapagos Rise 35 J18
Galashiels 10 F6
Galaţi 15 B13
Galax 43 G5
Galcaio 24 E3
Galdhøpiggen 7 E5
Galela 23 C4
Galena 36 C4
Galesburg 40 E9
Galicia □ 13 A2
Galina Pt. 44 a
Galiuro Mts. 39 K8
Gallan Hd. 10 C1
Gallatin 43 G2
Galle 25 E7
Galley Hd. 11 E3
Gallipoli = Gelibolu 15 D12
Gallipolis 42 F4
Gällivare 7 D8
Galloway 10 F4
Galloway △ 10 F4
Galloway, Mull of 10 G4
Gallup 39 J9
Galty Mts. 11 D3
Galtymore 11 D3
Galva 40 E9
Galveston 41 L7
Galveston B. 41 L7
Galway 11 C2
Galway □ 11 C2
Galway B. 11 C2
Gambia ■ 26 F2
Gambia → 26 F2
Gambier, Îs. 35 K14
Gambier Is. 32 C2
Gammon Ranges △ 32 B2
Gan Jiang → 21 D6
Ganado 39 J9
Gäncä 17 B7
Gander 37 E14
Ganga → 25 C8
Ganges = Ganga → 25 C8
Gani 23 D4
Gannett Peak 38 E9
Gansu □ 20 C5
Gantheaume, C. 32 C2
Ganzhou 21 D6
Gao 26 E5
Gap 12 D7
Gar 20 C2
Gara, L. 11 C3
Garagum 18 F6
Garah 32 A4
Garberville 38 F2
Garda, L. di 14 B4
Garden City, *Ga., U.S.A.* 43 J5
Garden City, *Kans., U.S.A.* 41 G4
Garden City, *Tex., U.S.A.* 41 K4
Gardēz 25 B5
Gardiner, *Maine, U.S.A.* 43 C11
Gardiner, *Mont., U.S.A.* 38 D8
Gardnerville 38 G4
Gardo 24 E3
Garfield 38 C5
Garforth 8 D6
Gargantua, C. 42 B3
Garland, *Tex., U.S.A.* 41 J6
Garland, *Utah, U.S.A.* 38 F7
Garner 40 D8
Garnett 40 F7
Garoe 24 E3
Garonne → 12 D3
Garrison, *Mont., U.S.A.* 38 C7
Garrison, *N. Dak., U.S.A.* 40 B4
Garron Pt. 11 A6
Garry → 10 E5
Garry, L. 36 C9
Garstang 8 D5
Garvie Mts. 33 L2
Gary 42 E2
Garzê 20 C5
Gascogne 12 E4
Gascogne, G. de 12 D2
Gaspé 37 E13
Gaspésie, Pén. de la 37 E13
Gastonia 43 H5
Gatehouse of Fleet 10 G4
Gateshead 8 C6
Gatesville 41 K6
Gatineau 42 C8
Gatton 32 A5
Gatwick, London (LGW) 9 F7
Gau 33 D8
Gaua 31 C12
Gävle 7 E7
Gawler 32 B2
Gaxun Nur 20 B5
Gaya 25 C7
Gaylord 42 C3
Gayndah 32 A5
Gaza 17 D4
Gaza Strip ■ 24 B2
Gaziantep 17 C5
Gcuwa 29 L5
Gdańsk 16 A9
Gdańska, Zatoka 16 A9
Gdynia 16 A9
Gebe 23 C4
Gedser 7 G6
Geelong 32 C3
Gejiu 20 D5
Gelib 24 E3
Gelibolu 15 D12
Gelsenkirchen 16 C3
General Santos 23 C4
Genesee 38 C5
Genesee → 42 D7
Geneseo, *Ill., U.S.A.* 40 E9
Geneseo, *N.Y., U.S.A.* 42 D7
Geneva = Genève 12 C7
Geneva, *Ala., U.S.A.* 43 K3
Geneva, *N.Y., U.S.A.* 42 D7
Geneva, *Nebr., U.S.A.* 40 E6
Geneva, *Ohio, U.S.A.* 42 E5
Genève 12 C7
Gennargentu, Mti. del 14 D3
Genoa = Génova 12 D8
Genoa, *Australia* 32 C4
Genoa, *U.S.A.* 40 E6
Génova 12 D8
Gent 16 C1
George 29 L4
George → 37 D13
George, L., *N.S.W., Australia* 32 C4
George, L., *S. Austral., Australia* 32 C3
George, L., *Fla., U.S.A.* 43 L5
George, L., *N.Y., U.S.A.* 42 D9
George Sound 33 L1
George Town, *Australia* 32 D4
George Town, *Malaysia* 23 C2
George V Land 6 D14
George West 41 L5
Georgetown, *Guyana* 46 B7
Georgetown, *Colo., U.S.A.* 38 G11
Georgetown, *Ky., U.S.A.* 42 F3
Georgetown, *Ohio, U.S.A.* 42 F4
Georgetown, *S.C., U.S.A.* 43 J6
Georgetown, *Tex., U.S.A.* 41 K6
Georgia □ 43 K5
Georgian B. 37 E11
Gera 16 C6
Geraldine 38 C8
Geraldton 30 F1
Gereshk 24 B5
Gering 40 E3
Gerlach 38 F4
Germantown 41 M10
Germany ■ 16 C5
Germiston 29 K5
Gerona = Girona 13 B7
Getafe 13 B4
Gettysburg, *Pa., U.S.A.* 42 F7
Gettysburg, *S. Dak., U.S.A.* 40 C5
Geyser 38 C8
Ghana ■ 26 G5
Ghanzi 29 J4
Ghats, Eastern 25 D6
Ghats, Western 25 D6
Ghazâl, Bahr el → 27 G12
Ghaziabad 25 C6
Ghaznī 24 B5
Ghent = Gent 16 C1
Giant Sequoia △ 39 J4
Giants Causeway 11 A5
Gibbon 40 E5
Gibraltar ⧄ 13 D3
Gibraltar, Str. of 13 E3
Gibraltar Range △ 32 A5
Gibson Desert 30 E4
Giddings 41 K6
Gifu 22 F5
Gigha 10 F3
Gijón 13 A3
Gila → 39 K6
Gila Bend 39 K7
Gila Bend Mts. 39 K7
Gila Cliff Dwellings △ 39 K9
Gilbert Is. 31 A14
Gilgandra 32 B4
Gilgit 25 B6
Gillam 36 D10
Gilles, L. 32 B2
Gillette 40 C2
Gillingham 9 F8
Gilmer 41 J7
Gilroy 39 H3
Gimie, Mt 45 f
Gin Gin 32 A5
Giohar 24 E3
Girard 41 G7
Girdle Ness 10 D6
Girona 13 B7
Gironde → 12 D3
Girraween △ 32 A5
Girvan 10 F4
Gisborne 33 H7
Giuba → 24 E3
Giza = El Gîza 27 C12
Gizhiga 19 C17
Gjoa Haven 36 C10
Glace Bay 37 E14
Glacier △ 38 B7
Glacier Peak 38 B3
Gladewater 41 J7
Gladstone, *Queens., Australia* 30 E9
Gladstone, *S. Austral., Australia* 32 B2
Gladstone, *U.S.A.* 42 C2
Gladwin 42 D3
Glamorgan, Vale of □ 9 F4
Glasco 40 F6
Glasgow, *U.K.* 10 F4
Glasgow, *Ky., U.S.A.* 42 G3
Glasgow, *Mont., U.S.A.* 38 B10
Glasgow Int. (GLA) 10 F4
Glastonbury 9 F5
Glen Affric 10 D3
Glen Canyon 39 H8
Glen Canyon △ 39 H8
Glen Canyon Dam 39 H8
Glen Coe 10 E3
Glen Garry 10 D3
Glen Innes 32 A5
Glen Mor 10 D4
Glen More △ 10 D5
Glen Moriston 10 D4
Glen Spean 10 E4
Glen Ullin 40 B4
Glenallen 36 C5
Glenariff △ 11 A5
Glenbeigh 11 D2
Glencoe 40 C7
Glencolumbkille 11 B3
Glendale, *Ariz., U.S.A.* 39 K7
Glendale, *Calif., U.S.A.* 39 J4
Glendive 40 B2
Glendo 40 D2
Glenelg → 32 C3
Glengad Hd. 11 A4
Glengarriff 11 E2
Glenmorgan 32 A4
Glennamaddy 11 C3
Glenns Ferry 38 E6
Glenreagh 32 B5
Glenrock 38 E11
Glenrothes 10 E5
Glens Falls 42 D9
Glenties 11 B3
Glenveagh △ 11 A3
Glenville 42 F5
Glenwood, *Ark., U.S.A.* 41 H8
Glenwood, *Iowa, U.S.A.* 40 E7
Glenwood, *Minn., U.S.A.* 40 C7
Glenwood Springs 38 G10
Glin 11 D2
Gliwice 16 C9
Globe 39 K8
Głogów 16 C8
Glomma → 7 F6
Glossop 8 D6
Gloucester, *Australia* 32 B5
Gloucester, *U.K.* 9 F5
Gloucester Point 42 G7
Gloucestershire □ 9 F5
Gniezno 16 B8
Goa □ 25 D6
Goalen Hd. 32 C5
Goat Fell 10 F3
Gobabis 29 J3
Gobi 21 B5
Godalming 9 F7
Godavari → 25 D7
Gods → 36 D10
Gods L. 36 D10
Gogebic, L. 40 B10
Goiânia 47 G9
Goio-Erê 48 A6
Golconda 38 F5
Gold Beach 38 E1
Gold Coast, *Australia* 30 F9
Gold Coast, *W. Afr.* 26 H5
Gold Hill 38 E2
Golden B. 33 J4
Golden Gate 38 H2
Golden Spike △ 38 F7
Golden Vale 11 D3
Goldendale 38 D3
Goldfield 39 H5
Goldsboro 43 H7
Goldsmith 41 K3
Goldthwaite 41 K5
Goliad 41 L6
Golspie 10 D5
Gómez Palacio 44 B4
Gonābād 24 B4
Gonaïves 45 D10
Gongbei 21 G10
Gongga Shan 25 C9
Gonghe 20 C5
Gongming 21 F10
Gongolgon 32 B4
Gonzales, *Calif., U.S.A.* 39 H3
Gonzales, *Tex., U.S.A.* 41 L6
Good Hope, C. of 29 L3
Gooding 38 E6
Goodland 40 F4
Goodooga 32 A4
Goole 8 D7
Goolgowi 32 B4
Goomeri 32 A5
Goondiwindi 32 A5
Goose Creek 43 J5
Goose L. 38 F3
Gorakhpur 25 C7
Gordon 40 D3
Gordon → 32 D4
Gore 33 M2
Gorey 11 D5
Gorgān 24 B4
Gorleston 9 E9
Görlitz 16 C7
Gorontalo 23 C4
Gort 11 C3
Gorzów Wielkopolski 16 B7
Gosford 32 B5
Goshen 42 E3
Gosport 9 G6
Göta kanal 7 F7
Göteborg 7 F6
Gotha 16 C5
Gothenburg = Göteborg 7 F6
Gothenburg 40 E4
Gotland 7 F7
Göttingen 16 C4
Gouda 16 B2
Gouin, Rés. 37 E12
Goulburn 32 B4
Gourock 10 F4
Gouverneur 42 C8
Governador Valadares 47 G10
Gowanda 42 D6
Gower 9 F3
Gowna, L. 11 C4
Goyder Lagoon 32 A2
Gozo 14 F6
Graaff-Reinet 29 L4
Gracias a Dios, C. 45 E8
Grady 41 H3
Grafham Water 9 E7
Grafton, *Australia* 32 A5
Grafton, *N. Dak., U.S.A.* 40 A6
Grafton, *W. Va., U.S.A.* 42 F5
Graham 41 J5
Graham, Mt. 39 K9
Graham Land 6 D3
Grahamstown 29 L5
Grain Coast 26 H3
Grampian Mts. 10 E5
Grampians, The 32 C3
Gran Canaria 26 C2
Gran Chaco 48 B4
Gran Sasso d'Itália 14 C5
Granada, *Nic.* 44 E7
Granada, *Spain* 13 D4
Granada, *U.S.A.* 41 F3
Granard 11 C4
Granbury 41 J6
Granby, *Canada* 37 E12
Granby, *U.S.A.* 38 F11
Grand →, *Mo., U.S.A.* 40 F8
Grand →, *S. Dak., U.S.A.* 40 C4
Grand Bahama I. 45 B9
Grand-Bourg 44 b
Grand Canyon 39 H7
Grand Canyon △ 39 H7
Grand Canyon-Parashant △ 39 H7
Grand Cayman 45 D8
Grand Coulee 38 C4
Grand Coulee Dam 38 C4
Grand Falls 37 E13
Grand Falls-Windsor 37 E14
Grand Forks 40 B6
Grand Haven 42 D2
Grand I. 42 B2
Grand Island 40 E5
Grand Isle 41 L9
Grand Junction 39 G9
Grand L. 41 L8
Grand Lake 38 F11
Grand Marais 42 B3
Grand Portage 40 B10
Grand Prairie 41 J6
Grand Rapids, *Canada* 36 D10
Grand Rapids, *Mich., U.S.A.* 42 D2
Grand Rapids, *Minn., U.S.A.* 40 B8
Grand St-Bernard, Col du 12 D7
Grand Staircase-Escalante △ 39 H8
Grand Teton 38 E8
Grand Teton △ 38 D8
Grand Union Canal 9 E7
Grand-Vigie, Pte. de la 44 b
Grande, Rio → 41 N6
Grande Baleine, R. de la → 37 D12
Grande Prairie 36 D8
Grande-Terre 44 b
Grandfalls 41 K3
Grandview 38 C4
Grangemouth 10 E5
Granger 38 F9
Grangeville 38 D5
Granite City 40 F9
Granite Falls 40 C7
Granite Pk. 38 D9
Granity 33 J3
Grant 40 E4
Grant, Mt. 38 G4
Grant City 40 E7
Grant Range 39 G6
Grantham 8 E7
Grantown-on-Spey 10 D5
Grants 39 J10
Grants Pass 38 E2
Grantsville 38 F7
Granville, *N. Dak., U.S.A.* 40 A4
Granville, *N.Y., U.S.A.* 42 D9
Grass Range 38 C9
Grass Valley, *Calif., U.S.A.* 38 G3
Grass Valley, *Oreg., U.S.A.* 38 D3
Grasse 12 E7
Grassy 32 D3
Graulhet 12 E4
's-Gravenhage 16 B2
Gravesend, *Australia* 32 A5
Gravesend, *U.K.* 9 F8
Grayling 42 C3
Grays 9 F8
Grays Harbor 38 C1
Grays L. 38 E8
Graz 16 E7
Great Australian Bight 30 G5
Great Bahama Bank 44 B4
Great Barrier I. 33 G5
Great Barrier Reef 30 D8
Great Basin 38 G5
Great Basin △ 38 G6
Great Bear → 36 C7
Great Bear L. 36 C8
Great Bend 40 F5
Great Blasket I. 11 D1
Great Camanoe 45 e
Great Channel 25 E8
Great Dividing Ra. 30 E8
Great Exuma I. 45 C9
Great Falls 38 C8
Great Inagua I. 45 C10
Great Karoo 29 L4
Great Lake 32 D4
Great Malvern 9 E5
Great Miami → 42 F3
Great Ormes Head 8 D4
Great Ouse → 8 E8
Great Pedro Bluff 44 a
Great Pee Dee → 43 J6
Great Plains 2 C5
Great Salt L. 38 F7
Great Salt Lake Desert 38 F7
Great Salt Plains L. 41 G5
Great Sand Dunes △ 39 H11
Great Sandy △ 32 A5
Great Sandy Desert 30 E3
Great Skellig 11 E1
Great Slave L. 36 C8
Great Smoky Mts. △ 43 H4
Great Snow Mt. 36 D7
Great Victoria Desert 30 F4
Great Wall 21 C5
Great Whernside 8 C6
Great Yarmouth 9 E9
Greater Antilles 45 D10
Greater London □ 9 F7
Greater Manchester □ 8 D5
Greater Sunda Is. 23 D3
Greece ■ 15 E9
Greeley, *Colo., U.S.A.* 40 E2
Greeley, *Nebr., U.S.A.* 40 E5
Greely Fd. 37 B10
Greem-Bell, Ostrov 18 A7
Green →, *Ky., U.S.A.* 42 G2
Green →, *Utah, U.S.A.* 39 G9
Green B. 42 C2
Green Bay 42 C2
Green C. 32 C5
Green Cove Springs 43 L5
Green River, *Utah, U.S.A.* 39 G8
Green River, *Wyo., U.S.A.* 38 F9
Green Valley 39 L8
Greenbush 40 A6
Greencastle 42 F2
Greeneville 43 G4
Greenfield, *Ind., U.S.A.* 42 F3
Greenfield, *Iowa, U.S.A.* 40 E7
Greenfield, *Mass., U.S.A.* 42 D9
Greenfield, *Mo., U.S.A.* 41 G8
Greenland ⧄ 6 C4
Greenland Sea 6 B6
Greenock 10 F4
Greenore 11 B5
Greenore Pt. 11 D5
Greensboro, *Ga., U.S.A.* 43 J4
Greensboro, *N.C., U.S.A.* 43 G6
Greensburg, *Ind., U.S.A.* 42 F3
Greensburg, *Kans., U.S.A.* 41 G5
Greensburg, *Pa., U.S.A.* 42 E6
Greenstone Pt. 10 D3
Greenville, *Ala., U.S.A.* 43 K2
Greenville, *Calif., U.S.A.* 38 F3
Greenville, *Maine, U.S.A.* 43 C11
Greenville, *Mich., U.S.A.* 42 D3
Greenville, *Miss., U.S.A.* 41 J9
Greenville, *Mo., U.S.A.* 41 G9
Greenville, *N.C., U.S.A.* 43 H7
Greenville, *Ohio, U.S.A.* 42 E3
Greenville, *Pa., U.S.A.* 42 E5
Greenville, *S.C., U.S.A.* 43 H4
Greenville, *Tex., U.S.A.* 41 J6
Greenwich □ 9 F8
Greenwood, *Ark., U.S.A.* 41 H7
Greenwood, *Ind., U.S.A.* 42 F2
Greenwood, *Miss., U.S.A.* 41 J9
Greenwood, *S.C., U.S.A.* 43 H4
Gregory 40 D5
Gregory, L. 32 A2
Grenada 41 J10
Grenada ■ 45 E12
Grenfell 32 B4
Grenoble 12 D6
Gresham 38 D2
Gretna, *U.K.* 10 F5
Gretna, *U.S.A.* 41 L9
Grey → 33 K3
Grey Ra. 32 A3
Greybull 38 D9
Greymouth 33 K3
Greystones 11 C5
Greytown 33 J5
Gridley 38 G3
Griffin 43 J3
Griffith 32 B4
Grimsay 10 D1
Grimsby 8 D7
Grinnell 40 E8
Gris-Nez, C. 12 A4
Grise Fiord 37 B10
Groesbeck 41 K6
Groningen 16 B3
Groom 41 H4
Groote Eylandt 30 C6
Gros Islet 45 f
Gros Piton 45 f
Gros Piton Pt. 45 f
Grossglockner 16 E6
Groton 40 C5
Grove Hill 43 K2
Groves 41 L8
Groveton 42 C10
Groznyy 17 B7
Grudziądz 16 B9
Gruinard B. 10 D3
Grundy Center 40 D8
Gruver 41 G4
Guadalajara, *Mexico* 44 C4
Guadalajara, *Spain* 13 B4
Guadalcanal 31 B11
Guadalete → 13 D2
Guadalquivir → 13 D2
Guadalupe 39 J3
Guadalupe → 41 L6
Guadalupe Mts. △ 41 K2
Guadalupe Peak 41 K2
Guadarrama, Sierra de 13 B4
Guadeloupe ⧄ 44 b
Guadiana → 13 D2
Guadix 13 D4
Guam ⧄ 34 F6
Guamúchil 44 B3
Guana I. 45 e
Guanajuato 44 C4
Guane 45 C8
Guangdong □ 21 D6
Guangxi Zhuangzu Zizhiqu □ 21 D5
Guangyuan 25 B9
Guangzhou 21 D6
Guanica 45 d
Guantánamo 45 C9
Guaporé → 46 F5
Guarapuava 48 B6
Guatemala 44 E6
Guatemala ■ 44 D6
Guatemala Basin 35 F18
Guatemala Trench 35 F18
Guaviare → 46 C5
Guayama 45 d
Guayaquil 46 D3
Guayaquil, G. de 46 D2
Guaymas 44 B2
Guéret 12 C4
Guernsey, *U.K.* 9 H5
Guernsey, *U.S.A.* 40 D2
Guildford 9 F7
Guilin 21 D6
Guinea ■ 26 F3
Guinea, Gulf of 4 D10
Guinea-Bissau ■ 26 F3
Güines 45 C8
Guingamp 12 B2
Guiyang 20 D5
Guizhou □ 20 D5
Gujarat □ 25 C6
Gujranwala 25 C6
Gulbarga 25 D6
Gulf Islands △ 43 E2
Gulfport 41 K10
Gulgong 32 B4
Gunnbjørn Fjeld 6 C5
Gunnedah 32 B5
Gunnewin 32 A4
Gunningbar Cr. → 32 B4
Gunnison, *Colo., U.S.A.* 39 G10
Gunnison, *Utah, U.S.A.* 38 G8
Gunnison → 39 G9
Guntersville 43 H2
Guntur 25 D7
Gurdon 41 J8
Gurley 32 A4
Gusinoozersk 19 D11
Gustine 39 H3
Guthrie, *Okla., U.S.A.* 41 H6
Guthrie, *Tex., U.S.A.* 41 J4
Guttenberg 40 D9
Guwahati 20 D4
Guy Fawkes River △ 32 A5
Guyana ■ 46 C7
Guyenne 12 D4
Guymon 41 G4
Guyra 32 B5
Gwabegar 32 B4
Gwādar 24 C5
Gwalior 25 C6
Gwangju 21 C7
Gweebarra B. 11 B3
Gweedore 11 A3
Gweru 29 H5
Gwinn 42 B2
Gwydir → 32 A4
Gwynedd □ 8 E3
Gyaring Hu 20 C4
Gympie 32 A5
Győr 16 E8
Gyumri 17 B6

H

Ha Tinh 23 B2
Ha'apai Group 31 D16
Haarlem 16 B2
Haast → 33 K2
Hachinohe 22 C7
Ḥadd, Ra's al 24 C4
Haddington 10 F6
Ḥaḍramawt 24 D3
Hadrian's Wall 8 B5
Haeju 21 C7
Hafar al Bāţin 24 C3
Hagen 16 C3
Hagerman 41 J2
Hagerman Fossil Beds △ 38 E6
Hagerstown 42 F7
Hagondange 12 B7
Hags Hd. 11 D2
Hague, C. de la 12 B3
Hague, The = 's-Gravenhage 16 B2
Haguenau 12 B7
Haifa = Ḥefa 17 D5
Haikou 21 D6
Ḥā'il 24 C3
Hailar 21 B6
Hailey 38 E6
Hainan □ 21 E5
Haines 38 D5
Haines City 43 L5
Haines Junction 36 C6
Haiphong 20 D5
Haiti ■ 45 D10
Ḥajjah 24 D3
Hakodate 22 C7
Ḥalab 24 B2
Halberstadt 16 C5
Halcombe 33 J5
Halden 7 F6
Halesowen 9 E5
Halesworth 9 E9
Haleyville 43 H2
Halfmoon Bay 33 M2
Halifax, *Canada* 37 E13
Halifax, *U.K.* 8 D6
Halīl → 24 C4
Halkirk 10 C5
Hall Pen. 37 C13
Hallāniyat, Jazā'ir al 24 D4
Halle 16 C5
Hallett 32 B2
Hallettsville 41 L6
Hallock 40 A6
Halls Creek 30 D4
Halmahera 23 C4
Halmstad 7 F6
Halstead 9 F8
Halton □ 8 D5
Haltwhistle 8 C5
Hamadān 24 B3
Ḥamāh 24 B2
Hamamatsu 22 F5
Hamar 7 E6
Hamburg, *Germany* 16 B4
Hamburg, *Ark., U.S.A.* 41 J9
Hamburg, *N.Y., U.S.A.* 42 D6
Hämeenlinna 7 E8
Hameln 16 B4
Hamersley Ra. 30 E2
Hami 20 B4
Hamilton, *Australia* 32 C3
Hamilton, *Canada* 37 E12
Hamilton, *N.Z.* 33 G5
Hamilton, *U.K.* 10 F4
Hamilton, *Ala., U.S.A.* 43 H1
Hamilton, *Mont., U.S.A.* 38 C6
Hamilton, *N.Y., U.S.A.* 42 D8
Hamilton, *Ohio, U.S.A.* 42 F3
Hamilton, *Tex., U.S.A.* 41 K5
Hamilton → 32 A2
Hamlet 43 H6
Hamley Bridge 32 B2
Hamlin 41 J4
Hamm 16 C3
Hammerfest 7 C8
Hammond, *Ind., U.S.A.* 42 E2
Hammond, *La., U.S.A.* 41 K9
Hammonton 42 F8
Hampden 33 L3
Hampshire □ 9 F6
Hampshire Downs 9 F6
Hampton, *Ark., U.S.A.* 41 J8
Hampton, *Iowa, U.S.A.* 40 D8
Hampton, *S.C., U.S.A.* 43 J5
Hampton, *Va., U.S.A.* 42 G7
Hancock 40 B10
Handan 21 C6
Hanford 39 H4
Hanford Reach △ 38 C4
Hangayn Nuruu 20 B4
Hangzhou 21 C7
Hangzhou Wan 21 C7
Hankinson 40 B6
Hankö 7 F8
Hanksville 39 G8
Hanmer Springs 33 K4
Hanna, *Canada* 36 D8
Hanna, *U.S.A.* 38 F10
Hannibal 40 F9
Hannover 16 B4
Hanoi 20 D5
Hanover, *N.H., U.S.A.* 42 D9
Hanover, *Pa., U.S.A.* 42 F7
Hans Lollik I. 45 e
Hanson, L. 32 B2
Hanzhong 20 C5
Haora 25 C7
Haparanda 7 D8
Happy 41 H4
Happy Camp 38 F2
Happy Valley-Goose Bay 37 D13
Har Hu 20 C4
Har Us Nuur 20 B4
Ḥaraḍ 24 C3
Harare 29 H6
Harbin 21 B7
Harbor Beach 42 D4
Hardangerfjorden 7 E5
Hardin 38 D10
Hardy, Pte. 45 f
Harer 24 E3
Hargeisa 24 E3
Hari → 23 D2
Haridwar 25 C6
Harīrūd → 24 B5
Harlan, *Iowa, U.S.A.* 40 E7
Harlan, *Ky., U.S.A.* 43 G4
Harlech 8 E3
Harlem 38 B9
Harlingen 41 M6
Harlow 9 F8
Harlowton 38 C9
Harney Basin 38 E4
Harney L. 38 E4
Harney Peak 40 D3
Härnösand 7 E7
Haroldswick 10 A8
Harricana → 37 D12
Harriman 43 H3
Harris 10 D2
Harris, L. 32 B2
Harris, Sd. of 10 D1
Harrisburg, *Ill., U.S.A.* 41 G10
Harrisburg, *Nebr., U.S.A.* 40 E3
Harrisburg, *Pa., U.S.A.* 42 E7
Harrison, *Ark., U.S.A.* 41 G8
Harrison, *Nebr., U.S.A.* 40 D3
Harrison, C. 37 D14
Harrisonburg 42 F6
Harrisonville 40 F7
Harrisville 42 C4
Harrodsburg 42 G3
Harrogate 8 C6
Harrow □ 9 F7
Harry S. Truman Res. 40 F7
Hart 42 D2
Hart, L. 32 B2
Hartford, *Conn., U.S.A.* 42 E9
Hartford, *Ky., U.S.A.* 42 G2
Hartford, *S. Dak., U.S.A.* 40 D6
Hartford, *Wis., U.S.A.* 40 D10
Hartford City 42 E3
Hartland Pt. 9 F3
Hartlepool 8 C6
Hartselle 43 H2
Hartshorne 41 H7
Hartsville 43 H5
Hartwell 43 H4
Harvey, *Ill., U.S.A.* 42 E2
Harvey, *N. Dak., U.S.A.* 40 B5
Harwich 9 F9
Haryana □ 25 C6
Harz 16 C5
Hasa 24 C3
Haskell 41 J5
Haslemere 9 F7
Hastings, *N.Z.* 33 H6
Hastings, *U.K.* 9 G8
Hastings, *Mich., U.S.A.* 42 D3
Hastings, *Minn., U.S.A.* 40 C8
Hastings, *Nebr., U.S.A.* 40 E5
Hastings Ra. 32 B5
Hat Yai 23 C2
Hatay 17 C4
Hatch 39 K10
Hatfield P.O. 32 B3
Hatgal 20 A5
Hattah 32 B3
Hatteras, C. 43 H8
Hattiesburg 41 K10
Haugesund 7 F5
Hauraki G. 33 G5
Haut Atlas 26 B4
Havana = La Habana 44 B3
Havana 40 E9
Havant 9 G7
Havasu, L. 39 J6
Havel → 16 B6
Havelock, *N.Z.* 33 J4
Havelock, *U.S.A.* 43 H7
Haverfordwest 9 F3
Haverhill, *U.K.* 9 E8
Haverhill, *U.S.A.* 42 D10
Havre 38 B9
Havre-St.-Pierre 37 D13
Haw → 43 H6
Hawaiian Is. 35 E12
Hawaiian Ridge 35 E11
Hawarden 40 D6
Hawea, L. 33 L2
Hawera 33 H5
Hawick 10 F6
Hawke B. 33 H6
Hawker 32 B2
Hawkinsville 43 J4
Hawley 40 B6
Hawthorne 38 G4
Hay 32 B3
Hay → 36 C8
Hay-on-Wye 9 E4
Hay River 36 C8
Hay Springs 40 D3
Hayden 38 F10
Hayes 40 C4
Hayes → 36 D10
Hayle 9 G2
Hayling I. 9 G7
Haymā' 24 D4
Hays 40 F5
Hayward, *Calif., U.S.A.* 39 G2
Hayward, *Wis., U.S.A.* 40 B9
Haywards Heath 9 G7
Hazard 42 G4
Hazelton 40 B4
Hazen 40 B4
Hazlehurst, *Ga., U.S.A.* 43 K4
Hazlehurst, *Miss., U.S.A.* 41 K9
Hazleton 42 E8
Healdsburg 38 G2
Healdton 41 H6
Healesville 32 C4
Heard I. 5 G14
Hearne 41 K6
Hearst 37 E11
Heart → 40 B4
Heathrow, London (LHR) 9 F7
Heavener 41 H7
Hebbronville 41 M5
Hebei □ 21 C6
Hebel 32 A4
Heber Springs 41 H9
Hebgen L. 38 D8
Hebrides, Sea of the 10 D2
Hebron, *Canada* 37 D13
Hebron, *N. Dak., U.S.A.* 40 B3
Hebron, *Nebr., U.S.A.* 40 E6
Hecate Str. 36 D6
Hechi 20 D5
Hechuan 20 C5
Hecla 40 C5
Heerlen 12 A6
Ḥefa 17 D5
Hefei 21 C6
Hegang 21 B8
Hei Ling Chau 21 G11
Heidelberg 16 D4
Heilbronn 16 D4
Heilongjiang □ 21 B7
Hejaz = Ḥijāz 24 C3
Hekou 20 D5
Helena, *Ark., U.S.A.* 41 H9
Helena, *Mont., U.S.A.* 38 C7
Helensburgh 10 E4
Helensville 33 G5
Helgoland 16 A3
Hells Canyon △ 38 D5
Helmand → 24 B5
Helmsdale 10 C5
Helmsdale → 10 C5
Helper 38 G8
Helsingborg 7 F6
Helsinki 7 E9
Helston 9 G2
Helvellyn 8 C4
Hemel Hempstead 9 F7
Hemet 39 K5
Hemingford 40 D3
Hempstead 41 K6
Henan □ 21 C6
Henderson, *Ky., U.S.A.* 42 G2
Henderson, *N.C., U.S.A.* 43 G6
Henderson, *Nev., U.S.A.* 39 H6
Henderson, *Tenn., U.S.A.* 43 H1
Henderson, *Tex., U.S.A.* 41 J7
Henderson I. 35 K15
Hendersonville, *N.C., U.S.A.* 43 H4
Hendersonville, *Tenn., U.S.A.* 43 G2
Henggang 21 F11
Hengmen 21 F10
Hengqin Dao 21 G10
Hengyang 21 D6
Henley-on-Thames 9 F7
Henlopen, C. 42 F8
Hennessey 41 G6
Henrietta 41 J5
Henrietta Maria, C. 37 D11
Henry 40 E10
Henryetta 41 H7
Hentiyn Nuruu 21 B5
Henty 32 C4
Henzada 25 D8
Heppner 38 D4
Herāt 24 B5
Hereford, *U.K.* 9 E5
Hereford, *U.S.A.* 41 H3
Herefordshire □ 9 E5
Herford 16 B4
Herington 40 F6
Herkimer 42 D8
Herm 9 H5
Hermann 40 F9
Hermidale 32 B4
Hermiston 38 D4
Hermosillo 44 B2
Hernando 41 H10
Herne Bay 9 F9
Herreid 40 C4
Herrin 41 G10
Hertford 9 F7
Hertfordshire □ 9 F7
's-Hertogenbosch 16 C2
Hesperia 39 J5
Hessen □ 16 C4
Hettinger 40 C3
Hewitt 41 K6
Hexham 8 C5
Heysham 8 C5
Heywood 32 C3
Hialeah 43 N5
Hiawatha 40 F7
Hibbing 40 B8
Hibbs B. 32 D4
Hickman 41 G10
Hickory 43 H5
Hicks, Pt. 32 C4
Hidalgo del Parral 44 B3
Higashiōsaka 22 F4
Higgins 41 G4
High Island Res. 21 G11
High Level 36 D8
High Point 43 H6
High Prairie 36 D8
High River 36 D8
High Wycombe 9 F7
Highland □ 10 D4
Highland Park 42 D2
Highmore 40 C5
Ḥijāz 24 C3
Hiko 39 H6
Hikurangi, *Gisborne, N.Z.* 33 H6
Hikurangi, *Northland, N.Z.* 33 F5
Hildesheim 16 B4
Hill City, *Idaho, U.S.A.* 38 E6
Hill City, *Kans., U.S.A.* 40 F5
Hill City, *Minn., U.S.A.* 40 B8
Hill City, *S. Dak., U.S.A.* 40 D3
Hillaby, Mt. 45 g
Hillcrest 45 g
Hillsboro, *Kans., U.S.A.* 40 F6
Hillsboro, *N. Dak., U.S.A.* 40 B6
Hillsboro, *Ohio, U.S.A.* 42 F4
Hillsboro, *Tex., U.S.A.* 41 J6
Hillsborough 42 D10
Hillsdale 42 E3
Hillston 32 B4
Hilton Head Island 43 J5
Hilversum 16 B2
Himachal Pradesh □ 25 B6
Himalaya 25 C7
Himeji 22 F4
Ḥimş 24 B2
Hinckley, *U.K.* 9 E6
Hinckley, *U.S.A.* 40 B8
Hindmarsh, L. 32 C3
Hindu Kush 25 B6
Hinesville 43 K5
Hingham 38 B8
Hinton 42 G5
Hios 15 E12
Hirosaki 22 C7
Hiroshima 22 F3
Hispaniola 45 D10
Hitachi 22 E7
Hitchin 9 F7
Hiva Oa 35 H14
Hjälmaren 7 F7
Hoa Binh 23 A2
Hoare B. 37 C13
Hobart, *Australia* 32 D4
Hobart, *U.S.A.* 41 H5
Hobbs 41 J3
Hobe Sound 43 M5
Hodgson 36 D10
Hōfu 22 F2
Hogan Group 32 C4
Hohenwald 43 H2
Hohhot 21 B6
Hoisington 40 F5
Hokianga Harbour 33 F4
Hokitika 33 K3
Hokkaidō □ 22 B8
Holbrook, *Australia* 32 C4
Holbrook, *U.S.A.* 39 J8
Holden 38 G7
Holdenville 41 H6
Holdrege 40 E5
Holetown 45 g
Holguín 45 C9
Holland 42 D2
Hollandale 41 J9
Hollidaysburg 42 E6
Hollis 41 H5
Hollister, *Calif., U.S.A.* 39 H3
Hollister, *Idaho, U.S.A.* 38 E6
Holly Hill 43 L5
Holly Springs 41 H10
Hollywood 43 N5
Holman 36 B8
Holmen 40 D9
Holsworthy 9 G3
Holton 40 F7
Holtville 39 K6
Holy I., *Anglesey, U.K.* 8 D3
Holy I., *Northumberland, U.K.* 8 B6
Holyhead 8 D3
Holyoke, *Colo., U.S.A.* 40 E3
Holyoke, *Mass., U.S.A.* 42 D9
Home B. 37 C13
Homedale 38 E5
Homer, *Alaska, U.S.A.* 36 D4
Homer, *La., U.S.A.* 41 J8
Homestead 43 N5
Homestead △ 40 E6
Homs = Ḥimş 24 B2
Homyel 18 D4
Hondo 41 L5
Honduras ■ 44 E7
Honduras, G. de 44 D7
Honey L. 38 F3
Hong → 20 D5
Hong Gai 23 A2
Hong Kong □ 21 G11
Hong Kong I. 21 G11
Hong Kong Int. (HKG) 21 G10
Hongjiang 21 D5
Hongshui He → 21 D5
Hongze Hu 21 C6
Honiara 31 B10
Honiton 9 G4
Honolulu 35 E12
Honshū 22 F6
Hood, Mt. 38 D3
Hood River 38 D3
Hoodsport 38 C2
Hook Hd. 11 D5
Hooker 41 G4
Hooper Bay 36 C3
Hoopeston 42 E2
Hoorn 16 B2
Hoover 43 J2
Hoover Dam 39 J6
Hope 41 J8
Hope, L. 32 A2
Hopedale 37 D13
Hopetoun 32 C3
Hopewell 42 G7
Hopkinsville 43 G2
Hopland 38 G2
Hoquiam 38 C2
Horlivka 17 A5
Hormuz, Str. of 24 C4
Horn, Cape = Hornos, C. de 48 H3
Horn, Is. 31 C15
Horn Head 11 A3
Hornavan 7 D7
Hornbeck 41 K8
Hornbrook 38 F2
Horncastle 8 D7
Hornell 42 D7
Hornos, C. de 48 H3
Hornsea 8 D7
Horqin Youyi Qianqi 21 B7
Horse Cr. → 40 E3
Horsham, *Australia* 32 C3
Horsham, *U.K.* 9 F7
Horton 40 F7
Horton → 36 C7
Hot Creek Range 38 G6
Hot Springs, *Ark., U.S.A.* 41 H8
Hot Springs, *S. Dak., U.S.A.* 40 D3
Hot Springs △ 41 H8
Hotan 20 C2
Hotchkiss 39 G10
Hou Hai 21 F10
Houghton 40 B10
Houghton L. 42 C3
Houghton-le-Spring 8 C6
Houhora Heads 33 F4
Houlton 43 B12
Houma 41 L9
Houston, *Mo., U.S.A.* 41 G9
Houston, *Tex., U.S.A.* 41 L7
Hovd □ 20 B4
Hove 9 G7
Hovenweep △ 39 H9
Hövsgöl Nuur 20 A5
Howard, *Australia* 32 A5
Howard, *U.S.A.* 40 C6
Howe 38 E7
Howe, C. 32 C5
Howell 42 D4
Howitt, L. 32 A2
Howland I. 34 G10
Howrah = Haora 25 C7
Howth 11 C5
Howth Hd. 11 C5
Hoy 10 C5
Høyanger 7 E5
Hoylake 8 D4
Hradec Králové 16 C7
Hrodna 18 D3
Hron → 16 E9
Hsinchu 21 D7
Hua Hin 23 B1
Huahine, Î. 35 J12
Huai He → 21 C6
Huainan 21 C6
Huaiyin 21 C6
Hualapai Peak 39 J7
Huambo 29 G3
Huancayo 46 F3
Huang He → 21 C6
Huangshan 21 D5
Huangshi 21 C6
Huánuco 46 E3
Huascarán, Nevado 46 E3
Huatabampo 44 B3
Hubbard 41 K6
Hubei □ 21 C6
Hubli 25 D6
Hucknall 8 D6
Huddersfield 8 D6
Hudiksvall 7 E7
Hudson, *N.Y., U.S.A.* 42 D9
Hudson, *Wis., U.S.A.* 40 C8
Hudson, *Wyo., U.S.A.* 38 E9
Hudson → 42 E8
Hudson Bay 37 D11
Hudson Falls 42 D9
Hudson Str. 37 C13
Hue 23 B2
Huelva 13 D2
Huesca 13 A5
Hughenden 30 E7
Hugo, *Colo., U.S.A.* 40 F3
Hugo, *Okla., U.S.A.* 41 H7
Hugoton 41 G4
Huize 20 D5
Hull 37 E12
Hull → 8 D7
Hulun Nur 21 B6
Humacao 45 d
Humber → 8 D7
Humboldt, *Canada* 36 D9
Humboldt, *Iowa, U.S.A.* 40 D7
Humboldt, *Tenn., U.S.A.* 41 H10
Humboldt → 38 F4
Hume, L. 32 C4
Humen 21 F10
Humphreys Peak 39 J8
Hunan □ 21 D6
Hungary ■ 16 E9
Hungerford 32 A3
Hŭngnam 21 C7
Hunsrück 16 D3
Hunstanton 8 E8
Hunter I. 32 D3
Hunter Ra. 32 B5
Hunterville 33 H5
Huntingburg 42 F2
Huntingdon, *U.K.* 9 E7
Huntingdon, *U.S.A.* 42 E7
Huntington, *Ind., U.S.A.* 42 E3
Huntington, *Oreg., U.S.A.* 38 D5
Huntington, *Utah, U.S.A.* 38 G8
Huntington, *W. Va., U.S.A.* 42 F4
Huntington Beach 39 K5
Huntly, *N.Z.* 33 G5
Huntly, *U.K.* 10 D6
Huntsville, *Canada* 37 E12
Huntsville, *Ala., U.S.A.* 43 H2
Huntsville, *Tex., U.S.A.* 41 K7
Huonville 32 D4
Hurghada 24 C2
Hurley, *N. Mex., U.S.A.* 39 K9
Hurley, *Wis., U.S.A.* 40 B9
Huron 40 C5
Huron, L. 42 C4
Hurricane 39 H7
Hurunui → 33 K4
Hutchinson, *Kans., U.S.A.* 41 F6
Hutchinson, *Minn., U.S.A.* 40 C7
Hutton, Mt. 32 A4
Huzhou 21 C7
Hwang Ho = Huang He → 21 C6
Hyannis, *Mass., U.S.A.* 42 E10
Hyannis, *Nebr., U.S.A.* 40 E4
Hyargas Nuur 20 B4
Hyderabad, *India* 25 D6
Hyderabad, *Pakistan* 24 C5
Hyères 12 E7
Hyères, Îs. d' 12 E7
Hyndman Peak 38 E6
Hyrum 38 F8
Hysham 38 C10
Hythe 9 F9

I

Ialomiţa → 15 B12
Iaşi 17 A3
Ibadan 26 G6
Ibagué 46 C3
Ibb 24 D3
Iberian Peninsula 2 B9
Ibiza = Eivissa 13 C6
'Ibrī 24 C4
Ica 46 F3
İçel 17 C4
Iceland ■ 7 B2
Ichihara 22 F7
Ichinomiya 22 F5
Ida Grove 40 D7
Idabel 41 J7
Idaho □ 38 D7
Idaho City 38 E6
Idaho Falls 38 E7
Idar-Oberstein 16 D3
Ife 26 G6
Igarka 18 C9
Iglésias 14 E3
Igloolik 37 C11
Iguaçu, Cat. del 48 B6
Iguala 44 D5
Iisalmi 7 E9
IJsselmeer 16 B2
Ikaluktutiak 36 C9
Ikeda 22 F3
Ilagan 23 B4
Ile → 18 E8
Île-de-France □ 12 B5
Ilesha 26 G6
Ilfracombe 9 F3
Ilhéus 47 F11
Iliamna L. 36 D4
Iligan 23 C4
Ilkeston 8 E6
Ilkley 8 D6
Iller → 16 D4
Illinois □ 40 E10
Illinois → 40 F9
Iloilo 23 B4
Ilorin 26 G6
Imabari 22 F3
Imbil 32 A5
imeni Ismail Samani, Pik 18 F8
Imi 24 E3
Imlay 38 F4
Immingham 8 D7
Immokalee 43 M5
Imperatriz 47 E9
Imperial 40 E4
Imperial Dam 39 K6
Imphal 25 C8
Inangahua 33 J3
Inari 7 D9
Inarijärvi 7 D9
Incheon 21 C7
Incline Village 38 G4
Incomáti → 29 K6
Indalsälven → 7 E7
Independence, *Calif., U.S.A.* 39 H4
Independence, *Iowa, U.S.A.* 40 D9
Independence, *Kans., U.S.A.* 41 G7
Independence, *Ky., U.S.A.* 42 F3
Independence, *Mo., U.S.A.* 40 F7
Independence Mts. 38 F5
India ■ 25 C6
Indian → 43 M5
Indian Ocean 3 E14
Indian Springs 39 G6
Indiana 42 E6
Indiana □ 42 F3
Indianapolis 42 F2
Indianola, *Iowa, U.S.A.* 40 E8
Indianola, *Miss., U.S.A.* 41 J9
Indigirka → 19 B15
Indio 39 K5
Indo-China 23 B2
Indonesia ■ 23 D3
Indore 25 C6
Indravati → 25 D7
Indre → 12 C4
Indulkana 32 A1
Indus → 24 C5
Indus, Mouths of the 24 C5
Ingleborough 8 C5
Inglewood, *Queens., Australia* 32 A5
Inglewood, *Vic., Australia* 32 C3
Inglewood, *N.Z.* 33 H5
Inglewood, *U.S.A.* 39 K4
Ingolstadt 16 D5
Ingomar 38 C10
Inishbofin 11 C1
Inisheer 11 C2
Inishfree B. 11 A3
Inishkea North 11 B1
Inishkea South 11 B1
Inishmaan 11 C2
Inishmore 11 C2
Inishmurray I. 11 B3
Inishowen Pen. 11 A4
Inishshark 11 C1
Inishturk 11 C1
Inishvickillane 11 D1
Injune 32 A4
Inland Kaikoura Ra. 33 J4
Inn → 16 D6
Innamincka 32 A3
Inner Hebrides 10 E2
Inner Mongolia = Nei Monggol Zizhiqu □ 21 B6
Inner Sound 10 D3
Innsbruck 16 E5
Inny → 11 C4
Inowrocław 16 B9
Insein 25 D8
Interlaken 12 C7
International Falls 40 A8
Inukjuak 37 D12
Inuvik 36 C6
Inveraray 10 E3
Inverbervie 10 E6
Invercargill 33 M2
Inverclyde □ 10 F4
Inverell 32 A5
Invergordon 10 D4
Inverloch 32 C4
Inverness, *U.K.* 10 D4
Inverness, *U.S.A.* 43 L4
Inverurie 10 D6
Investigator Group 32 B1
Investigator Str. 32 C2
Inyo Mts. 39 H5
Inyokern 39 J5
Iola 41 G7
Iona 10 E2
Ione 38 G3
Ionia 42 D3
Ionian Is. = Ionioi Nisoi 15 E9
Ionian Sea 15 E7
Ionioi Nisoi 15 E9
Iowa □ 40 D8
Iowa → 40 E9
Iowa City 40 E9
Iowa Falls 40 D8
Iowa Park 41 J5
Ipatinga 47 G10
Ipoh 23 C2
Ipswich, *Australia* 32 A5
Ipswich, *U.K.* 9 E9
Ipswich, *U.S.A.* 40 C5
Iqaluit 37 C13
Iquique 46 H4
Iquitos 46 D4
Iraklio 15 G11
Iran ■ 24 B4
Irapuato 44 C4
Iraq ■ 24 B3
Ireland ■ 11 C4
Iringa 28 F7
Irish Republic ■ 11 C4
Irish Sea 8 D3
Irkutsk 19 D11
Iron Baron 32 B2
Iron Knob 32 B2
Iron Mountain 42 C1
Iron River 40 B10
Ironton, *Mo., U.S.A.* 41 G9
Ironton, *Ohio, U.S.A.* 42 F4
Ironwood 40 B9
Ironwood Forest △ 39 K8
Irrara Cr. → 32 A4
Irrawaddy → 25 D8
Irtysh → 18 C7
Irvine, *U.K.* 10 F4
Irvine, *U.S.A.* 42 G4
Irvinestown 11 B4
Irving 41 J6
Irymple 32 B3
Isabel 40 C4
Isabela 45 d
Isar → 16 D6
Isère → 12 D6
Isfahan = Eşfahān 24 B4
Ishim → 18 D8
Ishinomaki 22 D7
Ishpeming 42 B2
İskenderun 17 C5
Isla → 10 E5
Islamabad 25 B6
Island L. 36 D10
Island Lagoon 32 B2
Island Pond 42 C10
Islands, B. of 33 F5
Islay 10 F2
Isle of Wight □ 9 G6
Isle Royale △ 42 B1
Ismâ'ilîya 27 B12
Israel ■ 17 D4
Issoire 12 D5
İstanbul 15 D13
İstanbul Boğazı 15 D13
Istokpoga, L. 43 M5
Istra 14 B6
Istres 12 E6
Istria = Istra 14 B6
Itabuna 47 F11
Itaipú, Reprêsa de 48 B6
Italy ■ 14 C5
Itapipoca 47 D11
Itchen → 9 G6
Ithaca 42 D7
Ivanhoe, *Australia* 32 B3
Ivanhoe, *U.S.A.* 40 C6
Ivano-Frankivsk 18 E3
Ivanovo 18 D5
Ivory Coast ■ 26 G4
Ivujivik 37 C12
Ivybridge 9 G4
Iwaki 22 E7
Iwakuni 22 F3
Iwo 26 G6
Izhevsk 18 D6
Izkī 24 C4
İzmir 15 E12

J

J. Strom Thurmond L. 43 J4
Jabalpur 25 C6
Jaboatão 47 E11
Jackman 43 C10
Jacksboro 41 J5
Jackson, *Barbados* 45 g
Jackson, *Ala., U.S.A.* 43 K2
Jackson, *Calif., U.S.A.* 38 G3
Jackson, *Ky., U.S.A.* 42 G4
Jackson, *Mich., U.S.A.* 42 D3
Jackson, *Minn., U.S.A.* 40 D7
Jackson, *Miss., U.S.A.* 41 J9
Jackson, *Mo., U.S.A.* 41 G10
Jackson, *Ohio, U.S.A.* 42 F4
Jackson, *Tenn., U.S.A.* 43 H1
Jackson, *Wyo., U.S.A.* 38 E8
Jackson B. 33 K2
Jackson L. 38 E8
Jacksons 33 K3
Jacksonville, *Ala., U.S.A.* 43 J3
Jacksonville, *Ark., U.S.A.* 41 H8
Jacksonville, *Fla., U.S.A.* 43 K5
Jacksonville, *Ill., U.S.A.* 40 F9
Jacksonville, *N.C., U.S.A.* 43 H7
Jacksonville, *Tex., U.S.A.* 41 K7
Jacksonville Beach 43 K5
Jacmel 45 D10
Jacob Lake 39 H7
Jaén 13 D4
Jaffa = Tel Aviv-Yafo 17 D4
Jaffa, C. 32 C2
Jaffna 25 E7
Jagdalpur 25 D7
Jahrom 24 C4
Jaipur 25 C6
Jakarta 23 D2
Jal 41 J3
Jalna 25 D6
Jaluit I. 34 G8
Jamaica ■ 44 a
Jambi 23 D2
James →, *S. Dak., U.S.A.* 40 D6
James →, *Va., U.S.A.* 42 G7
James B. 37 D12
Jamestown, *Australia* 32 B2
Jamestown, *N. Dak., U.S.A.* 40 B5
Jamestown, *N.Y., U.S.A.* 42 D6
Jammu 25 B6
Jammu & Kashmir □ 25 B6
Jamnagar 25 C6
Jamshedpur 25 C7
Jan Mayen 6 B6
Jandowae 32 A5
Janesville 40 D10
Japan ■ 22 F5
Japan, Sea of 22 D4
Japan Trench 34 D6
Japurá → 46 D5
Jarvis I. 35 H12
Jäsk 24 C4
Jasper, *Canada* 36 D8
Jasper, *Ala., U.S.A.* 43 J2
Jasper, *Fla., U.S.A.* 43 K4
Jasper, *Ind., U.S.A.* 42 F2
Jasper, *Tex., U.S.A.* 41 K8
Jaunpur 25 C7
Java = Jawa 23 D3
Java Sea 23 D2
Java Trench 23 D2
Jawa 23 D3
Jaya, Puncak 23 D5
Jayton 41 J4
Jean 39 J6
Jeanerette 41 L9
Jebel, Bahr el → 27 G12
Jedburgh 10 F6
Jedda = Jiddah 24 C2
Jefferson, *Iowa, U.S.A.* 40 D7
Jefferson, *Tex., U.S.A.* 41 J7
Jefferson, Mt., *Nev., U.S.A.* 38 G5
Jefferson, Mt., *Oreg., U.S.A.* 38 D3
Jefferson City, *Mo., U.S.A.* 40 F8
Jefferson City, *Tenn., U.S.A.* 43 G4
Jeffersontown 42 F3
Jeffersonville 42 F3
Jeffrey City 38 E10
Jeju-do 21 C7
Jekyll I. 43 K5
Jelenia Góra 16 C7
Jena, *Germany* 16 C5
Jena, *U.S.A.* 41 K8
Jenkins 42 G4
Jennings 41 K8
Jeonju 21 C7
Jeparit 32 C3
Jequié 47 F10
Jérémie 45 D10
Jerez de la Frontera 13 D2
Jerilderie 32 C4
Jerome 38 E6
Jersey 9 H5
Jersey City 42 E8
Jersey Shore 42 E7
Jerseyville 40 F9
Jerusalem 17 D5
Jervis B. 32 C5
Jesup 43 K5
Jetmore 41 F5
Jhansi 25 C6
Jharkhand □ 25 C7
Jhelum → 25 B6

Jiamusi 21 B8
Ji'an 21 D6
Jiangcheng 20 D5
Jiangmen 21 D5
Jiangsu □ 21 C7
Jiangxi □ 21 D6
Jiaxing 21 C7
Jiddah 24 C2
Jihlava → 16 D8
Jijiga 24 E3
Jijuga 24 E3
Jilin 21 B7
Jilin □ 21 B7
Jiménez 21 C6
Jinan 21 C6
Jinchang 20 C5
Jindabyne 32 C4
Jinding 21 G10
Jingdezhen 21 D6
Jinggu 20 D5
Jinhua 21 D6
Jining,
 Nei Monggol Zizhiqu,
 China 21 B6
Jining, Shandong,
 China 21 C6
Jinja 28 D6
Jinsha Jiang → 20 D5
Jinzhou 21 B7
Jiujiang 21 D6
Jiwani 24 C5
Jixi 21 B8
Jīzān 24 D3
Jizzakh 24 A5
João Pessoa 47 E12
Jodhpur 25 C6
Johannesburg 29 K5
John Crow Mts. 44 a
John Day 38 D3
John Day → 38 D3
John Day Fossil
 Beds △ 38 D4
John H. Kerr Res. 43 G6
John o' Groats 10 C5
Johnson City,
 Kans., U.S.A. 41 G4
Johnson City,
 Tenn., U.S.A. 43 G4
Johnson City,
 U.S.A. 41 K5
Johnston I. 35 F11
Johnstown, Ireland 11 D4
Johnstown, N.Y.,
 U.S.A. 42 D8
Johnstown, Pa.,
 U.S.A. 42 E6
Johor Bahru 23 C2
Joinville 47 B6
Joliet 42 E2
Joliette 37 E12
Jolo 37 B10
Jones Sound 37 B10
Jonesboro, Ark.,
 U.S.A. 41 H9
Jonesboro, La.,
 U.S.A. 41 J8
Jönköping 7 F6
Jonquière 37 E12
Joplin 41 G7
Jordan 38 C10
Jordan ■ 24 D5
Jordan → 17 D5
Jos 26 G7
Joseph Bonaparte
 G. 30 C4
Joshua Tree △ 39 K5
Jost Van Dyke I. 45 e
Jotunheimen 7 E5
Juan de Fuca, Str
 of. 38 B1
Juan Fernández,
 Arch. de 35 L20
Juázeiro do Norte 47 E11
Júchitan de
 Zaragoza 44 D5
Judith → 38 C9
Judith Gap 38 C9
Juiz de Fora 47 H10
Juláesburg 40 E3
Juliaca 46 G4
Jullundur 25 D6
Junagadh 25 C6
Junction, Tex.,
 U.S.A. 41 K5
Junction, Utah,
 U.S.A. 39 G7
Junction City,
 Kans., U.S.A. 40 F6
Junction City,
 Oreg., U.S.A. 38 D2
Jundiaí 48 A7
Juneau 36 D6
Junee 32 B4
Junggar Pendi 20 B3
Juntura 38 D4
Jura 10 F3
Jura, Mts. du 12 C7
Jura, Sd. of 10 F3
Juruá → 46 D5
Jutland = Jylland 7 F5
Juventud, I. de la 45 C8
Jylland 7 F5
Jyväskylä 7 E9

K

K2 25 B6
Kabaena 23 D4
Kābul 24 B5
Kabwe 27 G5
Kachchh, Gulf of 25 C5
Kachin □ 20 D4
Kadavu 33 D8
Kadina 32 B2
Kaduna 26 F7
Kaesŏng 21 C7
Kagoshima 22 H2
Kahoka 42 F9
Kahramanmaraş 17 C5
Kahurangi △ 33 J4
Kai, Kepulauan 23 D5
Kaiapoi 33 K4
Kaifeng 21 C6
Kaikohe 33 H5
Kaikoura 33 K4
Kaimanawa Mts. 33 H5
Kaipara Harbour 33 H5
Kaiserslautern 14 D5
Kaitaia 33 H5
Kaitangata 33 M2
Kajaani 7 D9
Kajabbi 31 D3
Kakamega 28 D6
Kakinada 25 D7
Kalaallit Nunaat =
 Greenland ☑ 6 C4
Kalahari 29 J4
Kalamata 15 F10
Kalamazoo 42 D3
Kalemie 28 F5
Kalgoorlie-Boulder 30 G3
Kaliningrad 16 A10
Kalispell 38 B6
Kalisz 16 C9
Kalkaska 42 C3
Kalmar 7 F7
Kaluga 18 D4
Kamchatka,
 Poluostrov 19 D16
Kamiah 38 C5
Kamina 28 F4
Kamloops 36 D7
Kampala 28 D6
Kampong Saom 23 B2
Kampong
 Podlskyy 17 A3
Kamyshin 18 D5
Kanaaupscow 37 D12

Kanab 39 H7
Kanab Cr. → 39 H7
Kananga 28 F4
Kanawha → 42 F4
Kandos 32 B4
Kandahar 24 B4
Kandy 25 E7
Kane 42 E6
Kane Basin 6 B3
Kangaroo I. 32 C2
Kangean,
 Kepulauan 23 D3
Kangiqsualujjuaq 37 D13
Kangiqsujuaq 37 C12
Kangirsuk 37 D13
Kanin, Poluostrov 18 C5
Kankaanpää 7 E8
Kankakee 42 C3
Kankakee → 42 E1
Kankan 26 F4
Kannapolis 43 H5
Kano 26 F7
Kanpur 25 C7
Kansas □ 40 F5
Kansas → 40 F7
Kansas City,
 Kans., U.S.A. 40 F7
Kansas City, Mo.,
 U.S.A. 40 F7
Kansk 19 D10
Kanturk 11 D3
Kanye 29 J5
Kaohsiung 21 D7
Kaolack 26 F2
Kaposvár 16 E8
Kapiti I. 33 J5
Kapuas → 23 D2
Kapuas Hulu,
 Pegunungan 23 C3
Kapunda 32 B2
Kaputar, Mt. 32 B5
Kara Kum =
 Garagum 18 F6
Kara Sea 18 B7
Karachi 24 C5
Karaganda 18 E8
Karaj 24 B3
Karakol 20 B3
Karakoram Ra. 25 B6
Karamay 20 B3
Karamea Bight 33 J3
Karasburg 29 K3
Karasuk 18 D8
Karbalā' 24 B3
Karimata,
 Kepulauan 23 D2
Karimata, Selat 23 D2
Karimunjawa,
 Kepulauan 23 D3
Karlskrona 7 F7
Karlstad, Sweden 7 F6
Karlstad, U.S.A. 40 A6
Karnische Alpen 14 A5
Kärnten □ 16 E6
Karoonda 32 C2
Karora 24 D2
Karratha 30 D2
Karsakpay 18 E7
Karufa 23 D5
Kasai → 28 E3
Kasba L. 36 C9
Kasba Tadla 26 B4
Kashi 20 C2
Kaskaskia → 40 G10
Kassalâ 27 E13
Kassel 14 C4
Kasur 25 D6
Katahdin, Mt. 43 C11
Katanga □ 28 F4
Katanning 30 G2
Katha 20 D4
Katherine 30 C5
Katmandu 25 C7
Katoomba 32 B5
Katowice 16 C9
Katrine, L. 10 E4
Katsina 26 F7
Kattegat 7 F6
Kaufman 41 J6
Kaukauna 42 C1
Kaunas 18 D3
Kavala 15 D11
Kavieng 30 A9
Kavir, Dasht-e 24 B4
Kawagoe 22 F6
Kawaguchi 22 F6
Kawawachikamach 37 D13
Kawerau 33 H6
Kawhia 33 H5
Kawhia Harbour 33 H5
Kayan → 23 C3
Kaycee 38 E10
Kayenta 39 H8
Kayes 26 F3
Kayseri 17 C5
Kaysville 38 F8
Kazakhstan ■ 18 E7
Kazan 18 D5
Kazan-Rettō 34 E6
Kāzerūn 24 C4
Keady 11 B5
Kearney 40 E5
Kearny 39 K8
Kebnekaise 7 C7
Kebri Dehar 24 F3
Kecskemét 16 E9
Kediri 23 D3
Keeling Is. =
 Cocos Is. 23 E1
Keene 42 D9
Keeper Hill 11 D3
Keetmanshoop 29 K3
Kefalonia 15 E9
Keighley 8 D6
Keith, Australia 32 C3
Keith, U.K. 10 D6
Keizer 38 D2
Kelang 23 D2
Kellogg 38 C5
Kelowna 36 D8
Kelso, N.Z. 33 L2
Kelso, U.K. 10 F6
Kelso, U.S.A. 38 C2
Kemerovo 18 D9
Kemi 7 D8
Kemijoki → 7 D8
Kemmerer 38 F8
Kemp Land 5 C5
Kempsey 32 B5
Kempten 14 E6
Kenai 36 C4
Kendal, Australia 32 B5
Kendal, U.K. 8 C5
Kendall 43 N5
Kendallville 42 E3
Kendari 23 D4
Kenedy 41 L6
Kenema 26 G3
Kenitra 26 B4
Kenmare, Ireland 11 E2
Kenmare, U.S.A. 40 A3
Kenmare River 11 E2
Kennebunk 42 D10
Kennedy Town 21 a
Kennet → 9 F7
Kennett 41 G9
Kennewick 38 C4
Keno Hill 36 C6
Kenogami → 37 D11
Kenora 36 E10
Kenosha 42 D2
Kent, Tex., U.S.A. 41 K2
Kent, Wash.,
 U.S.A. 38 C2
Kent □ 9 F8
Kent Group 32 A4
Kent Pen. 36 C9
Kentland 42 E2
Kenton 42 E4

Kentucky □ 42 G3
Kentucky → 42 F3
Kentucky L. 43 G2
Kentville 37 E13
Kentwood 41 K9
Kenya ■ 28 D7
Kenya, Mt. 28 E7
Keokuk 40 E9
Kerala □ 25 D6
Kerang 32 C3
Kerch 17 A5
Kerguelen 5 G14
Kericho 28 E7
Kerinci 22 E2
Kermadec Is. 31 G15
Kermadec Trench 31 G15
Kermān 24 B4
Kermānshāh 24 B3
Kerrobert 36 D9
Kerrville 41 K5
Kerry □ 11 D2
Kerry Hd. 11 D2
Kerulen → 21 B6
Keswick 8 C4
Ketchikan 36 D6
Ketchum 38 E6
Kettering, U.K. 9 E7
Kettering, U.S.A. 42 F3
Kettle Falls 38 B4
Kewanee 40 E10
Kewaunee 42 C2
Keweenaw B. 42 B1
Keweenaw Pen. 42 B2
Keweenaw Pt. 42 B2
Key, L. 11 B3
Key Largo 43 N5
Key West 43 N4
Khabarovsk 19 E14
Khakassia □ 18 D9
Khambhat, G. of 25 C6
Khamis Mushayt 24 D3
Kharkiv 18 E4
Kharkov = Kharkiv 18 E4
Khartoum = El
 Khartûm 27 E12
Khaskovo 15 D11
Khatanga 19 B11
Kherson 17 A4
Kholm 24 B5
Khon Kaen 23 B2
Khorramābād 24 B3
Khorramshahr 24 B3
Khouribga 26 B4
Khūjand 18 E7
Khulna 25 D7
Khvoy 24 B3
Khyber Pass 25 B6
Kiama 32 B5
Kicking Horse
 Pass 36 D8
Kidderminster 9 E5
Kidnappers, C. 33 H6
Kidsgrove 8 D5
Kiel 14 A6
Kiel Canal = Nord-
 Ostsee-Kanal 16 A4
Kielce 16 C10
Kielder Water 8 B5
Kieler Bucht 14 A6
Kiev = Kyyiv 18 D5
Kigali 28 E6
Kigoma-Ujiji 28 E5
Kikwit 28 E3
Kilbrannan Sd. 10 F3
Kilcoy 32 A5
Kildare 11 C5
Kildare □ 11 C5
Kilfinnane 11 D3
Kilimanjaro 28 E7
Kilkee 11 D2
Kilkeel 11 B6
Kilkenny 11 D4
Kilkenny □ 11 D4
Kilkieran B. 11 C2
Killala 11 B2
Killala B. 11 B2
Killaloe 11 D3
Killarney, Australia 32 A5
Killarney, Ireland 11 D2
Killary Harbour 11 C2
Killdeer 40 B3
Killeen 41 K6
Killiney 11 C5
Killin 10 E4
Killorglin 11 D2
Killybegs 11 B3
Kilmarnock 10 F4
Kilmore 32 C3
Kilmore Quay 11 D5
Kilrush 11 D2
Kilwinning 10 F4
Kim 41 G3
Kimba 32 B2
Kimball, Nebr.,
 U.S.A. 40 E3
Kimball, S. Dak.,
 U.S.A. 40 D5
Kimberley,
 S. Africa 29 K4
Kimberley,
 Australia 30 C4
Kimberly 38 E6
Kimmirut 37 C13
Kinabalu, Gunung 23 C3
Kinder Scout 8 D6
Kindersley 36 D9
Kindu 28 E5
King City 39 H3
King George I. 5 C18
King George Is. 37 D11
King I. 31 H15
King William I. 36 C10
Kingaroy 31 F9
Kingfisher 41 H6
Kingman, Ariz.,
 U.S.A. 39 J6
Kingman, Kans.,
 U.S.A. 41 G5
Kingoonya 32 B1
Kings → 39 H4
Kings Canyon △ 39 H4
Kings Lynn 9 E8
Kings Peak 38 F8
Kingsbridge 9 G4
Kingscote 32 C2
Kingscourt 11 C5
Kingsland 43 K5
Kingsport 43 G4
Kingston, Canada 37 E12
Kingston, Jamaica 44 a
Kingston, N.Z. 33 L2
Kingston, Pa.,
 U.S.A. 42 E8
Kingston South
 East 32 C2
Kingston upon Hull 8 D7
Kingston-upon-
 Thames □ 9 F7
Kingstown 45 E12
Kingstree 43 J6
Kingsville 41 M6
Kingussie 10 D4
Kinlochleven 10 E4
Kinna 7 F6
Kinross 10 E5
Kinsale 11 E3
Kinsale, Old Hd. of 11 E3
Kinshasa 28 E3
Kinston 43 H7
Kintore Ra. 30 E5
Kintyre 10 F3
Kintyre, Mull of 10 F3
Kinvarra 11 C3

Kiowa, Kans.,
 U.S.A. 41 G5
Kiowa, Okla.,
 U.S.A. 41 H7
Kippure 11 C5
Kirghizia =
 Kyrgyzstan ■ 18 E8
Kiribati ■ 33 K12
Kırıkkale 17 C4
Kirinyaga =
 Kenya, Mt. 28 E7
Kiritimati 35 G12
Kirkby 8 D5
Kirkby-in-Ashfield 8 D6
Kirkby Lonsdale 8 C5
Kirkby Stephen 8 C5
Kirkcaldy 10 E5
Kirkcudbright 10 G4
Kirkintilloch 10 F4
Kirkland Lake 37 E11
Kirksville 40 E8
Kirkūk 24 B3
Kirkwall 10 C6
Kirov 18 D5
Kirovohrad 17 A4
Kirriemuir 10 E5
Kirtland 39 H9
Kiruna 7 D8
Kiryū 22 E6
Kisangani 28 D5
Kisii 28 E6
Kislovodsk 17 B6
Kissimmee 43 L5
Kissimmee → 43 M5
Kisumu 28 E6
Kitakyūshū 22 G2
Kitami 22 B8
Kitchener 37 E11
Kithira = Kythira 15 F10
Kittakittaooloo, L. 32 A2
Kittanning 42 E6
Kittery 43 D10
Kitwe 29 G5
Kivu, L. 28 E5
Kizil Irmak → 17 B5
Kladno 16 C7
Klagenfurt 16 E7
Klaipėda 18 D3
Klamath → 38 F1
Klamath Falls 38 E3
Klamath Mts. 38 F2
Klang = Kelang 23 D2
Klarälven → 7 F6
Klerksdorp 29 K5
Klickitat 38 D3
Kluane L. 36 C6
Klyuchevskaya,
 Gora 19 D17
Knaresborough 8 C6
Knighton 9 E4
Knock 11 C3
Knocknealdown
 Mts. 11 D4
Knossós 15 G11
Knox 42 E2
Knoxville, Iowa,
 U.S.A. 40 E8
Knoxville, Tenn.,
 U.S.A. 43 H4
Kōbe 22 F4
København 7 F6
Koblenz 14 C3
Kocaeli 17 B3
Kōchi 22 G3
Kodiak 36 D4
Kodiak I. 36 D4
Kokkola 7 E8
Kokomo 42 E4
Kökshetaū 18 D7
Koksoak → 37 D13
Kokstad 29 L5
Kolar 25 D6
Kolhapur 25 D6
Kolkata 25 D7
Köln 14 C3
Kolomna 18 D4
Kolomyya 16 D12
Kolskiy Poluostrov 7 D11
Kolwezi 28 G5
Kolyma → 19 C16
Kolymskoye
 Nagorye 19 C16
Komandorskiye
 Ostrova 19 D17
Komatsu 22 E5
Kompong Cham 23 B2
Kompong
 Somoolets, 23 B2
Komsomolets,
 Ostrov 19 A10
Komsomolsk 19 D14
Konin 16 B9
Konya 17 C4
Koocanusa, L. 38 B6
Kootenay → 38 B5
Kootenay △ 36 D8
Kooskia 38 C6
Kopet Dagh 24 B4
Kopi 32 B2
Korçë 15 D9
Korea, North ■ 21 C7
Korea, South ■ 21 C7
Korea Bay 21 C7
Korea Strait 21 C7
Korinthiakos
 Kolpos 15 E10
Kōriyama 22 E7
Koro 33 D8
Koro Sea 33 D9
Körös → 16 E10
Korosten 17 C4
Kortrijk 14 C2
Koš Chagyl 18 E6
Kos 15 F12
Kosciusko 41 J10
Kosciuszko, Mt. 32 C4
Kosovo ■ 15 C9
Kôstî 27 F12
Kostroma 18 D5
Koszalin 16 A8
Kota 25 C6
Kota Bharu 23 C2
Kota Kinabalu 23 C3
Kotabumi 23 D2
Kotka 7 F9
Kotor 22 H2
Kotri 24 C5
Kotuy → 19 B11
Kotzebue 36 C3
Kouchibouguac △ 37 E13
Kowloon 21 a
Kozhikode =
 Calicut 25 D6
Kra, Isthmus of 23 B1
Kra, Ko Khot 23 B1
Kragujevac 15 B9
Krakatau = Rakata,
 Pulau 23 D2
Kraków 16 C9
Kramatorsk 17 A5
Krasnodar 18 E4
Krasnoyarsk 19 D10
Krasnyy Luch 17 A5
Kremenchuk 17 A4
Kristiansand 7 G5
Kristiansund 7 E5
Kríti 15 G11
Krivoy Rog =
 Kryvyy Rih 17 A4
Kronshtadt 7 F9
Kroonstad 29 K5
Kropotkin 18 E5
Krugersdorp 29 K5
Kruševac 15 C9
Krymskyy
 Pivostriv 17 A4
Kryvyy Rih 17 A4
Kuala Belait 23 C3
Kuala Lumpur 23 D2
Kuala Terengganu 23 C2
Kuantan 23 C2
Kuban → 18 E4
Kuching 23 C3
Kudat 23 C3

Kugluktuk 36 C8
Kuichong 21 F11
Kuiwin 32 C3
Kumagaya 22 E6
Kumai 23 D3
Kumamoto 22 G2
Kumanovo 15 C9
Kumara 33 K3
Kumarl 30 G3
Kumasi 26 G5
Kumbakonam 25 D6
Kumbarilla 32 A5
Kunlun Shan 20 C3
Kunming 20 D5
Kuopio 7 E9
Kupang 23 E4
Kuqa 20 B3
Kür → 24 B3
Kura = Kür → 24 B3
Kure 22 F3
Kuril Is. =
 Kurilskiye
 Ostrova 19 E15
Kuril-Kamchatka
 Trench 34 C7
Kurilskiye Ostrova 19 E15
Kurnool 25 D6
Kurow 33 L3
Kurri Kurri 32 B5
Kursk 18 D4
Kuruktag 20 B3
Kuruman 29 K4
Kurume 22 G2
Kushiro 22 B9
Kuskokwim B. 36 C3
Kütahya 17 C4
Kutaisi 18 E5
Kutch, Gulf of =
 Kachchh, Gulf of 25 C5
Kuujjuaq 37 D13
Kuujjuarapik 37 D12
Kuwait = Al
 Kuwayt 24 C3
Kuwait ■ 24 C3
Kwajalein 34 G8
Kwakoegron 46 B4
KwaMashu 29 K6
Kwando → 28 H4
Kwangju 21 C7
Kwango → 28 E3
Kwinana 30 G2
Kwun Tong 21 a
Kyabram 32 C4
Kyancutta 32 B2
Kyaukse 20 D4
Kyle of Lochalsh 10 D3
Kyneton 32 C3
Kyoga, L. 28 D6
Kyōto 22 F4
Kyrgyzstan ■ 18 E8
Kythira 15 F10
Kyūshū 22 G2
Kyushu-Palau
 Ridge 34 F5
Kyyiv 18 D5
Kyzyl Kum 24 A5

L

La Barge 38 E8
La Belle 43 M5
La Ceiba 44 D7
La Coruña =
 A Coruña 13 A1
La Crescent 40 D9
La Crosse, Kans.,
 U.S.A. 40 F5
La Crosse, Wis.,
 U.S.A. 40 D9
La Désirade 45 D12
La Fayette 43 H3
La Follette 43 G3
La Grande 38 D4
La Grande → 37 D12
La Grange, Ga.,
 U.S.A. 43 J3
La Grange, Ky.,
 U.S.A. 42 F3
La Grange, Tex.,
 U.S.A. 41 L6
La Habana 45 C8
La Junta 41 F3
La Loche 36 D9
La Mancha 13 C4
La Mesa 39 K5
La Moure 40 B5
La Paz, Bolivia 46 G5
La Paz, Mexico 44 C2
La Perouse Str. 22 B8
La Plata 47 D5
La Porte 42 E2
La Push 38 C1
La Rioja 47 B3
La Roche-sur-Yon 12 C3
La Rochelle 12 C3
La Romana 45 D11
La Ronge 36 D9
La Salle 40 E10
La Spézia 12 D8
La Trinité 44 b
La Tuque 42 A9
La Vega 45 D10
Labasa 33 C8
Labé 26 F3
Labelle 45 j
Labrador City 37 D13
Labrador Sea 37 D14
Labyrinth, L. 32 B2
Lac La Biche 36 D8
Lacanau △ 40 B6
Lacepede B. 32 C2
Lachine 42 D9
Lachlan → 32 B3
Lackagh Hills 11 B3
Lacombe 36 D8
Laconia 43 D10
Ladakh Ra. 25 B6
Ladoga, L. =
 Ladozhskoye
 Ozero 7 E10
Ladysmith,
 S. Africa 29 K5
Ladysmith,
 U.S.A. 40 C9
Lae 30 B8
Lafayette, Ind.,
 U.S.A. 42 E4
Lafayette, La.,
 U.S.A. 41 K9
LaFayette, Tenn.,
 U.S.A. 43 G3
Lagan → 11 B6
Lagos, Nigeria 26 G6
Lagos, Portugal 13 D1
Laguna 48 B7
Lagunas 46 E3
Lahad Datu 23 C3
Lahat 23 D2
Lahn → 14 C3
Lahore 25 D6
Lahti 7 E9
Lairg 10 C4
Lajes 47 B5
Lake Andes 40 D5
Lake Arthur 41 K8
Lake Bindegolly △ 32 A3
Lake Cargelligo 32 B4
Lake Charles 41 K8
Lake City, Colo.,
 U.S.A. 39 G10
Lake City, Mich.,
 U.S.A. 42 C3
Lake City, Minn.,
 U.S.A. 40 C8
Lake City, S.C.,
 U.S.A. 43 J6
Lake District △ 8 C4
Lake Havasu City 39 J6
Lake Jackson 41 L7
Lake Mead △ 39 H6
Lake Meredith △ 41 H4
Lake Providence 41 J9
Lake Torrens 32 B2

Lake Village 41 J9
Lake Wales 43 M5
Lake Worth 43 M5
Lakeba 33 D9
Lakeland 43 M5
Lakeport 38 G2
Lakes Entrance 32 C4
Lakeside, Colo.,
 U.S.A. 40 F2
Lakeside, Ariz.,
 U.S.A. 39 J9
Lakeview 38 E3
Lakeville 40 C8
Lakewood, Colo.,
 U.S.A. 40 F2
Lakewood, Ohio,
 U.S.A. 42 E5
Lakshadweep Is. 25 E6
Lamar, Colo.,
 U.S.A. 41 G7
Lamar, Mo., U.S.A. 41 G7
Lambay I. 11 C5
Lame Deer 38 D10
Lamesa 41 J4
Lamington △ 32 A5
Lammermuir Hills 10 F6
Lamon B. 23 B4
Lampang 23 B1
Lampasas 41 K5
Lampeter 9 E3
Lamy 39 J11
Lanark 10 F5
Lancang Jiang → 20 D5
Lancashire □ 8 D5
Lancaster, U.K. 8 C5
Lancaster, Calif.,
 U.S.A. 39 J4
Lancaster, Ky.,
 U.S.A. 42 G3
Lancaster, N.H.,
 U.S.A. 42 C10
Lancaster, Ohio,
 U.S.A. 42 F4
Lancaster, Pa.,
 U.S.A. 42 E7
Lancaster, S.C.,
 U.S.A. 43 H5
Lancaster, Wis.,
 U.S.A. 40 D9
Lancaster Sd. 37 B11
Land Between the
 Lakes △ 43 G1
Lander 38 E9
Landes 12 D3
Land's End 9 G2
Lanett 43 J3
Langdon 40 A5
Langholm 10 F5
Langres 12 C6
Langres, Plateau
 de 12 C6
Langsa 23 C1
Langtry 41 L4
Languedoc 12 E5
Langwang 21 F9
Lannion 12 B2
Lansdowne 32 B5
L'Anse 42 B1
Lansing 42 D3
Lantau I. 21 G10
Lanzhou 20 C5
Lao Bao 23 B3
Laoag 23 B4
Laois □ 11 D4
Laon 12 B5
Laona 42 C1
Laos ■ 23 B2
Lapeer 42 D4
LaPorte 42 E2
Lapland =
 Lappland 7 B8
Lappland 7 B8
Laptev Sea 19 B13
Laramie 38 F11
Laramie Mts. 40 E2
Laredo 41 M5
Largo 43 M4
Largs 10 F4
Larimore 40 B6
Larino 13 E10
Larkana 24 C5
Larne 11 B6
Larned 40 F5
Larrimah 30 C5
Larvik 7 G6
Las Animas 41 G7
Las Anod 24 F4
Las Cruces 39 K10
Las Palmas 26 C1
Las Piedras 47 C5
Las Tunas 45 C9
Las Vegas,
 N. Mex., U.S.A. 39 J11
Las Vegas, Nev.,
 U.S.A. 39 H6
Lassen Pk. 38 F3
Lassen Volcanic △ 38 F3
Lata 31 D16
Latina 13 D5
Latium = Lazio □ 14 C5
Latrobe 32 D4
Latur 25 D6
Latvia ■ 7 F8
Lauchhammer 14 C7
Launceston,
 Australia 32 D4
Launceston, U.K. 9 G3
Laune → 11 D2
Laurel, Miss.,
 U.S.A. 41 K10
Laurel, Mont.,
 U.S.A. 38 D9
Laurencekirk 10 E6
Laurens 43 H4
Laurinburg 43 H6
Laurium 42 B1
Laut, Pulau 23 D3
Laut Kecil,
 Kepulauan 23 D3
Laval 12 B3
Lavagh More 11 B3
Laverton 30 F3
Lawas 23 C3
Lawng Pit 20 D4
Lawrence, N.Z. 33 L2
Lawrence, Ind.,
 U.S.A. 42 F2
Lawrence, Kans.,
 U.S.A. 40 F7
Lawrence, Mass.,
 U.S.A. 43 D10
Lawrenceburg,
 Ind., U.S.A. 42 F3
Lawrenceburg,
 Tenn., U.S.A. 43 H2
Lawrenceville 43 J4
Lawton 41 H5
Laxford, L. 10 C3
Laylá 24 C4
Laylan 24 B3
Layton 38 F7
Laytonville 38 G2
Lazio □ 14 C5
Le Creusot 12 C6
Le François 44 b
Le Havre 12 B4
Le Mans 12 C4
Le Marin 44 b
Le Moule 45 C12
Le Moyne, L. 37 D13
Le Prêcheur 44 b
Le Puy-en-Velay 12 D5
Le St-Esprit 44 b
Leadhills 10 F5
Leadville 39 G10
Leaf → 41 K10
Leamington 42 D4
Leane, L. 11 D2
Learmonth 30 D1
Leavenworth,
 Kans., U.S.A. 40 F7

Leavenworth,
 Wash., U.S.A. 38 C3
Leawood 40 F7
Lebanon, Ind.,
 U.S.A. 42 E2
Lebanon, Kans.,
 U.S.A. 40 F5
Lebanon, Ky.,
 U.S.A. 42 G3
Lebanon, Mo.,
 U.S.A. 41 G8
Lebanon, N.H.,
 U.S.A. 43 D9
Lebanon, Oreg.,
 U.S.A. 38 D2
Lebanon, Pa.,
 U.S.A. 42 E7
Lebanon, Tenn.,
 U.S.A. 43 G3
Lebanon ■ 17 D5
Lecce 15 D8
Lecco 12 D8
Lee → 11 E3
Lee Vining 38 H7
Leech L. 40 B7
Leeds, U.K. 8 D6
Leeds, U.S.A. 43 J2
Leek 8 D5
Leesburg 43 L5
Leesville 41 K8
Leeton 32 B4
Leeuwarden 14 B3
Leeuwin, C. 30 G2
Leeward Is. 45 D12
Lefkada 15 E9
Leganés 13 B4
Legazpi 23 B4
Legnica 16 C8
Lehigh Acres 43 M5
Leicester 9 E6
Leicestershire □ 9 E6
Leiden 14 B3
Leine → 14 B5
Leinster 30 E3
Leinster □ 11 C4
Leinster, Mt. 11 D5
Leipzig 16 C6
Leith 10 F5
Leith Hill 9 F7
Leitrim 11 B3
Leitrim □ 11 B4
Leizhou Bandao 21 D6
Léman, L. 12 C7
Lena → 19 B13
Lenadoon Pt. 11 B2
Leninogorsk 18 D9
Leninsk-
 Kuznetskiy 18 D9
Lennox 40 D6
Lenoir 43 H5
Lenoir City 43 H3
Lenora 12 a
Leola 40 C5
Leominster, U.K. 9 E5
Leominster, U.S.A. 42 D10
León, Mexico 44 C4
León, Nic. 44 E7
León, Spain 13 A3
Leon, U.S.A. 40 E8
Leon → 41 K6
Leonardtown 42 F7
Leongatha 32 C4
Leoti 40 F4
Lerwick 10 A7
Les Cayes 45 D10
Les Sables-
 d'Olonne 12 C3
Lesbos = Lesvos 15 E12
Leskovac 15 C9
Lesotho ■ 29 K5
Lesser Antilles 45 D12
Lesser Slave L. 36 D8
Lesser Sunda Is. 23 D3
Leszno 16 C8
Letchworth 9 F7
Lethbridge 36 D8
Leti, Kepulauan 23 D4
Letterkenny 11 B4
Leuven 14 C3
Levelland 41 J3
Leven 10 E6
Leven, L. 10 E5
Levin 33 J5
Lévis 37 E12
Levittown 42 E8
Lewes, U.K. 9 G8
Lewes, U.S.A. 42 F8
Lewis 10 C2
Lewis, Butt of 10 C2
Lewis Range 38 B7
Lewisburg, Pa.,
 U.S.A. 42 E7
Lewisburg, Tenn.,
 U.S.A. 43 H2
Lewisburg, W. Va.,
 U.S.A. 42 G5
Lewisporte 37 E14
Lewiston, Idaho,
 U.S.A. 38 C5
Lewiston, Maine,
 U.S.A. 43 C11
Lewistown, Mont.,
 U.S.A. 38 C9
Lewistown, Pa.,
 U.S.A. 42 E7
Lexington, Ill.,
 U.S.A. 40 E10
Lexington, Ky.,
 U.S.A. 42 F3
Lexington, Mo.,
 U.S.A. 40 F8
Lexington, N.C.,
 U.S.A. 43 H5
Lexington, Nebr.,
 U.S.A. 40 E5
Lexington, Tenn.,
 U.S.A. 43 H1
Lexington Park 42 F7
Leyburn 8 C6
Leyland 8 D5
Leyte 23 B4
Lezhë 15 C8
Lhasa 20 D4
Lhazê 20 D3
L'Hospitalet de
 Llobregat 13 B7
Lianyungang 21 C6
Liaoning □ 21 B7
Liaoyang 21 B7
Liaoyuan 21 B7
Liard → 36 C7
Liberal 41 G4
Liberec 16 C7
Liberia ■ 26 G4
Liberty, Mo.,
 U.S.A. 40 F7
Liberty, N.Y.,
 U.S.A. 42 E8
Liberty, Tex.,
 U.S.A. 41 K7
Lîbîya, Sahrâ' 27 C10
Libourne 12 D3
Libreville 28 D1
Libya ■ 27 C9
Libyan Desert =
 Lîbîya, Sahrâ' 27 C10
Licata 14 F5
Lichinga 27 G7
Lichtenburg 29 K5
Licking → 42 F3
Lida 7 H8
Liechtenstein ■ 14 E5
Liège 14 C3
Lienz 14 E7
Liepāja 7 F8
Liffey → 11 C5
Lifford 11 B4
Lightning Ridge 32 A4
Liguria □ 12 D8
Ligurian Sea 12 E8
Likasi 28 G5
Lille 12 A5

Lillehammer 7 E6
Lilongwe 29 G6
Lima, Peru 46 F3
Lima, Mont.,
 U.S.A. 38 D7
Lima, Ohio, U.S.A. 42 E3
Limassol 17 E5
Limavady 11 A5
Limburg □ 14 C3
Limeira 48 A7
Limerick 11 D3
Limerick □ 11 D3
Limfjorden 7 F5
Límnos 15 E11
Limoges 12 D4
Limón, Costa Rica 45 F8
Limon, U.S.A. 40 F3
Limousin 12 D4
Limoux 12 E5
Limpopo → 29 K6
Linares, Chile 47 F2
Linares, Mexico 44 C5
Linares, Spain 13 C4
Lincoln, N.Z. 33 K4
Lincoln, U.K. 8 D7
Lincoln, Ill., U.S.A. 40 E10
Lincoln, Maine,
 U.S.A. 43 C11
Lincoln, N. Mex.,
 U.S.A. 39 K11
Lincoln, Nebr.,
 U.S.A. 40 E6
Lincoln City 38 D1
Lincoln Sea 6 A4
Lincolnshire □ 8 D7
Lincolnshire Wolds 8 D7
Lincolnton 43 H5
Linden, Ala.,
 U.S.A. 43 J2
Linden, Tex.,
 U.S.A. 41 J7
Lindesnes 7 F5
Lindi 28 F7
Lindsay, Calif.,
 U.S.A. 39 H4
Lindsay, Okla.,
 U.S.A. 41 H6
Line Islands 35 H12
Linfen 21 C6
Lingayen 23 B4
Lingga, Kepulauan 23 D2
Linhares 47 G10
Linköping 7 F7
Linnhe, L. 10 E3
Linosa 14 G5
Linton, Ind.,
 U.S.A. 42 F2
Linton, N. Dak.,
 U.S.A. 40 B4
Linxia 20 C5
Linz 16 D7
Lipa 23 B4
Lipetsk 18 D4
Lippe → 14 C4
Lipscomb 41 G4
Liptrap, C. 32 C4
Liquillo, Sierra de 45 d
Lircay 46 F4
Lisboa 13 C1
Lisbon = Lisboa 13 C1
Lisbon Falls 43 D11
Lisburn 11 B5
Liscannor B. 11 D2
Lisdoonvarna 11 C2
Lisianski I. 34 E10
Lisieux 12 B4
Liski 18 D4
Lismore, Australia 31 F9
Lismore, Ireland 11 D4
Liston 32 A5
Listowel 11 D2
Litchfield, Ill.,
 U.S.A. 40 F10
Litchfield, Minn.,
 U.S.A. 40 C7
Lithgow 32 B5
Lithinon, Akra 15 G11
Lithuania ■ 7 F8
Little Abaco I. 45 B9
Little Andaman I. 25 D8
Little Barrier I. 33 H6
Little Belt Mts. 38 C8
Little Bighorn
 Battlefield △ 38 D10
Little Blue → 40 E6
Little Colorado → 39 H8
Little Current 42 B5
Little Falls, Minn.,
 U.S.A. 40 C7
Little Falls, N.Y.,
 U.S.A. 42 D8
Little Humboldt → 38 F5
Little Karoo 29 L4
Little Lake 39 J5
Little Minch 10 D2
Little Missouri → 40 B3
Little Ouse → 9 E9
Little Red → 41 H9
Little River 33 K4
Little Rock 41 H8
Little Sioux → 40 D6
Little Snake → 38 F9
Little Wabash → 42 G1
Little White → 40 D4
Littlefield 41 J3
Littlehampton 9 G7
Littleton 42 C10
Liupanshui 20 D5
Liuzhou 20 D5
Live Oak 43 K4
Liverpool, Canada 37 E13
Liverpool, U.K. 8 D5
Liverpool Ra. 32 B5
Livingston, U.K. 10 F5
Livingston, Calif.,
 U.S.A. 38 H3
Livingston, Mont.,
 U.S.A. 38 D8
Livingston, Tenn.,
 U.S.A. 43 G3
Livingstone 29 G5
Livonia 42 D4
Livorno 12 E8
Liwale 28 F7
Lizard Pt. 9 H2
Ljubljana 14 E8
Ljungan → 7 E7
Ljusnan → 7 E7
Llandeilo 9 F4
Llandovery 9 F4
Llandrindod Wells 9 E4
Llandudno 8 D4
Llanelli 9 F3
Llangollen 8 E4
Llanidloes 9 E4
Llano 41 K5
Llano → 41 K5
Llano Estacado 41 J3
Llanos 46 C4
Lleida 13 B6
Llevn Peninsula 8 E3
Lloret de Mar 13 B7
Lloydminster 36 D9
Lobatse 29 K5
Lobería 47 D5
Lobito 29 G2
Loc Ninh 23 B2
Loch Garman =
 Wexford 11 D5
Lochaber 10 E4
Lochboisdale 10 D1
Loches 12 C4
Lochgilphead 10 E3
Lochinver 10 C3
Lochnagar 10 E5
Lochy, L. 10 E4
Lock 32 B2
Lock Haven 42 E7
Lockhart 41 L6
Lockney 41 H4
Lockport 42 D6
Lodge Grass 38 D10

Lodgepole Cr. → 40 E2
Lodi 38 G3
Łódź 16 C9
Lofoten 7 D6
Logan, Iowa,
 U.S.A. 40 E7
Logan, Ohio,
 U.S.A. 42 F4
Logan, Utah,
 U.S.A. 38 F8
Logan, W. Va.,
 U.S.A. 42 G5
Logansport, Ind.,
 U.S.A. 42 E2
Logansport, La.,
 U.S.A. 41 K8
Logroño 13 A4
Loir → 12 C3
Loire → 12 C2
Loja 46 D3
Loma 38 C8
Lomas de Zamora 47 C5
Lombardía □ 12 D8
Lomblen 23 D4
Lombok 23 D3
Lomé 26 G6
Lomela → 28 E4
Lomond, L. 10 E4
Łomża 16 B11
London, Canada 37 E11
London, U.S.A. 42 G3
London, Greater □ 9 F7
London, Ky.,
 U.S.A. 42 G3
London, Ohio,
 U.S.A. 42 F4
London Gatwick
 (LGW) 9 F7
London Heathrow
 (LHR) 9 F7
London Stansted
 (STN) 9 F8
Londonderry 11 B4
Londonderry □ 11 B4
Londonderry, C. 30 B4
Londrina 47 A6
Lone Pine 39 H4
Long Beach, Calif.,
 U.S.A. 39 K4
Long Beach,
 Wash., U.S.A. 38 C1
Long Branch 42 E9
Long Creek 38 D4
Long Eaton 8 E6
Long I., Bahamas 45 C9
Long I., Ireland 11 E2
Long I., U.S.A. 42 E9
Long Island Sd. 42 E9
Long Lake 42 D8
Long Prairie 40 C7
Long Prairie → 40 C7
Long Xuyen 23 B2
Longbenton 8 B6
Longboat Key 43 M4
Longford, Australia 32 D4
Longford, Ireland 11 C4
Longford □ 11 C4
Longhua 21 F11
Longlac 37 E11
Longmeadow 42 D9
Longmont 40 E2
Longnawan 23 C3
Longreach 31 E3
Longton 8 D5
Longview, Tex.,
 U.S.A. 41 J7
Longview, Wash.,
 U.S.A. 38 C2
Lons-le-Saunier 12 C6
Looc 23 B4
Lookout, C. 43 H6
Loop Hd. 11 D2
Lop Nur 20 B4
Lopez, C. 28 E1
Lora Cr. → 32 A2
Lorain 42 E5
Lorca 13 D5
Lord Howe I. 34 K8
Lord Howe Rise 34 L8
Lordsburg 39 K9
Lorestan □ 24 B3
Lorient 12 C2
Lorne 32 C3
Lorraine 12 B7
Los Alamos 39 J10
Los Ángeles, Chile 47 F2
Los Angeles,
 U.S.A. 39 J5
Los Lunas 39 J10
Los Mochis 44 B3
Lossiemouth 10 D5
Lostwithiel 9 G3
Loughborough 8 E6
Loughrea 11 C3
Loughros More B. 11 B3
Louis Trichardt 29 J5
Louisa 42 F4
Louisburgh 11 C2
Louisiade Arch. 30 C9
Louisiana □ 41 K9
Louisville, Ky.,
 U.S.A. 42 F3
Louisville, Miss.,
 U.S.A. 41 J10
Loup → 40 E5
Lourdes 12 E3
Louth, Australia 32 B4
Louth, Ireland 11 C5
Louth, U.K. 8 D7
Louth □ 11 C5
Loveland 40 E2
Lovell 38 D9
Lovelock 38 F5
Loving 41 J2
Lovington 41 J3
Lowell 43 D10
Lower California =
 Baja California 44 A1
Lower Hutt 33 J5
Lower Saxony =
 Niedersachsen □ 14 B5
Lowestoft 9 E9
Łowicz 16 B9
Lowville 42 D8
Loxton 32 B3
Loyalty Is. =
 Loyauté, Îs. 31 E12
Luala → 28 F6
Luan Xian 21 C6
Luanda 28 F2
Luang Prabang 23 B2
Luangwa → 29 G6
Luanshya 29 G5
Luapula → 28 G5
Lubalo 28 G5
Lubango 29 G2
Lubbock 41 J4
Lübeck 14 B6
Lublin 16 C11
Lubumbashi 29 G5
Lucca 12 E8
Luce Bay 10 G4
Lucea 44 a
Lucena 23 B4
Lucerne = Luzern 14 E5
Lucknow 25 C7
Lüderitz 29 K3
Ludhiana 25 D6
Ludington 42 D2
Ludlow 9 E5
Ludwigshafen 14 D5

Luleå 7 D8
Luleälven → 7 D8
Lüleburgaz 17 B2
Lumberton 43 H6
Lumsden 33 L2
Lundy 9 F3
Lüneburger Heide 16 B5
Lunéville 12 B7
Luni → 25 C6
Luning 38 G5
Luoyang 21 C6
Luray 42 F6
Lurgan 11 B5
Lusaka 29 G5
Lusk 38 E11
Lüt, Dasht-e 24 B4
Luton 9 F7
Łutselk'e 36 C8
Luverne, Ala.,
 U.S.A. 43 K2
Luverne, Minn.,
 U.S.A. 40 D6
Luvua → 28 F5
Luxembourg 12 B7
Luxembourg ■ 14 D4
Luxi 20 D4
Luzhou 20 D5
Luziânia 47 G9
Luzon 23 B4
Lviv 17 D2
Lyakhovskiye,
 Ostrova 19 B15
Lybster 10 C5
Lydenburg 29 K6
Lyell 33 J4
Lyme B. 9 G5
Lyme Regis 9 G5
Lymington 9 G6
Lynchburg 42 G6
Lynd Ra. 32 A4
Lynden 38 B2
Lyndhurst 32 B2
Lyndonville 42 C9
Lynn 43 D10
Lynn Haven 43 K3
Lynn Lake 36 D9
Lynton 9 F4
Lyon 12 D6
Lyonnais 12 D6
Lyons, Ga., U.S.A. 43 J4
Lyons, Kans., U.S.A. 40 F5
Lysychansk 17 A5
Lytham St. Anne's 8 D4
Lyttelton 33 K4

M

Ma'ān 24 B2
Ma'anshan 21 C6
Maas → 14 C3
Maastricht 14 C3
Mablethorpe 8 D8
McAlester 41 H7
McAllen 41 M5
MacAlpine L. 36 C9
Macapá 47 C8
Macau 47 E11
Macau □ 21 G10
Macauley I. 31 G15
McCall 38 D5
McCamey 41 K3
McCammon 38 E7
McCarthy 36 C5
M'Clintock Chan. 36 B9
McCloud 38 F2
McClure Str. 37 B1
McComb 41 K9
McCook 40 E4
McDermitt 38 F5
McDonald Is. 5 G14
McDonnell
 Ranges 30 E5
Macduff 10 D6
Macedonia ■ 15 D9
Macedonia □ 15 D10
Maceió 47 E11
McGehee 41 J9
McGill 38 G6
McGillycuddy's
 Reeks 11 E2
MacGregor 40 A5
MacGregor Ra. 32 A3
Machakos 28 E7
Machala 46 D3
Machias 43 C12
Machilipatnam 25 D7
Machupicchu 46 F4
Macintyre → 32 A5
Mackay, Australia 31 E8
Mackay, U.S.A. 38 E7
Mackay, L. 30 E4
McKeesport 42 E6
McKenzie 43 G1
Mackenzie → 36 B6
Mackenzie City =
 Linden 46 B7
Mackenzie King I. 37 B8
Mackenzie Mts. 36 C6
Mackinaw City 42 C3
McKinley, Mt. 36 C4
McKinley Sea 6 A6
McKinney 41 J6
McLaughlin 40 C4
Maclean 32 A5
McLean 41 H4
McLeansboro 40 G10
Macleay → 32 B5
McLennan 36 D8
McLeod, L. 30 E1
Macmillan → 36 C6
McMinnville,
 Oreg., U.S.A. 38 D2
McMinnville,
 Tenn., U.S.A. 43 H3
McMurdo Sd. 5 D11
Macomb 40 E9
Macon, France 12 C6
Macon, Ga., U.S.A. 43 J4
Macon, Miss.,
 U.S.A. 43 J1
Macon, Mo., U.S.A. 40 F8
Macquarie → 32 B4
Macquarie
 Harbour 32 D3
Macquarie Is. 34 N7
Macroom 11 E3
Madawaska → 42 A7
Madeira 26 B2
Madeira → 46 D7
Madeleine, Î. de la 37 E13
Madera 39 H3
Madha 25 D6
Madhya
 Pradesh □ 25 C6
Madison, Fla.,
 U.S.A. 43 K4
Madison, Ind.,
 U.S.A. 42 F3
Madison, Nebr.,
 U.S.A. 40 E6
Madison, S. Dak.,
 U.S.A. 40 C6
Madison, Wis.,
 U.S.A. 40 D10
Madison → 38 D8
Madison Heights 42 G6
Madisonville, Ky.,
 U.S.A. 42 G2

Madisonville, Tex.,
 U.S.A. 41 K7
Madiun 23 D3
Madrakah, Ra's al 24 D4
Madras = Chennai 25 D7
Madras 38 D3
Madre, L. 41 M6
Madre de Dios → 46 F5
Madre de Dios, I. 48 G1
Madre Occidental,
 Sierra 44 B3
Madre Oriental,
 Sierra 44 C5
Madrid 13 B4
Madura 23 D3
Madurai 25 E6
Maebashi 22 E6
Mafeking = Mafikeng 29 K5
Mafeteng 29 K5
Maffra 32 C4
Mafikeng 29 K5
Magadan 19 D16
Magadi 28 E7
Magallanes,
 Estrecho de 48 G2
Magdalena 39 J10
Magdalena → 46 A4
Magdeburg 16 B6
Magee 41 K10
Magelang 23 D3
Magellan's Str. =
 Magallanes,
 Estrecho de 48 G2
Maggiore, Lago 12 D8
Magherafelt 11 B5
Magnetic Pole
 (North) 37 B9
Magnetic Pole
 (South) 5 D13
Magnitogorsk 18 D6
Magnolia, Ark.,
 U.S.A. 41 K9
Magnolia, Miss.,
 U.S.A. 41 K9
Mahabharat Lekh 25 C7
Mahakam → 23 D3
Mahalapye 29 J5
Mahanadi → 25 C7
Maharashtra □ 25 D6
Maheno 33 L3
Mahia Pen. 33 H6
Mahilyow 17 B6
Mahinerangi, L. 33 L3
Mahnomen 40 B7
Maidenhead 9 F7
Maidstone 9 F8
Maiduguri 27 F8
Main → 14 D5
Main →, U.K. 11 B5
Main Range △ 32 A5
Maine 12 C3
Maine □ 43 C11
Maine → 11 D2
Mainland, Orkney,
 U.K. 10 C5
Mainland, Shet.,
 U.K. 10 A7
Mainz 16 C4
Maitland, N.S.W.,
 Australia 32 B5
Maitland,
 S. Austral.,
 Australia 32 B2
Majorca =
 Mallorca 13 C7
Majuro 34 G9
Makale 23 D4
Makasar = Ujung
 Pandang 23 D3
Makasar, Selat 23 D3
Makgadikgadi Salt
 Pans 29 J5
Makhachkala 18 F6
Makhado 29 J5
Makkah 24 C2
Mai B. 11 C2
Makó 16 E10
Makurdi 26 G7
Malabar Coast 25 D6
Malacca, Straits of 23 C1
Malad City 38 E7
Málaga 13 D3
Malahide 11 C5
Malakal 27 G12
Malang 23 D3
Malanje 28 F3
Mälaren 7 F7
Malatya 17 C6
Malawi ■ 29 G6
Malawi, L. 28 G6
Malay Pen. 23 C2
Malaysia ■ 23 C3
Malbork 16 A9
Malden 40 G10
Maldives ■ 25 F8
Maldon 9 F8
Maldonado 47 C5
Malé 25 F8
Malegaon 25 C6
Malheur → 38 D5
Mali ■ 26 E5
Malin Hd. 11 A4
Malin Pen. 11 A4
Mallacoota Inlet 32 C4
Mallaig 10 D3
Mallorca 13 C7
Mallow 11 D3
Malmö 7 F6
Malone 42 C8
Malpelo, I. de 35 D7
Malta, Mont.,
 U.S.A. 38 B10
Malta, Idaho,
 U.S.A. 38 E7
Malta ■ 14 G6
Maltahöhe 29 J3
Malton 8 C7
Maluku 23 D4
Malvern, U.K. 9 E5
Malvern, U.S.A. 41 H8
Malvern Hills 9 E5
Malvinas, Is. =
 Falkland Is. ☑ 48 G5
Mammoth 39 K8
Mammoth Cave △ 42 G3
Man 26 G4
Man, I. of 8 C3
Manado 23 C4
Managua 44 E7
Manahawkin 42 F8
Manakara 33 J9
Manama = Al
 Manāmah 24 C4
Mananjary 33 J9
Manaus 46 D7
Manchester, U.K. 8 D5
Manchester, Ga.,
 U.S.A. 43 J3
Manchester, Iowa,
 U.S.A. 40 D9
Manchester, Ky.,
 U.S.A. 42 G4
Manchester, N.H.,
 U.S.A. 43 D10
Manchester, Tenn.,
 U.S.A. 43 H2
Manchuria =
 Dongbei 21 B7
Mandal 7 F5
Mandalay 20 D4
Mandan 40 B4
Mandeville 44 a
Mandvi 25 C5
Manfredónia 14 D6
Mangalore 25 D6
Mangaweka 33 H6
Mangla Dam 25 B6
Mangnai 20 C4
Mangole 23 D4
Manhattan 40 F6
Manhiça 29 K6
Manica 29 H6
Manicoré 46 E7
Manicouagan → 37 E13
Manila 23 B4
Manipur □ 25 C8
Manisa 17 C2
Manistee 42 C2
Manistee → 42 C2
Manistique 42 C2
Manizales 46 B3
Mankato, Kans.,
 U.S.A. 40 F5
Mankato, Minn.,
 U.S.A. 40 C7
Manmad 25 C6
Mannar 25 E6
Mannheim 14 D5
Manning 43 J5
Mannum 32 B2
Manokwari 23 D5
Manono 28 F5
Manresa 13 B6
Mansel I. 37 C11
Mansfield, Australia 32 C4
Mansfield, U.K. 8 D6
Mansfield, La.,
 U.S.A. 41 J8
Mansfield, Ohio,
 U.S.A. 42 E4
Mansfield, Pa.,
 U.S.A. 42 E7
Mansfield, Mt. 42 C9
Manta 46 D2
Mantua = Mántova 12 D9
Manui 23 D4
Manukau 33 H5
Manus I. 30 A9
Manych → 18 E5
Manzanares 13 C4
Manzanillo, Cuba 45 C9
Manzanillo, Mexico 44 D4
Manzhouli 21 B6
Maó 13 C8
Maoke, Pegunungan 23 D5
Maoming 21 D6
Mapam Yumco 25 C7
Maputo 29 K6

Manila, *Phil.*, 23 B4
Manila, *U.S.A.*, 38 F9
Manila B., 23 B4
Manila □, 23 B4
Manipur □, 25 C8
Manistee, 42 C2
Manistee →, 42 C2
Manistique, 42 C2
Manitoba □, 36 D10
Manitoba, L., 36 D10
Manitou Is., 42 C2
Manitou Springs, 40 F2
Manitoulin I., 37 E11
Manizales, 46 B3
Mankato, *Kans., U.S.A.*, 40 F5
Mankato, *Minn., U.S.A.*, 40 C8
Mannahill, 32 B2
Mannar, 25 E6
Mannar, G. of, 25 E6
Mannheim, 16 D5
Manning, *Canada*, 36 D8
Manning, *U.S.A.*, 43 J5
Manokwari, 23 D5
Manorhamilton, 11 B3
Manosque, 12 E6
Manra, 31 A16
Mansel I., 37 C12
Mansfield, *Australia*, 32 C4
Mansfield, *U.K.*, 8 D6
Mansfield, *La., U.S.A.*, 41 J8
Mansfield, *Ohio, U.S.A.*, 42 E4
Mansfield, *Tex., U.S.A.*, 41 J6
Mantalingajan, Mt., 23 C3
Mantes-la-Jolie, 12 B4
Manti, 38 G8
Manton, 42 C3
Mantova, 14 B4
Manu'a Is., 33 B14
Manukau, 33 G5
Many, 41 K8
Manzanillo, *Cuba*, 45 C9
Manzanillo, *Mexico*, 44 D4
Manzano Mts., 41 J10
Manzhouli, 21 B6
Maoming, 21 D6
Mapam Yumco, 20 C3
Mapia, Kepulauan, 23 C5
Mapleton, 38 D2
Maputo, 29 K6
Maquoketa, 40 D9
Mar Chiquita, L., 48 C4
Mar del Plata, 48 D5
Marabá, 46 A4
Maracaibo, 46 A4
Maracaibo, L. de, 46 B4
Maracay, 46 A5
Marajó, I. de, 47 D9
Marana, 39 K8
Maranoa →, 32 D4
Marañón →, 46 D4
Marathon, 41 K3
Marbella, 13 D3
Marble Falls, 41 K5
Marche, 9 E8
Marco Island, 43 N5
Mardan, 25 B6
Maré, Î., 31 E12
Maree, L., 10 D3
Marengo, 40 E8
Marfa, 41 K2
Margarita, I. de, 46 A6
Margate, 9 F9
Mårgow, Dasht-e, 24 D2
Mari □, 18 D9
Maria I., 32 D4
Maria Island △, 32 D4
Maria van Diemen, C., 33 F4
Mariala △, 32 D4
Mariana Trench, 34 F6
Marianna, *Ark., U.S.A.*, 41 H9
Marianna, *Fla., U.S.A.*, 43 K3
Marías →, 38 C8
Maribor, 16 E8
Maricopa, *Ariz., U.S.A.*, 39 K7
Maricopa, *Calif., U.S.A.*, 39 J4
Marie Byrd Land, 5 E18
Marie-Galante, 44 b
Mariental, 29 J3
Marietta, *Ga., U.S.A.*, 43 J3
Marietta, *Ohio, U.S.A.*, 42 F5
Marília, 47 H9
Marinette, 42 C2
Maringá, 48 A6
Marion, *Ill., U.S.A.*, 41 G10
Marion, *Ind., U.S.A.*, 42 E3
Marion, *Iowa, U.S.A.*, 40 D9
Marion, *Kans., U.S.A.*, 40 F6
Marion, *N.C., U.S.A.*, 43 H5
Marion, *Ohio, U.S.A.*, 42 E4
Marion, *S.C., U.S.A.*, 43 H6
Marion, L., 43 J5
Maritimes, Alpes, 12 D7
Mariupol, 17 A5
Marked Tree, 41 H9
Market Drayton, 8 E5
Market Harborough, 9 E7
Market Rasen, 8 D7
Markham, Mt., 5 F15
Marksville, 41 K8
Marla, 32 A1
Marlborough, 9 F6
Marlborough Downs, 9 F6
Marlin, 41 K6
Marlow, *U.K.*, 9 F7
Marlow, *U.S.A.*, 41 H6
Marmara Denizi, 15 D13
Marne →, 12 B5
Maroochydore, 32 D5
Maroona, 32 C3
Marquesas Fracture Zone, 35 H15
Marquette, 42 B2
Marquis, 45 f
Marquises, Îs., 35 H14
Marrakech, 26 B4
Marrawah, 32 D3
Marree, 32 A2
Marrowie Cr. →, 32 B4
Mars Hill, 43 B12
Marsden, 32 B4
Marseille, 12 E6
Marsh I., 41 L9
Marshall, *Ark., U.S.A.*, 41 H8
Marshall, *Mich., U.S.A.*, 42 D3
Marshall, *Minn., U.S.A.*, 40 C7
Marshall, *Mo., U.S.A.*, 40 F8
Marshall, *Tex., U.S.A.*, 41 J7
Marshall Is. ■, 34 G9
Marshalltown, 40 D8
Marshfield, *Mo., U.S.A.*, 41 G8
Marshfield, *Wis., U.S.A.*, 40 C9

Mart, 41 K6
Martaban, G. of, 25 D8
Martapura, 23 D3
Martha's Vineyard, 42 E10
Martigues, 12 E6
Martin, *S. Dak., U.S.A.*, 40 D4
Martin, *Tenn., U.S.A.*, 41 G10
Martin L., 43 J3
Martinborough, 33 J5
Martinez, 33 J4
Martinique ☑, 44 c
Martins Ferry, 42 E5
Martinsburg, 42 F7
Martinsville, *Ind., U.S.A.*, 42 F2
Martinsville, *Va., U.S.A.*, 43 G6
Marton, 33 J5
Martos, 13 D4
Marudi, 22 C5
Maryborough, *Queens., Australia*, 32 A5
Maryborough, *Vic., Australia*, 32 C3
Maryland □, 42 F7
Maryport, 8 C4
Marystown, 37 E14
Marysville, *Calif., U.S.A.*, 38 G3
Marysville, *Kans., U.S.A.*, 40 F6
Marysville, *Ohio, U.S.A.*, 42 E4
Maryville, *Mo., U.S.A.*, 40 E7
Maryville, *Tenn., U.S.A.*, 43 H4
Masan, 21 C7
Masaya, 44 E7
Masbate, 23 B4
Maseru, 29 K5
Mashhad, 24 B4
Masjid-e Soleymān? , 11 C2
Mask, L., 11 C2
Mason, 41 K5
Mason City, 40 D8
Masqat, 24 C4
Massachusetts □, 42 D10
Massena, 42 C8
Massiah Street, 45 g
Massif Central, 12 D5
Massillon, 42 E5
Masterton, 33 J5
Masvingo, 29 J6
Matachewan, 37 E12
Matadi, 28 F2
Matagalpa, 44 E7
Matagami, 37 E12
Matagami, L., 37 E12
Matagorda I., 41 L6
Matamoros, *Coahuila, Mexico*, 44 B5
Matamoros, *Tamaulipas, Mexico*, 44 B5
Matane, 37 E13
Matanzas, 45 C8
Mataró, 13 B7
Matera, 14 D7
Mathis, 41 L6
Mathura, 25 F7
Matlock, 8 D6
Mato Grosso □, 46 F7
Mato Grosso, Planalto do, 47 G8
Matopo Hills, 29 J5
Matrûh, 27 B11
Matsue, 22 F3
Matsumoto, 22 F5
Matsusaka, 22 F5
Matsuyama, 22 G3
Mattagami →, 37 D11
Mattancheri, 25 F6
Matterhorn, 12 D7
Matthew, Î., 31 E13
Maturín, 46 B6
Maubeuge, 12 A6
Maud, 41 H6
Maude, 32 B3
Maudin Sun, 25 D8
Maughold Hd., 8 C3
Maumee, 42 E4
Maumee →, 42 E4
Maun, 29 H4
Maupin, 38 D3
Mauritania ■, 26 D3
Mauritius ■, 5 F13
Mauston, 40 D9
Max, 40 B4
May Pen, 44 a
Mayaguana, 45 C10
Mayagüez, 45 d
Maybell, 38 F9
Maydena, 32 D4
Mayenne, 12 B3
Mayfield, 41 G1
Mayhill, 39 K11
Maykop, 17 A7
Maynooth, 11 C5
Mayo, 36 B6
Mayo □, 11 C2
Mayo →, 37 D6
Mayor I., 33 G6
Mayotte ☑, 5 F9
Mayville, 40 B6
Mazabuka, 29 H5
Mazar-e Sharif, 24 B5
Mazatlán, 44 C3
Mbabane, 29 K6
Mbandaka, 28 D3
Mbanza Ngungu, 28 F2
Mbeya, 28 F6
Mbuji-Mayi, 28 F4
McKean, 31 A16
Mead, L., 39 H6
Meade, 41 G4
Meadow Lake, 36 C9
Meadow Valley Wash →, 39 H6
Meaford, 42 C5
Mealy Mts., 37 B8
Meares, C., 38 D2
Mearim →, 47 D10
Meath □, 11 C5
Meaux, 12 B5
Mecca = Makkah, 24 C2
Mechelen, 11 C4
Mecklenburg, 16 B6
Medan, 23 D1
Médéa, 26 A6
Medellín, 46 B3
Medford, *Oreg., U.S.A.*, 38 E2
Medford, *Wis., U.S.A.*, 40 C9
Medicine Bow, 38 F10
Medicine Bow Mts., 38 F10
Medicine Bow Pk., 38 F10
Medicine Hat, 36 D8
Medicine Lodge, 41 G5
Medina = Al Madinah, 24 C2
Medina, *N. Dak., U.S.A.*, 40 B5
Medina, *N.Y., U.S.A.*, 42 D6
Medina, *Ohio, U.S.A.*, 42 E5
Medina →, 41 L5
Mediterranean Sea, 3 C11
Medway □, 9 F8
Medway →, 9 F8
Meekatharra, 30 F2

Meeker, 38 F10
Meerut, 25 C6
Meeteetse, 38 D9
Meghalaya □, 25 C8
Mehlville, 40 F9
Meighen I., 37 A10
Meiktila, 25 C8
Meizhou, 21 D6
Mekele, 24 D2
Mekong →, 23 C2
Melaka, 23 C2
Melanesia, 31 A14
Melanesian Basin, 34 G8
Melbourne, *Australia*, 32 C4
Melbourne, *U.S.A.*, 43 L5
Mélèzes →, 37 D12
Melfort, 36 C9
Melitopol, 17 A6
Melksham, 9 F5
Mellette, 40 C5
Melrose, *Australia*, 32 B4
Melrose, *U.K.*, 10 F6
Melrose, *N. Mex., U.S.A.*, 40 C7
Melstone, 38 C10
Melton Mowbray, 8 E7
Melun, 12 B5
Melville, 36 C9
Melville, L., 37 B8
Melville I., *Australia*, 30 B5
Melville I., *Canada*, 37 B9
Melville Pen., 37 C11
Melvin, Lough, 11 B3
Memba, 29 G8
Memel →, 32 C5
Memmingen, 16 E6
Memphis, *Tenn., U.S.A.*, 41 H10
Memphis, *Tex., U.S.A.*, 41 H4
Mena, 41 H7
Menai Strait, 8 D3
Menard, 41 K5
Menard Fracture Zone, 35 M18
Mendaña Fracture Zone, 35 J18
Mende, 12 D5
Mendip Hills, 9 F5
Mendocino, 38 F1
Mendocino, C., 38 F1
Mendota, *Calif., U.S.A.*, 39 H3
Mendota, *Ill., U.S.A.*, 40 E10
Mendoza, 48 C3
Mene Grande, 46 B4
Menemen, 15 E12
Menfi, 14 F5
Mengzi, 20 D5
Menindee, 32 B3
Menindee L., 32 B3
Meningie, 32 C2
Menominee, 42 C2
Menominee →, 42 C2
Menomonie, 40 C9
Menorca, 13 C8
Mentawai, Kepulauan, 23 D1
Mentor, 42 E5
Merbein, 32 B3
Merca, 24 D3
Merced, 39 H3
Mercedes →, 48 C4
Mercy, C., 37 C13
Mere, 9 F5
Meredith, L., 41 H4
Mergui, 23 B1
Mérida, *Mexico*, 44 C7
Mérida, *Spain*, 13 C2
Mérida, *Venezuela*, 46 B4
Mérida, Cord. de, 46 B4
Meriden, *U.K.*, 9 E6
Meriden, *U.S.A.*, 42 E9
Meridian, *Miss., U.S.A.*, 43 J1
Merkel, 41 J4
Merredin, 30 G2
Merrill, *Oreg., U.S.A.*, 38 E3
Merrill, *Wis., U.S.A.*, 40 C10
Merritt, 36 C7
Merritt Island, 43 L5
Merriwa, 32 B5
Merry →, 9 F8
Merseyside □, 8 D4
Mersin = İçel, 25 G5
Merthyr Tydfil, 9 F4
Mertzon, 41 K4
Mesa, 39 K8
Mesa Verde △, 39 H9
Mesopotamia = Al Jazirah, 24 B3
Mesquite, 39 H6
Messina, 14 E6
Messina, Str. di, 14 F6
Messini, 15 F10
Meta →, 46 B5
Meta Incognita Pen., 37 C13
Metairie, 41 L9
Metaline Falls, 38 B5
Methven, 33 K3
Metlakatla, 36 C6
Metropolis, 41 G10
Metz, 12 B7
Meulaboh, 23 C1
Meuse →, 11 C5
Mexia, 41 K6
Mexicali, 44 A1
Mexican Water, 39 H9
México, *Mexico*, 44 D5
Mexico, *N.Y., U.S.A.*, 42 D8
Mexico □, 44 C4
México, Ciudad de, 44 D5
Mexico, G. of, 44 B7
Meymaneh, 24 B5
Mezen, 18 C5
Miami, *Fla., U.S.A.*, 43 N5
Miami, *Okla., U.S.A.*, 41 G7
Miami, *Tex., U.S.A.*, 41 H4
Miami Beach, 43 N5
Mianchi, 21 C6
Miandrivazo, 29 H9
Mianwali, 25 C5
Miass, 18 D10
Michigan □, 42 C3
Michigan, L., 42 D2
Michigan City, 42 E2
Micoud, 45 f
Micronesia, 34 G7
Micronesia, Federated States of ■, 34 G7
Middelburg, 29 K5
Middle Alkali L., 38 F3
Middle East, 4 E3
Middle Loup →, 40 E5
Middlebury, 42 C9
Middleport, 42 F4
Middlesboro, 41 G12
Middlesbrough, 8 C6
Middlesbrough □, 8 C6
Middleton, *U.K.*, 8 D5
Middletown, *N.Y., U.S.A.*, 42 E8
Middletown, *Ohio, U.S.A.*, 42 F3
Midhurst, 9 G7
Midi, Canal du →, 12 E4
Midland, *Mich., U.S.A.*, 42 D3
Midland, *Tex., U.S.A.*, 41 K3
Midleton, 11 E3
Midlothian □, 10 F5
Midway Is., 34 E10
Midwest, 38 E10
Midwest City, 41 H6
Mikkeli, 6 F12
Milaca, 40 C8
Milan = Milano, 14 B3
Milan, *Mo., U.S.A.*, 40 E8
Milan, *Tenn., U.S.A.*, 43 H1

Milano, 12 D8
Milbank, 40 C6
Mildenhall, 9 E8
Mildura, 32 B3
Miles, 32 A5
Miles City, 40 B2
Milford, *Del., U.S.A.*, 42 F8
Milford, *Utah, U.S.A.*, 39 G7
Milford Haven, 9 F2
Milford Sound, 33 L1
Millau, 12 D5
Milledgeville, 43 J4
Millen, 43 J5
Millennium I. = Caroline I., 35 H12
Miller, 40 C5
Millet, 45 f
Millicent, 32 C3
Millington, 41 H10
Millinocket, 43 C11
Millmerran, 32 A5
Millom, 8 C4
Millstreet, 11 D2
Milltown Malbay, 11 D2
Millville, 42 F8
Millwood L., 41 J8
Milmilana, 32 A3
Milton, *N.Z.*, 33 M2
Milton, *Fla., U.S.A.*, 43 K2
Milton, *Pa., U.S.A.*, 42 E7
Milton-Freewater, 38 D4
Milton Keynes, 9 E7
Milwaukee, 42 D2
Milwaukee Deep, 45 d
Milwaukie, 38 D2
Min Jiang →, *Fujian, China*, 21 D6
Min Jiang →, *Sichuan, China*, 20 D5
Minami-Tori-Shima, 34 E7
Minas Gerais □, 47 G9
Minatitlán, 44 D6
Minbu, 25 C8
Mindanao, 23 C4
Mindanao Trench, 23 B4
Minden, *Ger.*, 16 B5
Minden, *La., U.S.A.*, 41 J8
Minden, *Nev., U.S.A.*, 38 G4
Mindoro, 23 B4
Mindoro Str., 23 B4
Minehead, 9 F4
Mineola, 41 J7
Mineral Wells, 41 J5
Minidoka, 38 E7
Minneapolis, *Kans., U.S.A.*, 40 F6
Minneapolis, *Minn., U.S.A.*, 40 C8
Minnedosa, 36 D10
Minnesota □, 40 B8
Minnesota →, 40 C8
Minnewaukan, 40 A5
Minnipa, 32 B2
Minorca = Menorca, 13 C8
Minot, 40 A4
Minsk, 18 D3
Mintaka Pass, 25 A6
Minto, L., 37 D12
Minton, 38 B10
Minturn, 38 G10
Minzhong, 21 F10
Miquelon, 37 E14
Miramichi, 37 E13
Miranda de Ebro, 13 A4
Miri, 23 C3
Mirjaveh, 24 C5
Mirpur Khas, 25 C5
Mirzapur, 25 C7
Mishan, 21 B8
Mishawaka, 42 E2
Misool, 23 D5
Misrata, 27 B9
Missinaibi →, 37 D11
Mission, *S. Dak., U.S.A.*, 40 D4
Mission, *Tex., U.S.A.*, 41 M5
Mission Viejo, 39 K5
Mississippi □, 41 J10
Mississippi →, 41 L10
Mississippi River Delta, 41 L10
Mississippi Sd., 41 K10
Missoula, 38 C6
Missouri □, 40 F8
Missouri →, 40 F9
Missouri City, 41 L7
Missouri Valley, 40 E7
Mistassini →, 37 D12
Mitchell, *Australia*, 32 A4
Mitchell, *Oreg., U.S.A.*, 38 D3
Mitchell, *S. Dak., U.S.A.*, 40 D5
Mitchell →, 30 D7
Mitchell, Mt., 43 H4
Mitchelstown, 11 D3
Mito, 22 F6
Mittagong, 32 B5
Mitumba, Mts., 28 F5
Miyakonojō, 22 H2
Miyazaki, 22 H2
Mizen Hd., *Cork, Ireland*, 11 E2
Mizen Hd., *Wicklow, Ireland*, 11 D5
Mizoram □, 25 C8
Mjøsa, 6 F10
Mmabatho, 29 K5
Mo i Rana, 6 C10
Moa, L., 47 E11
Moab, 39 G9
Moala, 31 D8
Moama, 32 C3
Moate, 11 C4
Moberly, 40 F8
Mobile, 43 K1
Mobile B., 43 K1
Mobridge, 40 C4
Moçambique, 29 H8
Mochudi, 29 J5
Mocoa, 46 C3
Modena, *Italy*, 14 B4
Modena, *U.S.A.*, 39 H7
Modesto, 39 H3
Modimolle, 29 J5
Moe, 32 C4
Moffat, 10 F5
Mogadishu = Muqdisho, 24 D3
Mogi das Cruzes, 48 A7
Mogollon Rim, 39 J8
Mohall, 40 A4
Mohave, L., 39 J6
Moher, Cliffs of, 11 D2
Moidart, L., 10 E3
Mojave, 39 J4
Mojave →, 39 J5
Mojave Desert, 39 J5
Mokai, 33 H5
Mokopane, 29 J5
Mold, 8 D4
Moldova ■, 17 E15
Mole →, 9 F7
Molepolole, 29 J5
Moline, 40 E9
Molokai, 37 H16
Molokai Fracture Zone, 35 E15
Molong, 32 B4
Molopo →, 29 K4
Molucca Sea, 23 D4
Moluccas = Maluku, 23 D4
Mombasa, 28 E7
Mona Passage, 45 D11
Monaco ■, 12 E7

Monadhliath Mts., 10 D4
Monaghan, 11 B5
Monaghan □, 11 B5
Monahans, 41 K3
Monar, L., 10 D3
Monarch Mt., 36 C7
Monastir = Bitola, 15 D9
Mönchengladbach, 16 C4
Moncks Corner, 43 J5
Monclova, 44 B4
Moncton, 37 E13
Mondego →, 13 B1
Moneague, 44 a
Monessen, 42 E6
Monett, 41 G8
Moneymore, 11 B5
Monforte de Lemos, 13 A2
Mongolia ■, 20 B5
Mongu, 29 H4
Monifieth, 10 E6
Monmouth, *U.K.*, 9 F5
Monmouth, *U.S.A.*, 40 E9
Monmouthshire □, 9 F5
Mono, L., 39 H4
Monroe, *Ga., U.S.A.*, 43 J4
Monroe, *La., U.S.A.*, 41 J8
Monroe, *Mich., U.S.A.*, 42 E4
Monroe, *N.C., U.S.A.*, 43 H5
Monroe, *Utah, U.S.A.*, 39 G7
Monroe, *Wis., U.S.A.*, 40 D10
Monroe City, 40 F9
Monroeville, 43 K2
Monrovia, 26 G3
Mons, 16 C1
Mont-de-Marsan, 12 E3
Mont-Laurier, 37 E12
Montana □, 38 C9
Montargis, 12 C5
Montauban, 12 D4
Montauk Pt., 42 E10
Montbéliard, 12 C7
Montceau-les-Mines, 12 C6
Monte-Carlo, 12 E7
Monte Cristi, 45 D10
Monte Vista, 39 H10
Montego Bay, 44 a
Montélimar, 12 D6
Montello, 40 D10
Montemorelos, 44 B5
Montenegro ■, 15 C8
Montería, 46 B3
Monterrey, 44 B4
Montes Claros, 47 G10
Montesano, 38 C2
Montevideo, *Uruguay*, 48 C5
Montevideo, *U.S.A.*, 40 C7
Montezuma, 40 E8
Montezuma Castle △, 39 J8
Montgomery, *U.K.*, 9 E4
Montgomery, *Ala., U.S.A.*, 43 J2
Montgomery, *W. Va., U.S.A.*, 42 F5
Montgomery City, 40 F9
Monticello, *Ark., U.S.A.*, 41 J9
Monticello, *Ind., U.S.A.*, 42 E2
Monticello, *Iowa, U.S.A.*, 40 D9
Monticello, *Ky., U.S.A.*, 43 G3
Monticello, *Minn., U.S.A.*, 40 C8
Monticello, *Miss., U.S.A.*, 41 K9
Monticello, *Utah, U.S.A.*, 39 H9
Montluçon, 12 C5
Montmagny, 37 E12
Montmorillon, 12 C4
Montpelier, *Idaho, U.S.A.*, 38 E8
Montpelier, *Vt., U.S.A.*, 42 C9
Montpellier, 12 E5
Montréal, 37 E12
Montreux, 12 C7
Montrose, *U.K.*, 10 E6
Montrose, *U.S.A.*, 39 G10
Montserrat ☑, 44 b
Monywa, 25 C8
Monza, 12 D8
Moonie, 32 A5
Moonie →, 32 A4
Moonta, 32 B2
Moorcroft, 40 C2
Moorefield, 42 F6
Moorfoot Hills, 10 F5
Moorhead, 40 B6
Mooresville, 43 H5
Moose →, 37 D11
Moose Jaw, 36 D9
Moose Lake, 40 B8
Mooselookmeguntic L., 42 C10
Moosomin, 36 D9
Moosonee, 37 D11
Mopti, 26 F5
Mora, *Sweden*, 6 F10
Mora, *Minn., U.S.A.*, 40 C8
Mora, *N. Mex., U.S.A.*, 40 C8
Moradabad, 25 C7
Moran, *Kans., U.S.A.*, 40 F7
Moran, *Wyo., U.S.A.*, 38 E8
Morar, L., 10 E3
Morava →, *Serbia*, 15 B9
Morava →, *Slovak Rep.*, 16 D9
Morawa, 30 E2
Moray □, 10 D5
Moray Firth, 10 D5
Morden, 36 D10
Mordvinia □, 18 D5
Moreau →, 40 C4
Morecambe, 8 C5
Morecambe B., 8 C4
Moree, 32 A4
Morehead, 42 F4
Morehead City, 43 H7
Morelia, 44 D4
Morena, Sierra, 13 C3
Moresby I., 36 C6
Moreton I., 32 A5
Morgan, 32 B2
Morgan City, 41 L9
Morganfield, 42 G2
Morganton, 43 H5
Morgantown, 42 F6
Moriarty, 39 J10
Morioka, 22 E7
Morlaix, 12 B2
Mornington, 32 C4
Mornington I., 30 C6
Morocco ■, 26 B4
Morogoro, 28 F7
Moroni, 29 G4
Morotai, 23 C4
Morpeth, 8 B6
Morrilton, 41 H8
Morris, *Ill., U.S.A.*, 40 E10
Morris, *Minn., U.S.A.*, 40 C7
Morristown, *Ariz., U.S.A.*, 39 K7
Morristown, *Tenn., U.S.A.*, 43 G4
Morro Bay, 39 J3

Mortlake, 32 C3
Morton, *Tex., U.S.A.*, 41 J3
Morton, *Wash., U.S.A.*, 38 C2
Moruya, 32 C5
Morvan, 12 C6
Morven, 10 A4
Morvern, 10 E3
Morwell, 32 C4
Moscow = Moskva, 18 C6
Moscow, *U.S.A.*, 38 C5
Mosel →, 12 A7
Moses Lake, 38 C4
Moshi, 28 E7
Moskva, 18 C6
Moss Vale, 32 B5
Mossbank, 38 B9
Mossburn, 33 L2
Mosselbaai, 29 L4
Mossgiel, 32 B3
Mossoró, 47 E11
Most, 16 C6
Mostaganem, 26 A6
Mostar, 16 H8
Motherwell, 10 F5
Motueka, 33 J4
Motueka →, 33 J4
Moul à Chique, C., 45 f
Moulins, 12 C5
Moultrie, 43 K4
Mound City, *Mo., U.S.A.*, 40 E7
Mound City, *S. Dak., U.S.A.*, 40 C4
Moundsville, 42 F5
Mount Airy, 43 G5
Mount Aspiring △, 33 L2
Mount Barker, 30 G2
Mount Bellew Bridge, 11 C3
Mount Burr, 32 C3
Mount Carmel, 42 F2
Mount Desert I., 43 C11
Mount Field △, 32 D4
Mount Gambier, 32 C3
Mount Hagen, 30 B7
Mount Hope, *N.S.W., Australia*, 32 B4
Mount Isa, 30 E6
Mount Kaputar △, 32 B5
Mount Lofty Ranges, 32 B2
Mount Magnet, 30 E2
Mount Maunganui, 33 G6
Mount Perry, 32 A5
Mount Pleasant, *Iowa, U.S.A.*, 40 E9
Mount Pleasant, *Mich., U.S.A.*, 42 D3
Mount Pleasant, *S.C., U.S.A.*, 43 J6
Mount Pleasant, *Tenn., U.S.A.*, 43 H2
Mount Pleasant, *Tex., U.S.A.*, 41 J7
Mount Rainier △, 38 C3
Mount St. Helens △, 38 C2
Mount Shasta, 38 F2
Mount Sterling, *Ill., U.S.A.*, 40 F9
Mount Sterling, *Ky., U.S.A.*, 42 F4
Mount Vernon, *Ill., U.S.A.*, 40 F1
Mount Vernon, *Ind., U.S.A.*, 42 G2
Mount Vernon, *Ohio, U.S.A.*, 42 E4
Mount Vernon, *Wash., U.S.A.*, 38 B2
Mount William △, 32 D4
Mountain Ash, 9 F4
Mountain City, *Nev., U.S.A.*, 38 F6
Mountain City, *Tenn., U.S.A.*, 43 G5
Mountain Grove, 41 G8
Mountain Home, *Ark., U.S.A.*, 41 G8
Mountain Home, *Idaho, U.S.A.*, 38 E6
Mountain View, 41 H8
Mountmellick, 11 C4
Mountnessing, 11 A4
Mourne →, 11 B4
Mourne Mts., 11 B5
Moville, 11 A4
Moy →, 11 B2
Moyale, 28 D7
Moyen Atlas, 26 B4
Mozambique ■, 29 H7
Mozambique Chan., 3 C10
Mpumalanga □, 29 K6
Msaken, 27 A8
Mtwara, 28 G8
Mu Us Shamo, 21 C5
Muar, 23 C2
Muck, 10 E2
Muckadilla, 32 A4
Muckle Flugga, 10 A8
Mudanjiang, 21 B7
Muddy Cr. →, 39 H8
Mudgee, 32 B4
Mufulira, 29 G5
Muhammad Qol, 24 C2
Muine Bheag, 11 D5
Muir Wo, 21 D5
Mukdahan, 23 A2
Mukinbudin, 30 F2
Mulde →, 16 C7
Mule Creek Junction, 40 D2
Muleshoe, 41 H3
Mulgrave, 37 E13
Mulhacén, 13 D4
Mulhouse, 12 C7
Mull, 10 E3
Mull, Sound of, 10 E3
Mullen, 40 D4
Muller, Pegunungan, 23 C3
Mullet Pen., 11 B1
Mullewa, 30 F2
Mulligan →, 30 E6
Mullingar, 11 C4
Mullins, 43 H6
Mullumbimby, 32 A5
Mulroy B., 11 A4
Multan, 25 D5
Mumbai, 25 D5
Muncie, 42 E3
Munciena? , 41 J6
Mundesley, 8 E9
Munger, 25 C7
Munich = München, 16 D6
Munising, 42 B2
Muñoz Gamero, Pen., 48 G2
Münster, 16 C4
Muonio, 6 C12
Muqdisho, 24 D3
Mur →, 16 E8
Murallón, Cerro, 48 F2
Murang'a, 28 E7
Murcia, 13 D5
Murcia □, 13 D5
Murdo, 40 D4
Mures →, 17 E11
Murfreesboro, *N.C., U.S.A.*, 43 G7
Murfreesboro, *Tenn., U.S.A.*, 43 H2
Murgab →, 24 B4
Murgon, 32 A5
Murmansk, 7 D10

Murom, 18 D5
Murphy, 38 E5
Murray, *Ky., U.S.A.*, 43 G1
Murray, *Utah, U.S.A.*, 38 F8
Murray →, 32 C2
Murray, L., 43 H5
Murray Bridge, 32 C2
Murray Fracture Zone, 35 D14
Murray River △, 32 B2
Murrumbidgee →, 32 B3
Murrumburrah, 32 B4
Murrurundi, 32 B5
Murtoa, 32 C3
Murupara, 33 H6
Mururoa, 35 K14
Murwara, 25 C7
Murwillumbah, 32 A5
Mûsa, Gebel, 24 C2
Muscat = Masqat, 24 C4
Muscatine, 40 E9
Muscle Shoals, 43 H2
Musgrave Ranges, 30 F5
Musi →, 23 D2
Musina, 29 J6
Muskegon, 42 D2
Muskegon →, 42 D2
Muskegon Heights, 42 D2
Muskogee, 41 H7
Musselburgh, 10 F5
Musselshell →, 38 C10
Muswellbrook, 32 B5
Mût, 27 C11
Mutare, 29 H6
Mutton I., 11 D2
Mwanza, 28 E6
Mweelrea, 11 C2
Mweru, L., 28 F5
My Tho, 23 B2
Myanmar = Burma ■, 25 C8
Myeik Kyunzu, 23 B1
Myingyan, 25 C8
Myitkyina, 25 C8
Mymensingh, 25 C8
Mynydd Du, 9 F4
Myrtle Beach, 43 J6
Myrtle Creek, 38 E2
Myrtle Point, 38 E1
Mysore, 25 D6

N

Naab →, 16 D6
Naas, 11 C5
Naberezhnyye Chelny, 18 D6
Naches, 38 C3
Nacimiento L., 39 J3
Nacogdoches, 41 K7
Nacozari de García, 44 A3
Nadi, 33 C7
Naga, 23 B4
Nagaland □, 25 C8
Nagano, 22 E6
Nagaoka, 22 E6
Nagappattinam, 25 E6
Nagasaki, 22 G1
Nagaur, 25 C5
Nagercoil, 25 F6
Nagles Mts., 11 D3
Nagorno-Karabakh □, 19 F8
Nagoya, 22 F5
Nagpur, 25 D6
Naha, 21 d
Nahanni △, 36 B7
Nain, 37 C13
Nairn, 10 D5
Nairobi, 28 E7
Najafabad, 24 B4
Najd, 24 C3
Najibabad, 25 C6
Najin, 21 B8
Najran, 24 D3
Nakhodka, 19 E14
Nakhon Ratchasima, 23 B2
Nakhon Sawan, 23 B2
Nakhon Si Thammarat, 23 C2
Nakuru, 28 E7
Nalchik, 19 F7
Nam Co, 20 C4
Namak, 24 B4
Namaland, 29 J3
Namangan, 18 E8
Namao, 32 B5
Nambour, 32 A5
Nambucca Heads, 32 B5
Namcha Barwa, 20 D4
Namib Desert, 29 J2
Namibe, 29 H2
Namibia ■, 29 J3
Namlea, 23 D4
Namoi →, 32 B4
Nampa, 38 E5
Nampo, 21 C7
Nampula, 29 H7
Namur, 16 C2
Namwala, 29 H5
Nan →, 23 A2
Nanaimo, 36 D7
Nanango, 32 A5
Nanchang, 21 D6
Nanchong, 20 C5
Nancy, 12 B7
Nanda Devi, 25 B6
Nanded, 25 D6
Nandewar Ra., 32 B5
Nandurbar, 25 D6
Nanga Parbat, 25 B6
Nanjing, 21 C6
Nanning, 20 D5
Nannup, 30 G2
Nanping, 21 D6
Nansei-Shotō, 21 M2
Nansen Sd., 4 A
Nantes, 12 C3
Nanticoke, 42 E7
Nantong, 21 C7
Nantucket I., 42 E10
Nantwich, 8 D5
Nanuque, 47 G10
Nanusa, Kepulauan, 23 C4
Nanyang, 21 C6
Nanyuki, 28 D7
Nao, C. de la, 13 C6
Napa, 38 G2
Napanee, 42 D7
Napier, 33 H6
Naples = Napoli, 14 D6
Naples, *U.S.A.*, 43 N5
Napo →, 46 D4
Napoleon, *N. Dak., U.S.A.*, 40 B5
Napoleon, *Ohio, U.S.A.*, 42 E3
Napoli, 14 D6
Nara, *Mali*, 26 E4
Nara, *Japan*, 22 F4
Nara Visa, 41 H3
Naracoorte, 32 C3
Naradhan, 32 B4
Narathiwat, 23 C2
Narayanganj, 25 C8
Narbonne, 12 E5
Nardò, 14 D8
Narew →, 16 B11
Narmada →, 25 D5
Narooma, 32 C5
Narrabri, 32 B4
Narran →, 32 A4
Narrandera, 32 B4
Narromine, 32 B4
Naruto, 22 F4
Narva, 7 F11
Narvik, 6 B11
Naryan-Mar, 18 C6
Naseby, 33 L3
Naser, Buheirat en, 27 D12
Nashua, *Mont., U.S.A.*, 38 B10
Nashua, *N.H., U.S.A.*, 42 D10
Nashville, *Ark., U.S.A.*, 41 J8
Nashville, *Tenn., U.S.A.*, 43 G2
Nasik, 25 D5
Nasirabad, 25 C5
Nassau, 45 B9
Nassau, B., 48 H3
Natal, 47 E11
Natashquan, 37 D13
Natchez, 41 K9
Natchitoches, 41 K8
Nathalia, 32 C4
Natitingou, 26 F6
Natkyizin, 23 B1
Natron, L., 28 E7
Natuna Besar, Kepulauan, 23 C2
Natuna Selatan, Kepulauan, 23 C2

Natural Bridges △, 39 H8
Naturaliste, C., 32 D4
Naturaliste Plateau, 34 M3
Nauru ■, 34 H8
Navajo Res., 39 H10
Navarra □, 13 A5
Navasota, 41 K6
Naver →, 10 C4
Navojoa, 44 B3
Nawabshah, 25 C5
Nawoiy, 24 A5
Naxos, 15 F11
Nazas →, 44 B4
Nazca Ridge, 35 K19
Naze, The, 9 F9
Ndjamena, 27 F8
Ndola, 29 G5
Neagh, Lough, 11 B5
Neah Bay, 38 B1
Neales →, 32 A2
Near Is., 36 C1
Neath, 9 F4
Neath →, 9 F4
Nebine Cr. →, 32 A4
Nebraska □, 40 E5
Nebraska City, 40 E7
Necedah, 40 C9
Neches →, 41 K8
Neckar →, 16 D5
Needles, 39 J6
Needles, The, 9 G6
Neenah, 42 C1
Neepawa, 36 D10
Negaunee, 42 B2
Negele, 24 D2
Negombo, 25 F6
Negra, Pta., 46 E2
Negril, 44 a
Negro →, *Argentina*, 48 E4
Negro →, *Brazil*, 46 D7
Negros, 23 C4
Nei Monggol Zizhiqu □, 21 B6
Neijiang, 20 D5
Neillsville, 40 C9
Neilton, 38 C2
Neiva, 46 C3
Neligh, 40 D5
Nelson, *Canada*, 36 D8
Nelson, *U.K.*, 8 D5
Nelson, *N.Z.*, 33 J4
Nelson →, 36 C10
Nelson, C., 32 C3
Nelson Lakes △, 33 J4
Nelspruit, 29 K6
Nemunas →, 18 D3
Nen Jiang →, 21 B7
Nenagh, 11 D3
Nene →, 9 E8
Nenjiang, 21 B7
Neodesha, 41 G7
Neosho, 41 G7
Neosho →, 41 H7
Nepal ■, 25 C7
Nepalganj, 25 C7
Nephi, 38 G8
Nephin, 11 B2
Nephin Beg Range, 11 B2
Nerang, 32 A5
Ness, L., 10 D4
Ness City, 40 F5
Netanya, 24 B2
Netherlands ■, 16 C3
Netherlands Antilles ☑, 45 E11
Nettilling L., 37 C12
Neuchâtel, 12 C7
Neuchâtel, Lac de, 12 C7
Neuse →, 43 H7
Neusiedler See, 16 E9
Neva →, 4 D10
Nevada, *Iowa, U.S.A.*, 40 D8
Nevada, *Mo., U.S.A.*, 41 G7
Nevada □, 38 G5
Nevada City, 38 G3
Nevers, 12 C5
Nevertire, 32 B4
Nevinnomyssk, 19 E7
New →, 42 F5
New Albany, *Ind., U.S.A.*, 42 F3
New Albany, *Miss., U.S.A.*, 41 H10
New Amsterdam, 46 B7
New Angledool, 32 A4
New Bedford, 42 E10
New Bern, 43 H7
New Boston, 41 J7
New Braunfels, 41 L5
New Britain, *Papua N.G.*, 34 H7
New Britain, *U.S.A.*, 42 E9
New Britain Trench, 34 H7
New Brunswick, 42 E8
New Brunswick □, 37 E13
New Caledonia ☑, 31 E12
New Caledonia Trough, 34 L8
New Castle, *Ind., U.S.A.*, 42 F3
New Castle, *Pa., U.S.A.*, 42 E5
New Delhi, 25 C6
New England Ra., 32 B5
New Forest, 9 G6
New Galloway, 10 F4
New Georgia Is., 31 B7
New Glasgow, 37 E13
New Guinea, 34 H6
New Hampshire □, 42 D10
New Hampton, 40 D8
New Haven, 42 E9
New Hebrides = Vanuatu ■, 31 C12
New Iberia, 41 K9
New Ireland, 34 H7
New Jersey □, 42 E8
New Lexington, 42 F4
New Liskeard, 37 E12
New London, *Conn., U.S.A.*, 42 E9
New London, *Wis., U.S.A.*, 40 C10
New Madrid, 41 G10
New Meadows, 38 D5
New Mexico □, 39 J10
New Norfolk, 32 D4
New Orleans, 41 L9
New Philadelphia, 42 E5
New Plymouth, 33 H5
New Port Richey, 43 L4
New Providence, 45 B9
New Richmond, 40 C8
New River Gorge △, 42 G5
New Roads, 41 K9
New Rockford, 40 B5
New Ross, 11 D5
New Salem, 40 B4
New Smyrna Beach, 43 L5
New South Wales □, 32 B4
New Town, 40 B3
New Ulm, 40 C7
New Westminster, 38 A4
New York, 42 E9
New York □, 42 D8
New Zealand ■, 33 J5
Newark, *N.J., U.S.A.*, 42 E8

Newark, *N.Y., U.S.A.*, 42 D7
Newark, *Ohio, U.S.A.*, 42 E4
Newark-on-Trent, 8 D7
Newberg, 38 D2
Newberry, *Mich., U.S.A.*, 42 B3
Newberry, *S.C., U.S.A.*, 43 H5
Newburgh, 42 E8
Newbury, 9 F6
Newburyport, 43 D10
Newcastle, *Australia*, 32 B5
Newcastle, *S. Africa*, 29 K5
Newcastle, *U.S.A.*, 40 D2
Newcastle Emlyn, 9 E3
Newcastle-under-Lyme, 8 D5
Newcastle-upon-Tyne, 8 C6
Newcastle Waters, 30 D5
Newcastle West, 11 D2
Newfoundland & Labrador □, 37 D14
Newhaven, 9 G8
Newkirk, 41 G6
Newman, 30 E2
Newmarket, *Ireland*, 11 D2
Newmarket, *U.K.*, 9 E8
Newnan, 43 J3
Newport, *Ireland*, 11 C2
Newport, *I. of W., U.K.*, 9 G6
Newport, *Newport, U.K.*, 9 F5
Newport, *Ark., U.S.A.*, 41 H9
Newport, *Ky., U.S.A.*, 42 F3
Newport, *N.H., U.S.A.*, 42 D9
Newport, *Oreg., U.S.A.*, 38 D1
Newport, *R.I., U.S.A.*, 42 E10
Newport, *Tenn., U.S.A.*, 43 H4
Newport, *Vt., U.S.A.*, 42 C9
Newport, *Wash., U.S.A.*, 38 B5
Newport Beach, 39 K5
Newport News, 42 G7
Newport Pagnell, 9 E7
Newquay, 9 G2
Newry, 11 B5
Newton, *Ill., U.S.A.*, 40 F10
Newton, *Iowa, U.S.A.*, 40 E8
Newton, *Kans., U.S.A.*, 40 F6
Newton, *Mass., U.S.A.*, 42 D10
Newton, *Miss., U.S.A.*, 41 J10
Newton, *N.C., U.S.A.*, 43 H5
Newton, *Tex., U.S.A.*, 41 K8
Newton Abbot, 9 G4
Newton Aycliffe, 8 C6
Newton Stewart, 10 G4
Newtonmore, 10 D4
Newtown, 9 E4
Newtownabbey, 11 B6
Newtownards, 11 B6
Newtownstewart, 11 B4
Neyshabur, 24 B4
Nezperce, 38 C5
Ngapara, 33 L3
Ngaoundéré, 27 G7
Ngoring Hu, 20 C4
Nha Trang, 23 B2
Nhill, 32 C3
Niagara Falls, *Canada*, 37 E12
Niagara Falls, *U.S.A.*, 42 D6
Niamey, 26 F6
Nias, 23 C1
Nicaragua ■, 44 E7
Nicaragua, L. de, 44 E7
Nice, 12 E7
Niceville, 43 K2
Nicholasville, 42 G3
Nicobar Is., 25 F8
Nicosia, 25 G5
Nicoya, Pen. de, 44 F7
Niedersachsen □, 16 B5
Niemen = Nemunas →, 18 D3
Niers →, 16 C3
Niger ■, 26 E7
Niger →, 26 G7
Nigeria ■, 26 G7
Nightcaps, 33 L2
Niigata, 22 E6
Nijmegen, 16 C3
Nikiniki, 23 F4
Nikolayevsk-na-Amur, 19 D15
Nikumaroro, 31 A16
Nikunau, 31 A14
Nîkshahr, 24 C5
Nil el Azraq →, 27 E12
Nîl, Nahr en →, 27 B12
Niland, 39 K6
Nile = Nîl, Nahr en →, 27 B12
Niles, 42 E2
Nîmes, 12 E6
Nimmitabel, 32 C4
Nindigully, 32 A4
Ninepin Group, 21 G11
Ningbo, 21 D7
Ningxia Huizu Zizhiqu □, 20 C5
Niobrara, 40 D5
Niobrara →, 40 D6
Niort, 12 C3
Nipawin, 36 C9
Nipigon, 37 D11
Nipigon, L., 37 D11
Nipissing, L., 37 E12
Nipomo, 39 J3
Niš, 15 C9
Nishinomiya, 22 F4
Niterói, 47 H10
Nith →, *U.K.*, 10 F5
Nitra, 16 D10
Nitra →, 16 E10
Niue ☑, 35 J11
Niut, 22 D4
Nivernais, 12 C5
Nizamabad, 25 D6
Nizhniy Novgorod, 18 D5
Nizhniy Tagil, 18 D10
Nizwá, 24 C4
Nkongsamba, 27 H6
Nobeoka, 22 H2
Nogales, *Mexico*, 44 A2
Nogales, *U.S.A.*, 39 L8
Noirmoutier, Î. de, 12 C2
Nola, 28 D3
Nome, 36 B3
Nord-Ostsee-Kanal, 16 A5
Nordfriesische Inseln, 16 A5
Nordkapp, 6 A11
Nordrhein-Westfalen □, 16 C4
Nordvik, 19 B12
Nore →, 11 D4
Norfolk, *Canada*, 42 D7

Norfolk, *Nebr., U.S.A.*, 40 D6
Norfolk, *Va., U.S.A.*, 42 G7
Norfolk I., 34 K8
Norfolk Basin, 31 G13
Norfolk Ridge, 34 K8
Norilsk, 19 C10
Norman, 41 H6
Norman Wells, 36 B7
Normandie, 12 B4
Normanton, 30 D7
Norquay, 36 C9
Norrköping, 6 G11
Norrland, 6 E10
Norseman, 30 G3
Norsk, 19 D14
North Adams, 42 D9
North Ayrshire □, 10 F4
North Battleford, 36 C9
North Bay, 37 E12
North Bend, 38 E1
North Berwick, 10 E6
North C., 33 F4
North Canadian →, 41 H7
North Cape = Nordkapp, 6 A11
North Carolina □, 43 H6
North Cascades △, 38 B3
North Channel, 10 F3
North Charleston, 43 J6
North Chicago, 42 D2
North Dakota □, 40 B5
North Downs, 9 F8
North East Lincolnshire □, 8 D7
North Esk →, 10 E6
North European Plain, 3 B12
North Foreland, 9 F9
North Fork →, 40 G3
North Fork Red →, 41 H5
North Frisian Is. = Nordfriesische Inseln, 16 A5
North Korea ■, 21 C7
North Lanarkshire □, 10 F5
North Las Vegas, 39 H6
North Little Rock, 41 H8
North Loup →, 40 E5
North Magnetic Pole, 37 B9
North Mankato, 40 C8
North Minch, 10 C3
North Myrtle Beach, 43 J6
North Palisade, 39 H4
North Platte, 40 E4
North Platte →, 40 E4
North Pole, 4 A
North Powder, 38 D5
North Ronaldsay, 10 B6
North Saskatchewan →, 36 C8
North Sea, 3 D10
North Somerset □, 9 F5
North Taranaki Bight, 33 H5
North Thompson →, 36 D7
North Tonawanda, 42 D6
North Tyne →, 8 B5
North Uist, 10 D1
North Vernon, 42 F3
North Walsham, 8 E9
North West C., 30 E1
North West Frontier □, 25 B6
North West Highlands, 10 D4
North West River, 37 B8
North Wildwood, 42 F8
North York Moors △, 8 C7
North Yorkshire □, 8 C6
Northallerton, 8 C6
Northam, 30 G2
Northampton, *U.K.*, 9 E7
Northampton, *U.S.A.*, 42 D9
Northamptonshire □, 9 E7
Northeast Pacific Basin, 35 D13
Northern Ireland □, 11 B5
Northern Marianas ☑, 34 F6
Northern Territory □, 30 D5
Northfield, 40 C8
Northland □, 33 F4
Northport, *Ala., U.S.A.*, 43 J2
Northport, *Wash., U.S.A.*, 38 B5
Northumberland □, 8 B6
Northumberland, C., 32 C3
Northumberland Str., 37 E13
Northwest Pacific Basin, 34 D8
Northwest Territories □, 36 B8
Northwich, 8 D5
Northwood, *Iowa, U.S.A.*, 40 D8
Northwood, *N. Dak., U.S.A.*, 40 B6
Norton, *U.S.A.*, 40 F5
Norton Sd., 36 B3
Norwalk, *Conn., U.S.A.*, 42 E9
Norwalk, *Ohio, U.S.A.*, 42 E4
Norway ■, 6 E10
Norway, *Maine, U.S.A.*, 43 C10
Norway, *Mich., U.S.A.*, 42 C2
Norway House, 36 C10
Norwegian B., 37 B10
Norwegian Sea, 4 C8
Norwich, *U.K.*, 8 E9
Norwich, *Conn., U.S.A.*, 42 E9
Norwich, *N.Y., U.S.A.*, 42 D8
Noss Hd., 10 C5
Nossob →, 29 K4
Notre Dame B., 37 E14
Nottawasaga B., 42 C5
Nottaway →, 37 D12
Nottingham, 8 E6
Nottingham City □, 8 E6
Nottinghamshire □, 8 D6
Nouâdhibou, 26 D2
Nouâdhibou, Ras, 26 D2
Nouakchott, 26 E2
Nouméa, 31 E12
Nova Friburgo, 47 H10
Nova Iguaçu, 47 H10
Nova Scotia □, 37 E13
Novara, 12 D8
Novaya Zemlya, 18 B7
Novgorod, 18 C4
Novi Sad, 15 B8
Novocherkassk, 19 E7
Novokuznetsk, 18 D9
Novomoskovsk, 18 D6

Novorossiysk, 17 B6
Novoshakhtinsk, 17 A5
Novosibirsk, 18 D9
Novosibirskiye Ostrova, 19 B15
Novotroitsk, 18 D10
Nowata, 41 G7
Nowra, 32 B5
Nowshak, 25 A6
Nowy Sącz, 16 D11
Nu Jiang →, 20 D4
Nu Shan, 20 D4
Nûbîya, Es Sahrâ en, 27 D12
Nueces →, 41 M6
Nueltin L., 36 C10
Nueva Rosita, 44 B4
Nuevitas, 45 C9
Nuevo Laredo, 44 B5
Nugget Pt., 33 M2
Nuhaka, 33 H6
Nui, 34 H9
Nukey Bluff, 32 B2
Nuku Hiva, 35 H14
Nuku'alofa, 31 E11
Nukualofa, 34 K10
Nukulaelae, 34 H9
Nukus, 18 E7
Nullarbor Plain, 30 G4
Numalla, L., 32 A3
Numazu, 22 F6
Numurkah, 32 C4
Nunap Isua, 37 C15
Nunavut □, 37 C11
Nuneaton, 9 E6
Nunivak I., 36 B3
Nuremberg = Nürnberg, 16 D6
Nürnberg, 16 D6
Nushki, 24 C5
Nuuk, 37 B14
Nuweveldberge, 29 L4
Nuyts Arch., 32 B1
Nyagan, 18 C8
Nyaingentanglha Shan, 20 D4
Nyasa, L. = Malawi, L., 29 G6
Nymagee, 32 B4
Nymboida →, 32 A5
Nyssa, 38 E5

O

Oa, Mull of, 10 F2
Oacoma, 40 D5
Oahe, Dam, 40 C4
Oahe, L., 40 C4
Oak Harbor, 42 E4
Oak Hill, 42 G5
Oak Island, 43 J6
Oak Ridge, 43 G3
Oakdale, *Calif., U.S.A.*, 39 H3
Oakengates, 8 E5
Oakesdale, 38 C5
Oakey, 32 A5
Oakham, 9 E7
Oakland, 38 H2
Oakley, *Idaho, U.S.A.*, 38 E7
Oakley, *Kans., U.S.A.*, 40 F4
Oakridge, 38 E2
Oakville, 42 D5
Oamaru, 33 L3
Oaxaca, 44 D5
Ob →, 18 C8
Oba, 37 E11
Oban, 10 E3
Obbia, 24 D3
Oberhausen, 16 C4
Oberlin, *Kans., U.S.A.*, 40 F4
Oberlin, *La., U.S.A.*, 41 K8
Oberon, 32 B4
Obi, Kepulauan, 23 D4
Óbidos, 46 D7
Obihiro, 22 D8
Obozerskiy, 18 C5
Occidental, Cordillera, 46 C3
Ocean City, *Md., U.S.A.*, 42 F8
Ocean City, *N.J., U.S.A.*, 42 F8
Ocean Park, 38 C1
Oceanside, 39 K5
Ochil Hills, 10 E5
Ocho Rios, 44 a
Ocilla, 43 K4
Ocmulgee →, 43 K4
Oconee →, 43 K5
Oconomowoc, 40 D10
Oconto, 42 C2
Oconto Falls, 42 C1
Odawara, 22 F6
Odense, 6 G10
Oder →, 16 B8
Odesa, 17 E16
Odessa, *Tex., U.S.A.*, 41 K3
Odessa, *Wash., U.S.A.*, 38 C4
Odienné, 26 G4
O'Donnell, 41 J4
Oelwein, 40 D9
Offa, 26 G6
Offaly □, 11 C4
Offenbach, 16 C5
Ogaden, 24 D3
Ogaki, 22 F5
Ogallala, 40 E4
Ogasawara Gunto, 34 E7
Ogbomosho, 26 G6
Ogden, 38 F8
Ogdensburg, 42 C8
Ogeechee →, 43 K5
Ogoki →, 37 D11
Ohai, 33 L2
Ohakune, 33 H5
Ohata, 22 D7
Ohau, L., 33 L2
Ohio □, 42 E4
Ohio →, 41 G10
Ohře →, 16 C7
Ohrid, 15 D9
Ohridsko Jezero, 15 D9
Oil City, 42 E6
Oise →, 12 B5
Ōita, 22 G2
Ojai, 39 J4
Ojinaga, 44 B4
Ojos del Salado, Cerro, 48 B3
Oka →, 18 D5
Okahandja, 29 J3
Okanogan →, 38 B4
Okara, 25 C5
Okavango Delta, 29 H4
Okaya, 22 F6
Okayama, 22 F3
Okazaki, 22 F5
Okeechobee, 43 M5
Okeechobee, L., 43 M5
Okefenokee Swamp, 43 K4
Okehampton, 9 G4
Okha, 19 D15
Okhotsk, 19 D15
Okhotsk, Sea of, 19 D15
Okinawa-Jima, 21 d
Oklahoma □, 41 H6
Oklahoma City, 41 H6
Okmulgee, 41 H7
Oktyabrsk, 19 E9
Öland, 6 G11
Olary, 32 B3
Olathe, 40 F7
Olavarría, 48 D4
Olbia, 14 D3
Old Crow, 36 B6
Oldcastle, 11 C4
Oldenburg, 16 B5
Oldham, 8 D5
Olds, 36 C8
Olean, 42 D6
Olekminsk, 19 C13
Oléron, Î. d', 12 D3
Olga, L., 37 D12
Olimbos, Óros, 15 D10
Olinda, 47 E12
Oliva, 13 C5
Olney, *Ill., U.S.A.*, 40 F10
Olney, *Tex., U.S.A.*, 41 J5
Olomouc, 16 D9
Olongapo, 23 B4
Olsztyn, 16 B11
Olt →, 17 G13
Olympia, *Greece*, 15 F9
Olympia, *U.S.A.*, 38 C2
Olympic △, 38 C2
Olympus, Mt. = Olimbos, 15 D10
Omagh, 11 B4
Omaha, 40 E7
Omak, 38 B4
Oman ■, 24 C4
Oman, G. of, 24 C4
Omaruru, 29 J3
Omdurmân, 27 E12
Ometepe, I. de, 44 E7
Ōmiya, 22 F6
Ommen, 16 B4
Omsk, 18 D8
Omu, 22 D8
Omura, 22 H1
Omuta, 22 G2
Ondangwa, 29 H3
Öndörhaan, 20 B6
Onega, 18 C4
Oneida, 42 D8
Oneida L., 42 D8
O'Neill, 40 D5
Oneonta, 42 D8
Onezhskoye Ozero, 18 C6
Ongole, 25 D7
Onida, 40 C4
Onitsha, 26 G7
Onslow, 30 E2
Ontario, *Calif., U.S.A.*, 39 K5
Ontario, *Oreg., U.S.A.*, 38 D5
Ontario □, 37 D11
Ontario, L., 42 D7
Ontonagon, 40 B10
Oodnadatta, 30 F6
Ooldea, 30 G5
Opala, 28 E4
Opelika, 43 J3
Opelousas, 41 K8
Opotiki, 33 H6
Opp, 43 K2
Oradea, 16 E11
Orai, 25 C7
Oral, 19 D9
Oran, 26 A5
Orange, *Australia*, 32 B4
Orange, *France*, 12 D6
Orange, *Tex., U.S.A.*, 41 K8
Orange →, 29 K3
Orange, C., 46 C8
Orangeburg, 43 J5
Orangeville, 42 D7

 AFGHANISTAN
 ALBANIA
 ALGERIA
 ANDORRA
 ANGOLA
 ANTIGUA & BARBUDA
 ARGENTINA

 BARBADOS
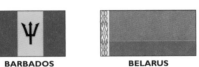 BELARUS
 BELGIUM
 BELIZE
 BENIN
 BHUTAN
 BOLIVIA

 BURUNDI
 CAMBODIA
 CAMEROON
 CANADA
 CAPE VERDE
 CENTRAL AFRICAN REP.
 CHAD

 CROATIA
 CUBA
 CYPRUS
 CZECH REPUBLIC
 DENMARK
 DJIBOUTI
 DOMINICA

 ESTONIA
 ETHIOPIA
 FIJI ISLANDS
 FINLAND
 FRANCE
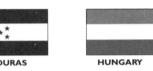 GABON
 GAMBIA

 GUINEA
 GUINEA-BISSAU
 GUYANA
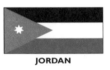 HAITI
 HONDURAS
 HUNGARY
 ICELAND

 IVORY COAST
 JAMAICA
 JAPAN
 JORDAN
 KAZAKHSTAN
 KENYA
 KIRIBATI

 LESOTHO
 LIBERIA
 LIBYA
 LIECHTENSTEIN
 LITHUANIA
 LUXEMBOURG
 MACEDONIA

 MARSHALL ISLANDS
 MAURITANIA
 MAURITIUS
 MEXICO
 MICRONESIA
 MOLDOVA
 MONACO

 NEW ZEALAND
 NICARAGUA
 NIGER
 NIGERIA
 NORTHERN MARIANAS
 NORWAY
 OMAN

 PORTUGAL
 PUERTO RICO
 QATAR
 ROMANIA
 RUSSIA
 RWANDA
 SAMOA

 SINGAPORE
 SLOVAK REPUBLIC
 SLOVENIA
 SOLOMON ISLANDS
 SOMALIA
 SOUTH AFRICA
 SPAIN

 SWEDEN
 SWITZERLAND
 SYRIA
 TAIWAN
 TAJIKISTAN
 TANZANIA
 THAILAND

 UGANDA
 UKRAINE
 UNITED ARAB EMIRATES
 UNITED KINGDOM
 UNITED STATES
URUGUAY
UZBEKISTAN